THE SPLIT SKY

A JOURNEY OF DISCOVERY IN UTAH'S NINE MILE CANYON

THE SPLIT SKY

A JOURNEY OF DISCOVERY
IN UTAH'S NINE MILE CANYON

by

Tom McCourt

Southpaw Publications ™

Copyright © 2002 by Tom McCourt
All rights reserved.

No Part of this book may be reproduced in any form without permission from the author, whether by graphic, visual, electronic, or by any other means, except for brief passages embodied in critical reviews and articles.

Second Edition
First Southpaw Publications printing: September 2003

ISBN: 0-9741568-1-7
Previously published by Bonneville Books ISBN:1-55517-636-4

Library of Congress Control Number: 2003096755

Created, published, and distributed by:

Southpaw Publications
400 East 3000 South
Price, Utah 84501
(435) 637-4544
southpaw@afnetinc.com

SOUTHPAW PUBLICATIONS ™

Printed By:
Peczuh Printing Co.
P.O. Box 1024 · Price, UT 84501

The darkness overwhelmed the light, suffocating it, pushing it back and stamping out the sparks as if jealous to share the heavens. Darkness prevailed everywhere—and from deep in the depths of the darkness came the voice of the storm, a deep and persistent wild-animal growl of thunder, the voice of a dragon, alive and threatening.

I was standing in a field of sunshine. Everything around me was lit with the brilliant hues of the rainbow. The contrast was startling. I looked up at the heavens. The sky was split in two.

To Jeannie,

the light of my life

About the cover photo

The author's son, Austin Wade, took the cover photo in 1985 when he was nine years old. The picture was taken on the San Rafael Swell. The author shot two rolls of film with an expensive 35MM camera in an attempt to capture the essence of the sunset against the rock spires. (Tom's four sons still call the place Mount Fuji in honor of all the Fuji film he wasted.) Austin shot a single frame from a little $12 Vivitar and the result is the cover photo.

TABLE OF CONTENTS

Acknowledgments	xi
Author's Introduction	xiii

Chapter 1: Into the Storm

Into the Storm	1
The Dragon's Den	8

Chapter 2: The Introduction

Breakfast of Champions	20
Bitter Disappointment	32
The Weeds of Wrath	38

Chapter 3: Getting Acquainted

Trash Man	44
The Road to Understanding	50
A Cowgirl Named Goldie	53
Cowboys Close to Home	56
Tracking Geronimo	63
Sand Wash Hotel	68

Chapter 4: The Job

Wire and Water	73
The Mechanics of Making Hay	77
Tending Water	81
Killer Badgers	86

Chapter 5: The Situation

A Man's Job	91
Vermin	101
God Among the Junipers	107

Chapter 6: The Players

The Players	111
A Wolf on the Doorstep	132
Cooking School	135

Chapter 7: **Cowboys**
The King of the Cowboys	139
Pony Jingler	148
Trail Mix; Cows and Raw Eggs	155
The End of the Trail	160

Chapter 8: **Incidentals**
The Lay of the Land	162
Old Hunkus	166
A Chance to Own The Ranch	170

Chapter 9: **A Trip To Town**
Pioneer Day	174
A Trip To Town	178
The Rodeo	185
Breaking Up Is Hard To Do	191

Chapter 10: **Wilderness**
Treasures of the Canyon	197
Alone in the Ledges	208
Aborigines	210
Spooks	220

Chapter 11: **Guns**
Guns	229
The Poacher	244

Chapter 12: **Water**
Water from the Sky	253
Mud People	257
Flood Poker	263

Chapter 13: **Gaining Control**
The Road to Myton	269
Slaying the Dragon	280

Chapter 14: **Salutation**
The Split Sky	285
Saying Goodbye	290

Epilogue 293

ACKNOWLEDGMENTS

I owe a debt of gratitude to several people who helped me write this story. I've picked the brains and winnowed the chaff of the collective memories of Arnold Adair, Don Gonzales, George Cook and Willis Hammerschmid. They were all so very good to talk to me about their remembrances and adventures on the Nutter Ranch.

I'm grateful for my parents who allowed me to stretch my wings and have such adventures as a boy.

I'm grateful to my brother Jack, the genealogist of the family, who helped me with research and putting together some of the facts.

A special thank you to my son, Austin Wade, who took the cover photograph in 1985 when he was nine years old.

I'm grateful to the Plateau Mining Corporation who laid me off and turned me out after almost thirty years. They gave me the opportunity to do something I've always wanted to do.

I'm grateful to my pretty wife Jeannie, who, true to her nature, gave me love, sympathy, encouragement, a shoulder to lean on, a reasonable time to mourn the loss of my job, and then kicked me in the butt and told me to cowboy up, get over it, and go write that book I'd always wanted to write.

AUTHOR'S INTRODUCTION

In the spring of 1963 I went to the Nutter Ranch in Nine Mile Canyon to be a cowboy. I was sixteen years old, starry-eyed and innocent as a baby lamb. I could never have dreamed of what lay before me in the weeks to come.

I climbed a mountain that summer, there on that ranch, among the hay fields, Indian ruins and cedar trees, and something remarkable and truly wonderful happened to me in the process. This book is all about it. It's the story of a young boy's quest to be a man and the dragons encountered on that rocky path; it's about living in wild country and loving the land; it's about overcoming adversity, learning to walk tall, and finding God and self in the wilderness. It's a true story.

This is a rough and tumble narrative, set on a wild and lonesome stage and beset with characters as coarse and diverse as the many species of cactus. It's a fun story to tell, and I've delighted in sharing it. At that time, Nine Mile Canyon was almost unknown to the outside world, and for those few glorious months I had it all to myself—a free spirit soaring in one of Utah's most wild and beautiful places. My heart grew strong there, and I found the pathway of my life among the ledges.

This adventure was lived by an inexperienced, naive and impressionable young man, but the story is being told by an older (but very well-preserved), world-wise and perceptive student of human behavior who has been dragged around a few rough corners and who now understands people, their motives and motivations, better than most. In the pages that follow you will find a blending of the two perspectives. They are almost the same person, that young cowboy and this well-preserved old Grandpa. Their worldview may be different, but they share a common heart.

I tell this story truthfully and as I remember it. All of the characters in this book are real people and all of the events described really happened. I've taken the liberty to move a couple of events from their proper time sequence to help the story flow. Doing so in no way changes the truth of the tale, but only makes the story easier to follow and understand. I have bravely resisted melancholy, and tiptoed through the minefields of sentimentalism by reverting to my true and basic nature. Some people find artistic expression in sculpting or painting; my medium has always been sarcasm and irreverent humor.

There was a great deal of obscene language in this story as I lived it, but I have culled the burrs and softened it considerably. In a few places where I couldn't effectively side-step the rough talk, I've borrowed a phrase from the transcripts of the Watergate tapes of President Nixon and his friends and added a few (expletives deleted). I think this actually adds to the humor in a few places and you will surely still get my point but without the vulgarities. Oh, I know all the words, and how to spell them too, but the world was such a better place when good people used restraint and good manners and didn't use those words in front of other good people.

The Nutter Ranch—the Preston Nutter Corporation—prospered for almost a hundred years in the Nine Mile country. I was there during the final high tide of the fortunes of the ranch and I saw it at its best. My time there was but the spark of a flashbulb when compared to the full history of the place, and I do not intend that this book be taken as a summary of what the ranch and the people were all about. This book is a snapshot, a pencil sketch, a Charlie Russell painting of the last days of the old West.

The author at age sixteen.

Chapter 1

Into The Storm

Into The Storm

The tire exploded with the sound of a shotgun blast and the Dodge fishtailed in the gravel and skidded to a stop in the dust alongside the road. Everything was quiet for a moment, and then dad slapped the steering wheel, jerked his door open and got out. The rag-tag little band of urchins peeked over the back of the seat, and then started to giggle and poke at each other again.

I felt like falling on my sword. What in the world was going to happen next? Everything that could go wrong had already happened at least twice and we were late already. Dad had told the Colonel that we would be there this afternoon and the day was almost gone. The evening shadows were creeping higher and higher up the canyon walls as the afternoon folded into darkness. The setting sun was kissing the tops of the mountains goodnight.

There in the gravel alongside the road, as we hurried to change the tire, I felt trapped in some all-encompassing cosmic conspiracy. It was like the demons of ill fortune had singled me out and were throwing obstacles in my path. Everything was working against me. I felt like some naked and exposed little cherub of a statue standing to my knees in the cold waters of the fountain while the pigeons used me for target practice. What next?

I was on my way to my first real job and I wanted so desperately to arrive with dignity, like a man should. I was sixteen and painfully self-conscious, and it was a difficult thing for me to sit like a child while my dad drove me to the ranch and my geeky little brothers tagged along. The anxiety of starting my first job and leaving home for the first time was causing me grief enough, and now I was enduring the humiliation of being delivered to the ranch like a little boy on his first day at school.

I had hoped that dad and I could go together, just the two of us, and I had hoped that he would let me drive so everyone could see that I was grown up and had a driver's license, but it was quickly apparent that it wasn't going to happen that way. I ask him if I could drive and he said no, it was late and we'd better hurry, and then he invited my little brothers to go along too. This was humiliation I was unprepared for. Nobody would ever expect a real cowboy to show up for a new job with his little brothers tagging along. I was crushed. I sat dejectedly on the front seat, mourning, while dad drove and my indifferent siblings made pandemonium on the back seat. I seethed with an inner turmoil that almost made me sick.

I saw my brothers as a band of unwashed little philistines, all snot-nosed and obnoxious, gumming up the windows with their sticky little paws. They were not at all the proper traveling companions for a real cowboy on his way to a real job. How in the world could I make a good first impression with this giggling, jostling, nose-picking band of gypsies hanging out of the car windows and mooing at every cow we passed? And dad wasn't much better. He could have worn his good hat and a better-looking shirt.

Dad had come home late, after six o'clock. He was still in his police uniform and looking sharp like he always did—a man of authority with a badge and a gun. He wore a drill sergeant's stiff campaign hat and a thick officer's belt and shining boots. He was a handsome trooper, every boy's ideal of what a man should look like. I was proud of him and I wanted to be just like him, but tonight I was impatient with him. I'd been waiting all afternoon and I was keyed-up like a racehorse. I was anxious, even desperate to be on our way. My bedroll and gear had been loaded in the Dodge hours before he got home and I was pacing the floor like a caged cat. I asked him to please hurry and he smiled and said that he would.

Dad went to change clothes and when he emerged from the bedroom he had undergone a startling transformation. He was ... seedy. He had put on work clothes! He was wearing old and faded Levis and a thin cotton shirt. His stiff brown Ranger hat had been replaced by his dusty, sweat-stained old work hat and I was appalled. I wanted to stomp my foot and make him go back and put on something better. He had a closet full of better clothes and a nice Stetson that he wore to town and on special occasions—like when he judged horse shows. I was disappointed and embarrassed for him. I wanted him to get all cleaned up so we would look sharp like rodeo cowboys when we went out to the ranch.

I was wearing my very best, just like I knew John Wayne would have done. I had on my best Levis, my favorite blue western shirt with white pearl snaps and my best pair of boots with a new shine. I was a little short in the hat department, but I wore the best I had, a pretty good straw hat, last year's model with the brim shaped to look like the hat James Dean wore in the movie *Giant*. I'd hoped that dad would to do the same. I wanted him to go back and at least get his good hat or put his police uniform back on. In his uniform he wouldn't look like a professional cowboy, but at least he'd look official.

I swallowed my disappointment. I knew better than to say anything. If I complained about his looks he'd only tease me and make me feel stupid and embarrassed. We'd been through it before. I chewed my lip and kept my anxieties to myself.

Things just weren't happening the way I hoped they would. For weeks, as I waited for school to end, I'd imagined myself arriving at the ranch like Gene Autry. I'd look sharp and I'd be cool and professional. I'd tip my hat to the Boss Lady and wrangle a fine horse and set out for the mountain to spend the summer punchin' them cows (that's right—them cows, that's how real cowboys talk). I'd ride tall and handsome. My spurs would jingle and I'd slap a coiled rope against my leg as I pushed them white-faced bovines to greener pastures. I'd played it all out in my mind many times. But now, as our traveling circus approached the ranch, I could see that my daydream and cold reality were on a collision course and I was powerless to stop it from happening.

All of my dreams were in tatters when we pulled up to the ranch house and the Colonel came out to meet us. We were late and it was growing dark. I was embarrassed and dying a thousand deaths. I desperately wanted this man to see me as an adult and a real cowboy; but there I was, my dad driving and my geeky little brothers spilling out from the back seat all giggles and pokes and stares, with dirty faces and Popsicle stained T-shirts. I wanted to cry out for the rocks to fall on me and hide my shame. I was deeply humiliated in that special way that only insecure teenagers can understand.

I was also completely intimidated. Here before me stood the man who owned the Nutter Ranch, an ex army officer, married to Virginia Nutter herself, an old guy in khaki shirt and pants, dripping with dignity, authority and poise—all of the things I wished I had at that moment. I tried to stand tall and make a good first impression. I wiped my sweaty palm on my pant leg so I could shake his hand and I reminded myself to look him in the eye when I introduced myself. I stood poised, waiting for him to reach out to me.

The Colonel ignored me. He gave me a passing glance, then

stepped past me and shook hands with my father.

I died.

I didn't hear what they said, something cordial I'm sure. I had retreated deep within myself to hide. I unplugged all sound and feeling.

The realization hit me like cold water. To this man I was just another of dad's kids, no different from the snot-nosed crowd from the back seat and not worthy to shake hands with a man who owned a ranch. The shock and humiliation numbed my senses. I could see their mouths moving but my young mind was stunned to unresponsiveness. I realized that I had come all the way out there to work at a man's job and the boss didn't see me as a man at all. My knees grew weak as the reality soaked in.

The Colonel and my dad talked for what seemed like a long time. They knew each other pretty well because of their professional relationship, the rich man with his ranch and my father working in law enforcement. Dad had helped the Colonel on several occasions with trespass and theft problems, and it was dad who had asked the Colonel to hire his oldest son for the summer. The Colonel had agreed, and now I was being delivered on his doorstep: western hat, baggage and bedroll.

This was something I had wanted very badly. I was the one who had goaded dad into asking the Colonel to hire me. I had dreamed of this moment for years. As a little boy growing up in Wellington, I knew there was no greater calling in life than to be a real cowboy. Cowboys were my heroes and I wanted to be one. I wanted to ride and rope and herd cows and sit by the campfire and strum my guitar and yodel at the moon. I wanted to wear a hat and chaps and boots with silver spurs and have the women cry when I left them. I wanted to be like Gene and Roy, Hop-Along Cassidy and The Lone Ranger.

As little boys, my cousins and neighbors and my brother

Reed and I attended the Saturday matinees at the Wellington show house, and we watched in fascination as our horse opera heroes beat up the bad guys and saved the pretty girls. We would soak up our thirty cents worth of entertainment and then retire to the Petersen Dairy Farm next door to where we lived, and with the owner's son Jim, we would reenact the scenes of violence and valor that we had witnessed at the show hall.

We would jump from the rafters into the grain bins, gut shot and dying like old Black Bart, and we would stage elaborate hand-to-hand combats in an old abandoned blacksmith shop that doubled as the Silver Dollar Saloon. We would spend hours playing "fist fight while the joint's on fire," and at least once a week we would make a pilgrimage to the Price River, to the willows, way down below the bottom of the fields, to cut stick horses and ride them back to the Silver Dollar Saloon—after an hour or two spent in breaking them to ride, of course.

We staged elaborate rodeos with an arena outlined with hay twine and willow sticks, and we even charged our parents admission—a nickel—to see us get bucked off from wild stick horses and ferocious shovel-handle bulls. We even had a clown. Brother Reed was too small to ride the rough stuff and so he told jokes and picked up the bull riders and dusted them off. It was great fun, and for us, being a cowboy was as good as it could get.

And now, not so many years since playing "fistfight while the joints' on fire," I stood with shaky knees in front of a man who hired and fired real cowboys, and I watched in silence as he spoke with my father. I felt so very small and pretentious, having been put in my place by his failure to offer me his hand. This rich and famous man owned the biggest private cattle ranch in the state and he had hired me to be a cowboy because my father had asked him to do so. I now fully understood for the first time that I was there only because this man knew and respected my father. The man hadn't hired me for who I was; I was just the baggage in a transaction between professional people. And to make matters worse, now that all the daydreams had evaporated and the cold reality was upon me, I had to face the fact that I wasn't really a cowboy after all. I could ride all right, and shoot too, but I had never roped a steer, or castrated a calf, or branded, or notched an ear . . . and soon the Colonel would know. The anxiety of it crushed me. At that moment I wanted to run away. I felt like I needed to throw up.

Finally, the Colonel turned to me and told me to take my gear into the bunkhouse and find a bed for the night and he'd talk with me in the morning. Yes! I was eager to do something—anything but just stand there in abject humiliation while my geeky little brothers giggled and poked at each other and made fools of themselves and me too.

I opened the trunk of the car and dug the bedroll out. I had been told to bring my own bedroll, and mother had insisted that I take plenty of blankets because it gets cold up on the mountain. As I hefted the great roll of blankets, sleeping bag and pillow on my shoulder, I saw immediately that I had made my first terrible mistake. The Colonel smiled scornfully when he saw the bulk of my bedroll—I froze like a rabbit on the freeway.

Of course, you stupid jerk, how are you going to pack this big roll of blankets all over the mountain following a herd of cows? I hadn't thought of that. There I stood, with that great bulk of embarrassing bedroll balanced on my shoulder, remembering how John Wayne slept with a single blanket and used his saddle for a pillow. How stupid of me. I should have known better. Dad should have said something. I should never have listened to mother; what does she know about being a cowboy?

I was glad the evening was growing dark so the Colonel and my dad couldn't see me blush. I felt so stupid. I tried to walk tall and pretend the mass of blankets wasn't really so big and heavy after all, but it was tough acting, the bedroll was a real monster.

I was going to stay all summer and so I had brought a large suitcase and a cardboard box full of clothes and books and personal items. Dad helped me carry these into the bunkhouse. It never occurred to me until then that the big suitcase and cardboard box might also be excessive baggage. I was confused, unsure of what I should have brought and what I should have left at home. I learned later that real cowboys keep their gear stowed in their pickup trucks or they carry duffel bags that are easier to handle than suitcases and cardboard boxes. I didn't have a pickup truck or a duffle bag and I had a lot to learn about the cowboy business.

The Dragon's Den

As I balanced my embarrassing bedroll on my back and staggered through the door of the small cinderblock building that served as the bunkhouse, I walked right into a renegade Apache. He was just inside the doorway and he was blocking my path. My breath sucked-up tight and my heart skidded to a stop high in my throat.

He was a white man, but his hair was long and wild and his eyes were dark and menacing. He looked like Geronimo. He was sitting on a kitchen chair, smoking a cigar and reading a newspaper. He sat solid and silent, his jaw set and his eyes all squinted up. He held the newspaper spread wide, making the bulk of him even bigger and the path around him even smaller. I was obviously about to intrude into his private space and he glared at me over the paper with the look a person might give a dog who has just soiled the rug. He didn't say anything; he just sat there belligerently, his lip curled up in a snarl. He was challenging me—daring me to ask him to move.

I quickly looked past him, away from his circle of reading light and into the depths of the darkening room, afraid, panicked, and avoiding the confrontation in his eyes. I struggled to get past him with awkward, apologetic and juvenile efforts. I had to squeeze around him to get into the building and he didn't offer to move an inch to give me the room to do so.

I was turned sideways, doing my best to get past the man without bumping him with my heavy bedroll, when dad walked in carrying my suitcase and cardboard box. At the sight of my dad, old Geronimo's attitude changed in a heartbeat and he quickly crumpled the newspaper and slid his chair back to make room for the man and his burdens.

" Hello Joe," dad said with a quiet familiarity that startled me.

"What you doin' out here Ned?" The wild Indian asked pleasantly.

I had to turn to be sure it was the same scowling face that spoke—and it wasn't. The pinched, angry face from just a second ago was gone and a tranquil, agreeable face had replaced it. Even the voice that spilled from the new face was all sugary and polite. The transformation was amazing.

I wasn't surprised that dad knew this angry, lost soul; my dad knew everybody. I wasn't surprised at the change in the old geezer's attitude when he saw dad either. Dad was a cop and he was tough as nails and even bad men respected him; I drew comfort from that fact. Dad had been a boxer in his younger years and there were very few men he couldn't take down if he put his mind to it. His reputation had preceded him and I could see that Injun Joe was afraid of him.

"This is my boy Tom and he's going to help you out for a while" dad said quietly.

"Take any bunk in the back there," the tranquil, agreeable face called out with an air of interest and concern.

"This corner here is mine and Humbert sleeps in that corner over there . . . anything else is yours."

I made my way to the back of the small, one-room building, as far away as I could get from that two-faced old jerk who now sat in rapt attention, visiting with my old man and smiling as pleasant as could be.

I pulled the tail of the hay string ripcord that held my bedroll together and the pile of blankets plopped open, completely covering the army surplus bunk that served as a bed. I set the suitcase and cardboard box on the floor near the foot of the bed and looked around at my new surroundings.

The place was as stark as a jail cell. There were no curtains on the windows and no decoration of any kind on the walls, just cold, gray cinderblock. There were no rugs or coverings on the cement floor and no dressers, end tables or lamps. A couple of stark and dusty light bulbs hung from the ceiling and were shielded with cheap tin shades. The man wearing the mask of a tranquil face occupied the one and only chair in the whole building.

It was clear that the two-faced man had lived in the building for a long time. He had built himself a dragon's nest and it was strewn with the bones and litter of his bleak existence. He had claimed a full quarter of the small building as his own and had provisioned himself like a Spartan soldier in the stark surroundings.

He had a bed covered with an ancient patchwork quilt and a couple of pillows. He had a small table with a reading lamp and the single kitchen chair. He had made bookshelves using cinderblocks and boards and these were weighted down with an unruly mass of dozens and dozens of cheap western novels and old newspapers. Some of the books and papers were in the dirt on the floor and others littered the table and even the bed. Here and there in the clutter, a *Life Magazine* or a *Reader's Digest* struggled to swim to the surface. He had a scratched-up old dresser and a rope stretched along one wall where work clothes dangled from wooden clothespins. His wardrobe was a collection of old man's clothes, long johns and bib overalls, white boot socks with red toes and heels. A calendar with the picture of a naked young lady was displayed prominently near his unadorned and dirty window. An ancient desktop radio sat covered with dust and a pair of greasy gloves on the window ledge. Several cardboard boxes peeked out from beneath his bed.

He had a bucket for an ashtray and it was nearly filled with cigar butts, spit and odd bits of trash. The whole building reeked with cigar smoke, and from somewhere, buried deep in the odious vapors, came the faint stink of vomit.

The man himself was the picture of excess, a poster boy for decadent living. His hair was very long and uncut, graying and dirty-looking. It hung down and hid the collar of his shirt and it stuck out over his ears in unruly waves. He was the first man I ever saw with hair that touched his shoulders and the sight startled me. Long hair was unnatural on a man, it seemed immoral and perverse to me. It made him look corrupted—a wild man beyond rules and civilization.

He looked like an old man to me but I found out later he was in his mid-forties. He looked older than his years. Decades of abuse, hard drinking and hard smoking were taking their toll. He wasn't a large man but he had been muscular in his youth and he still filled the shoulders of his flannel shirt quite well. He was growing paunchy and he had a three-day growth of gray whiskers bristling from his chin. The cigar smoke was curing his hide like a ham and his face was a wrinkled roadmap to every bar and cigar store he ever knew. His teeth were yellow and greasy.

It was easy to see that he made his living out-of-doors farming. His face, neck, and the backs of his hands were suntanned leather. There was a line around his forehead where his hat fit. Everything below the line, his eyebrows, nose, cheeks and chin, were brown, red, and wind burned. Everything above the line was white like a fish's belly, stark white, like boiled tripe. The whiteness extended up to the top of his head where the bleached and boiled skin showed through his dark and thinning hair. His hands looked dirty, stained with grease, tobacco, and God only knows what else.

I didn't know it at the time, and Dad hadn't warned me, but my dad had thrown this shipwrecked old pirate into the hoosegow on more than one occasion for being drunk and disorderly.

I walked with Dad back out to the car to say goodbye, and now that it was dark and no one could see me, I even said goodbye and was polite to my geeky little brothers. It was the first time we would be separated and I knew I was going to miss them, even though I would have suffered the tortures of the inquisition before admitting it.

Dad shook my hand, smiled bravely and patted me on the back, and then he gathered up the traveling circus and started for home. I watched the tail lights fade in the canyon. I was on my own. I took a deep breath and went back into the dragon's den.

The scowl was back. The chair was again in the doorway and I had to turn sideways to get through. The cold, dark eyes glared at me over the newspaper and the pinched-up mouth blew a great cloud of stinking cigar smoke in my direction. The angry face spoke and the voice was not the voice that had spoken to my father. This was a different voice, evil, malicious and intimidating, a voice that matched the ugly, hateful face of an old alligator.

He laid out the house rules using stark obscenities and immoral adjectives. I was made to understand that I was to stay completely away from him and his things. I was expected to be quiet and unobtrusive. Lights were out by ten o'clock and he didn't allow any of that rock and roll garbage on the radio. I was told plainly and with implied threats of violence that I was to use the other door, the back door, so as not to intrude on his private space and disturb his reading. I was put on notice that if anything, anything at all that belonged to him came up missing, or was even moved from its rightful place, there would be an unholy price to pay.

He got his point across. I was shocked numb. The vile obscenities slammed into my tender sensibilities like stones shot from a catapult. His attitude, posturing, and cold, reptilian eyes scared me to death. I had never had anyone speak to me like that before and I didn't know how to react. I had been taught to respect and obey older men. Older men were grandpas and schoolteachers and church leaders. Older men were not supposed to talk and act that way. This new reality filled me with uncertainty bordering on panic.

I stepped back, giving ground, and I managed to croak out a few faltering words.

"I'm goin' up on the mountain . . . to the cow camp . . . and I should be outta here by tomorrow."

"That so?" he snickered wickedly, "Good place for ya . . . we don't need no (strong expletive deleted) kids screwin' things up around here."

I quickly retreated to the bunk I had selected by the back door. I sat there for a while trying to sort it all out. My heart beat fast and my hands trembled. I was stunned by the barrage of threats and obscenities and I was unsure of what to do. What in the world did I do to that old goat to make him act like that? Does the Colonel know this man talks this way? What would dad do if he knew this old geezer was talking to me like this? Is this the way people on the ranch talk all of the time? What do I do if that old man actually tries to hit me or something? There was a lot to sort out.

The one thing for sure was that I was stuck with the old devil until tomorrow and I'd better make the best of it somehow. The Colonel had long since slipped away to the safety of his own house and dad and my brothers and everything familiar to me was gone in the blackness of the canyon. I was stranded on the dark side of the moon. I had no car, no telephone and no friend. It was time to be a real cowboy.

I looked at my watch. It was still early, just after nine o'clock. I was not sleepy at all but I didn't know what to do there by myself. I had expected the bunkhouse to be full of people and I wondered where everybody was. Surely, this one miserable old man couldn't be the only guy who worked for an outfit this size.

I had some books with my gear, but I was too apprehensive and too flustered to read. I had a million questions but no one to talk to. I sat for a while and stared at the cinderblock walls and fidgeted, and as I did, a thick blanket of gloom descended over me. I had never felt so alone and so vulnerable, and I began to feel sorry for myself.

My sense of loneliness and self-pity started to grow roots. Doubts and fears were creeping into my mind and my soul. This was not turning out the way I had imagined it. What was I doing here? Is this how I was going to spend my whole summer? Were the other men who worked here as mean and miserable as this one old geezer? I hadn't been at the ranch for an hour yet and already the Colonel had treated me with disrespect and the longhaired old Indian in the bunkhouse was treating me with hateful contempt. I'd been snubbed, challenged, shocked, intimidated, threatened and scared, and I hadn't been there long enough to open my suitcase yet. I was a kid, not a real cowboy . . . and I wanted to go home. I felt alone in a way I'd never experienced before, and I swallowed hard and stared at the stark cement floor. Maybe I'd made a big mistake? A rising panic was swelling up from deep inside me.

And then, somehow, in spite of myself, I began to be distracted from my misery by the sights, sounds and inferences of my new surroundings. I slowly became aware that through the screen door by my bed I could hear the sounds of the canyon in the night almost as well as if I were camping out. I listened . . . and I could hear peacocks in the trees outside, and crickets out in the weeds, and frogs down by the creek, and the occasional whoop of a nighthawk hunting bugs out over the fields. I raised my eyes to a dirty window and I could see pale moonlight playing over the canyon walls.

The effect was calming and reassuring. This was cowboy stuff. I remembered that I was in a bunkhouse on a big ranch and I actually had a job there now. This was something I'd always wanted and something I had dreamed about. Tonight, for the first time, I was a real cowboy—a timid one to be sure—but a real cowboy none-the-less. I drew fresh courage from my library of dreams. As I thought about it, the cold fear, raw doubts and sore humiliations took a back seat and the daydream came sneaking back.

With renewed courage, I watched old Joe for a while—on the sly. I hoped he wouldn't notice. My secret glances alternated between him and the picture of the naked girl on the wall just behind him. His back was quartered away from me and his attention seemed to be focused severely on his newspaper. He sat defiantly in front of the screen door, a squat and solid obstruction; his very presence challenging the free passage of people and air, a fat cigar clenched tightly in his greasy teeth.

I noticed with amusement that he was breathing and smoking like a steam engine. With every breath the cigar glowed brighter on the inhale stroke, and on the exhale stroke dirty smoke escaped from his nose and mouth. He breathed and smoked as a single act. There was a smooth and constant repetition in the pattern—a mechanical rhythm. The man was an absolute smoking machine.

My grandpa was a chain-smoker and addictively fond of Bull Durham cigarettes, but he didn't smoke like that. I had never seen a man smoke like Joe the Dragon and I was fascinated. He sucked on that cigar with the resolve and intensity of a lion at lunchtime, smacking and chewing, involving his whole face in the effort. He smoked like he was on a mission to save the world from clean air. He also coughed deeply and spit into his ashtray bucket at regular intervals.

I watched a continuous thin ribbon of dirty-brown cigar smoke pass slowly overhead near the ceiling, and I sat transfixed as it traveled the length of the room and then exited the screen door near my bed. I began to understand why the front doorway was the old buzzard's favorite roosting spot. It was there that he caught the light canyon breeze that squeezed in through the screen door. The thin trickle of cool night air washed the cigar smoke to the rear of the building and out the back screen door near my new bed. It was a good system for Joe, but I was on the downstream side of things, and I watched helplessly as the polluted river of brown smoke drifted slowly past and escaped into the night in a way that I could not.

It was obvious that Joe was working hard to ignore me, and after a while I grew tired of watching him. I slowly realized that I was exhausted from the ordeals of the day. It had been a day of intense mental and emotional turmoil for me. All of my senses, my sensibilities, my values, fears and dreams had all been tested, and now it was time to sleep.

As I started getting ready for bed, I noticed that there was something missing there in the bunkhouse, something important. Very timidly, and with a hesitant and squeaky voice, I interrupted the mechanical cigar-smoking machine with a necessary question.

"Where's the toilet Joe?"

There was a snort from behind the newspaper, a muffled growl, a whispered curse, and then the dragon's voice. He growled impatiently that the toilet was in the other building, and he used a very stark and obscene adjective to describe the other building. He didn't bother to tell me which other building, but he did add a small gem of helpful advice.

" Just go out in the weeds like a man."

He then sarcastically went into some detail about how the ranch didn't have a powder room for young ladies yet, and he covered the subject with ugly pornographic language and tasteless, anatomically correct descriptions.

Unbelievable . . . I cringed at the man's foul language. I'd never heard a grown man talk such trash. Every sentence he spoke was laced with rank obscenities and vile sexual innuendoes. My youthful sensibilities were undergoing shock treatment. I couldn't believe it. My mother would have staked me to an ant pile and filled my ears with jam for talking like that, and here this old buzzard, this "adult," was using words out loud that we kids only whispered in secret. I hadn't really considered until that very evening that an adult might actually say some of those words out loud.

And so . . . obediently, not knowing what else to do, I crept out the back door and wandered away from the building a respectable distance, feeling my way over the unfamiliar terrain in the dark, and there in the moonlight, I shed water on the Nutter Ranch—like a man.

The Split Sky

I didn't realize how noisy communal living in a bunkhouse could be until I tried to go to sleep that first night. I turned out the lights on my side of the bunkhouse, but I lay awake in the semi-darkness for what seemed like hours listening to the old buzzard cough his lungs up and spit and choke and then light another cigar.

At first I was annoyed, but then I squealed inwardly with delight, when in the depths of a deep cough the old dragon broke wind like a bucking horse. I chewed my pillow to try to keep from laughing out loud but my whole body shook and my eyes filled with tears. I was afraid old Joe was going to hear me laughing and come over and beat me up but I couldn't help myself. The situation was made even more hilarious because Joe the bucking horse had a cheering section. Every time he made a noise there was a great applauding chorus of squawks and honks from dozens of peacocks roosting in the nearby cottonwood trees.

I had seen the peacocks before, the ranch was famous for them, but I never dreamed they could be so noisy and stupid. With each of the old geezer's violent outbursts, from whichever end, the whole canyon reverberated with the yelps and honks and squawks of the stupid birds. I imagined them as a long chorus line of ugly, knot-kneed, bird-lady cheerleaders with pom-poms and gaudy feathers who danced and kicked and cheered old Joe on as he broke wind and coughed and strangled and choked. I almost smothered myself with my pillow, and I laughed silently and shook until I was truly exhausted. My pillow was soaked with happy tears and I knew I would never be able to see peacocks as distinguished and beautiful birds ever again.

If old Joe caught on that I was laughing at him he never let on. He didn't challenge me and I was probably lucky.

Finally, the strangling, smoke-stained, gassed-up and two-faced old fossil turned out his light and went to bed. Most of the disgusting noises were at least dampened by the covers now, and the birds were not quite so eager to celebrate each new outburst. I drifted off to sleep, dreaming about tomorrow when I would be a real cowboy, up in the cool pines and quakies on the mountain, ridin' a good horse and punchin' them Nutter cows.

Chapter 2

The Introduction

Breakfast Of Champions

I woke from a deep sleep and jerked myself up to a sitting position. I looked around at unfamiliar surroundings, my mind groping, catching up. It took just a moment to remember where I was and what I was doing there. The dirty windows were gray with the first blush of morning light and the room was still quite dark. I looked to see where the dragon was and found his bed empty. I was alone.

I dressed quickly, putting on work clothes for the day. I selected my best work clothes because I still hoped to make a good impression and I hadn't met Virginia Nutter yet. I put my cowboy duds from the night before into my big suitcase and then wrestled with my embarrassing bedroll, struggling to wrap it all up again. I worked quickly and with rising excitement. I was anxious to go up on the mountain with the cowboys and relieved that my one night in the bunkhouse with long-haired Injun Joe was over. I would be leaving soon, and the old dragon could have the whole place to himself again. It took a few minutes to roll the monster bedroll back together and suck it up tight with the hay twine.

I stacked my things just inside the back door like I was waiting for a taxi. I winced as I stood back and looked at the bulk of my gear. It did seem like an awful lot to be taking to a cow camp. I wondered if maybe I should leave about half of the blankets there in the bunkhouse to lighten the load, but then I wondered what mother would say if I went home without them. I hesitated and I fidgeted, unsure of what to do.

It was slowly getting light and I couldn't hear any sounds outside other than the morning chorus of birds. No machinery was running and I couldn't hear anyone talking. The whole ranch seemed to be still sleeping and I wondered where Joe had gone.

I timidly peeked out from the back door of the bunkhouse at the new morning. It was still quite dark but I could make out the essentials of my new surroundings. I immediately rejoiced in the smell of the freshness of the morning air. After spending a night in an ashtray, the smell of wet grass, sage and lilacs was heaven sent. A small cement pad served as a back porch to the bunkhouse and I stepped out and looked around.

The bunkhouse—back door view.

The ranch was nestled in a deep canyon, a ragged crack in the earth's surface that ran east and west. The walls of the canyon were formed by ascending layers of sandstone ledges, stacked like steps, that climbed higher and higher toward the sky until they reached the threshold of a high plateau many hundreds of feet above the canyon floor. My view from the bunkhouse was to the east, down the canyon and toward the morning sun. The sun was still hiding behind the far-off mountains but an orange glow lit the clouds above the canyon rim.

There was a row of ancient cottonwood trees just outside my door that marked the upper boundary of a hay field that extended toward the east for half a mile. The field was held captive by a stout barbed-wire fence. In the first blush of the morning light, a glistening blanket of dew made the dark hay appear liquid, and in the shadows it looked more like a lake than a field of grass.

To the right of the field I could see the path the creek followed as it meandered down the canyon. The channel was sunk below the level of the fields and its course was marked with cottonwood trees, willows and brush. It looked like a wild place, a thin strip of jungle interspersed with eroded banks and sandy defiles. The brush and tamarisk bushes were also glistening with cool morning dew and they looked fluffy and made-up like flocked Christmas trees sparkling with thousands of tiny lights.

To the left of the field, the Nine Mile Canyon road followed the contours of the fence, bending with the canyon. It disappeared and then reappeared as it touched the highs and lows of the canyon bottom. It stood out stark and empty in the morning light, an intrusion into the natural green and grayness of the canyon vegetation, a narrow and sinewy scar in the rocks and sage.

The air was electric with the excitement of the coming day. The canyon walls held the morning shadows close and the air was calm and cool. I shivered, more from anticipation than cold as I drank in the sights, smells and wonders of my first morning on the ranch.

I didn't know what to do or where to go. I knew nothing about the routines and expectations of my new job, and so I stayed put, expecting that someone would show up and tell me what to do. I knew that something must have been happening somewhere because the old dragon's bed was still empty.

Out in the damp grass, Blackbirds, Meadowlarks and Finches were practicing their vocal scales and waiting for the sun. High in the cottonwoods overhead, scruffy little sparrows argued and spit insults at each other. Peacocks walked clumsily on the ground and picked at the gravel with the chickens. I watched with some amusement as the stupid birds plodded around the yard. They were dim-eyed and comical creatures, like drawings from a Dr. Seuss cartoon. Once in a while one of them would throw his head back and let out a pitiful honk that would echo up through the ledges and then reverberate back down the canyon. I was still smiling about the peacock cheerleaders from the night before, and I was delighted to see that the old girls were wearing gray-feathered leotards, cut off at the knees, that fit right in with my imagined expectations.

I needed to pee. I anxiously pondered my predicament for a while, growing increasingly agitated. What did Joe say last night? The toilet was where? All I could remember was the swear words. I did remember that he told me to go water the weeds like a man and that looked like the only option again this morning; I couldn't see an outhouse anywhere. I was glad that Mister Sun was taking his time coming up; there were still a lot of shadows in the canyon.

Near the bunkhouse was an ancient shed that sheltered an old horse-drawn buggy. I couldn't see anyone around and everything was very quiet except for the birds. The shed would provide cover for my morning ritual. I sneaked over by the buggy and let 'er rip, and then tiptoed back to the bunkhouse, embarrassed. What if someone saw me? What if Virginia Nutter saw me do that? I decided I had better find the facilities soon because my conscience was going to kill me if I kept that up.

I sat on the bare bed frame and waited for someone to show up and tell me what to do. The thin, hardwood frame made an uncomfortable seat, but I didn't dare to even think about encroaching on the old buzzards roost, that kitchen chair that sat empty and inviting by the forbidden front door. That chair was the dragon's throne, and I would have sat on a carpet of tacks before defiling such a sacred object.

I sat waiting and watching as the room filled with light, and then the cool morning air that sneaked in through Joe's private screen door brought me the smell of frying bacon. Somewhere upwind, someone was cooking breakfast.

I was in the middle of my sixteenth year, growing like a weed and always ravenous. The smell of fried bacon was irresistible to me and I drank it in, savoring both the scent and the promise. I salivated like a dog and my flat little stomach growled with anticipation.

I was torn. I wanted to track the scent and discover the source, but I was afraid. The better soldier of my nature urged me to charge in boldly and claim the prize, but the insecure little boy that lurked in my shadow opted for caution. The bunkhouse was my one foothold of semi-familiarity in a brave new world of strangers and uncertainty, and I wanted to cling to it like a timid little rabbit in the shelter of his den. I hesitated and I fidgeted, but in the end, the smell of frying bacon was the siren's song I couldn't resist. The taste of the morning air compelled me to venture from the safety of my rabbit's hutch and cast my fate into the great unknown.

The cookhouse.

    I dutifully went out the back door, not wanting to violate Joe's space, even when he wasn't there, and I circled the building and followed the scented path of bacon to the cookhouse. I found the cookhouse to be another small, cinderblock building that stood only a few steps in front of the bunkhouse. It looked very similar to the bunkhouse, but it had a long front porch that spanned the width of the building, framing the front door.

    Part of my pay for working for the outfit was that my meals were furnished. I was supposed to get one hundred and fifty dollars a month and "found." I had asked dad what "found" meant and he told me it meant they would feed me. I felt embarrassed to be sneaking up on the cookhouse, hoping to be fed when I hadn't done any work yet, but I knew that even the chickens and cows would be fed this morning; one starving teen-aged boy shouldn't be too much of an imposition for a big outfit like the Nutter Ranch.

    With great trepidation, I opened the screen door to the cookhouse and walked in. The cookhouse was a single room set up with a long table and some metal kitchen chairs. There was a low partition built into one end of the room, and behind the partition was crowded a propane kitchen stove, a refrigerator, a set of cupboards and a large metal sink. The place was as stark and unadorned as the bunkhouse. There was only one other person in the building. There—standing over the stove and the precious bacon, his long hair wet and combed back severely, stood Joe the dragon.

He looked over at me as I entered the room. He sneered and then went back to his cooking without speaking. He stood there grinning like an alligator, slowly turning the sweet-smelling bacon. He was toying with me, cooking slowly and enjoying the game. I stood breathless with my mouth open, caught like a gopher in a trap. I sized the situation up and the implications quickly soaked in—I was screwed.

I turned and staggered back outside, out on the front porch and away from the evil grin and the atmosphere of doom. I was stunned. Where was everybody? Was I stranded on a desert island with this one hateful old lizard or what? I walked to each end of the porch and peeked around the corners. Everything was quiet. No other person was in sight.

There were a couple of beat up old chairs out there on the porch, just outside the cookhouse door. I sat down on one of them and watched as the sun came over the canyon rim. I was having adrenaline for breakfast. There was a knot in my stomach and my hands were all wet and sweaty. My heart was racing and I clenched my teeth tightly. The weight of the accumulated frustrations, humiliations, fear, apprehension, and misery of the past twenty-four hours engulfed me and I started to tremble.

"Don't bawl you damn baby . . . don't you dare let that old man see you cry."

I struggled to gain control of my emotions. I wrestled with the little boy that hid deep inside of me, that embarrassing little creature with tender sensibilities who hid in my shadow and wanted to cry and run away. I thought he had left me years ago and I was embarrassed to find him still there when I needed to be stronger than that. I was angry to find him back and I struck out at him with a vengeance. I whipped him soundly, but it was a battle; the fight took longer than it should have. I was shaken, bruised and bloodied . . . but I didn't cry.

The little boy of my childhood was forever banished. He walked away with a bloody nose and he never came back to embarrass me again. I replaced him with a circuit breaker, a ground wire, an electrical switch. After that day, whenever I was confronted with a lightning strike of high emotion, I flipped the switch, sending it to ground and deflecting it away from my vital parts, shielding myself while I dealt with an appropriate response. I wired the switch into the hole in my heart left by the little boy, and after a while I managed to sit still with an outward calm, the storm safely bottled up on the inside—like a man.

I was angry at the injustice of it. I hadn't done anything to old Joe and I didn't deserve to be treated the way he was treating me. I seethed in righteous indignation but I didn't dare say anything. I was still very much afraid of the old dragon and I wasn't about to confront him. I did resolve, however, that if he thought for one minute that I would beg him for something to eat, he was wrong. I wasn't about to humiliate myself anymore than had already been inflicted upon me. Joe would have to make the first move. If not invited to eat, I would do without; it was that simple.

The sun topped the canyon walls and swept the shadows from the ranch yard. The sparrows patched up their family feud, made peace and flew off to the labors of the day. The stupid peacocks chased bugs in the gravel and showed off their fancy tail feathers to each other. Barn Swallows darted in and out of little mud houses in the ledge above the corral and Joe rattled pots and pans and silverware in the kitchen. I refused to take the bait. I sat defiantly in the first warm rays of the morning sun and waited to be invited.

The morning calm was shattered when a truck came rattling noisily into the yard and stopped near the corral. It was a good-sized truck, bigger than a pickup and with a flat bed and a wooden stock rack. A severely crumpled old western hat peeked over the steering wheel. The face that wore the hat peeked through the steering wheel.

The crumpled old hat got out of the truck on the far side, where I couldn't see, and slammed the truck door. The sound echoed down the canyon, setting off a chorus of honks and squawks from the stupid peacocks. The hat came around from the back of the truck and I saw that there was a skinny little man beneath it. He walked quietly across the yard, coming through the gate and up to the cookhouse.

The skinny little man in the crumpled hat wore cowboy work clothes: Levis, boots and a long-sleeved cotton shirt. He looked clean and neat and well cared for, and as he got closer, I realized that he wasn't quite as small as he appeared to be; he just sort of slouched, which made him look smaller. He was about my size, five foot six or so. He had a pleasant, friendly face, not handsome by any stretch, but a decent, honest face. He was clean-shaven and he smelled of after-shave lotion. He walked up on the porch and extended his hand.

"You must be a new guy," he said with a smile that was honest, but strained and bashful.

"I'm Tom McCourt," I said, with an eagerness that surprised me.

"Naw," he giggled, "I know Tom McCourt and you're not him."

"He's my uncle," I said, "I'm Ned's kid."

"Ned the Sheriff?" he asked, with a raised eyebrow that showed he was impressed.

"Ned the Sheriff," I echoed back, warming up to his friendly face and his interest in my father.

"I'm Humbert Pressett," he smiled, "glad to know ya."

I had never met Humbert before that morning but I knew who he was. I had heard my dad and some of my young cowboy friends talk about him and the name had stuck with me. There couldn't be more than one person in the whole world named Humbert.

I was so excited to have another person to talk to, and so grateful that the little man seemed so open and friendly and interested enough to ask my name. I was relieved too, that someone had shown up that might intercede on my behalf with the sneering old dragon that guarded the bacon. I could have jumped up and hugged him when he opened the screen door and said, "Come on Tom, let's go get some breakfast . . . I'm starved." I was thrilled; the standoff with the dragon was over. I'd been invited to eat.

I followed my new friend back into the cookhouse, thankful and eager as a puppy to have someone to talk to and someone I could follow through the rituals and formalities of my first breakfast on the ranch.

I was startled and surprised when old Joe jumped on Humbert with almost the same venom he had shown me.

"Where you been you old (expletive deleted)? I been waitin' an hour for your sorry (crude expletives deleted again) and the eggs are gettin' cold."

I winced, expecting a major confrontation, and I was stunned when the little man answered back.

"Oh, go blow it out yer bloomer leg you ornery old (artfully descriptive expletive deleted). . . you probably burned the (expletive deleted) eggs anyway."

I was aghast. I looked back and forth at those two old geezers as they went about their business. It seemed that no offense was given and no offense was taken. Humbert went to the cupboard and pulled out some plates and silverware. He handed me a plate and a fork and nodded at a chair across the table. Joe the dragon set a skillet filled with fried eggs and a plate of bacon on the table and the two of them commenced to dig in. I was the little dog, and so I sat back hesitant, waiting for the big dogs to get their full share.

They piled their plates up high with bacon, eggs and toast, and then Humbert turned to me and said, "Hey . . . you better get in here . . . this flea-bit old coyote and sorry excuse for a cook will eat it all if you let him."

Joe snorted like an old buck sheep but he had his face filled with bacon and so he didn't say anything. I took the advice and did jump right in. There was plenty left and I filled my plate.

Joe stood up, chewing noisily and with the same intensity he demonstrated when he smoked, went to the stove and brought back a large pot of coffee. He poured himself a cup and set the pot in the middle of the table. Humbert went to the cupboard and fetched himself a cup, and then he hesitated, turned to me, and asked, "Do you want a cup of coffee?"

The question surprised me. I was a Mormon. My parents were Mormons. My whole family was Mormons. We lived the Word of Wisdom. We didn't use tobacco or alcohol, and tea and coffee were forbidden to us. For a second I hesitated. I really didn't want any, but the alternatives were humiliating. To ask for milk or orange juice would be like going into the Silver Dollar Saloon and ordering soda pop. If I drank water with my breakfast, or if I drank nothing at all, I would be setting myself apart from the men. If I did anything but drink coffee I would be different and I would draw unwanted attention and possible ridicule upon myself. I wanted desperately to fit in and be a part of the group, and so . . . I nodded my affirmation and reached out and took the forbidden cup.

I had tasted coffee before. My grandpa drank coffee by the gallon and I had sneaked a sip or two when he wasn't looking. I had also toyed with the forbidden brew at the homes of a couple of my boyhood friends and so I already knew I didn't like the taste of the stuff. I poured the thick, dark liquid into my cup and took my first timid sip. It smelled and tasted like crap. It was nasty stuff. The Church was right; coffee is bad for you. And to make matters worse, Injun Joe had made it as thick and black as liquid asphalt. I tried hard not to show how I felt about it; I tried to act like I drank coffee all the time. I puckered up at the bitterness of it and watched in amazement as the big dogs gulped it down by the pint—like it was good stuff. I managed to drink that first bitter cup, but I sure didn't enjoy it much.

I was persistent in my resolve to drink coffee and I stayed with it over the next several weeks and learned to drink the nasty stuff. I even came to look forward to it in the mornings. Joe and Humbert drank theirs black, like real men. I learned to make cocoa out of mine, half filling the cup with sugar and canned milk.

Coffee turned out to be the camel's nose under the tent for me. Once I had trampled on that one religious taboo it was easy for me to learn to smoke and drink. Some months after leaving the ranch I taught myself to do both of those things, and it was many years before I returned to full fellowship in the faith of my fathers.

We finished breakfast and Joe and Humbert got up and started to clean up the kitchen. Humbert gathered the plates, put them in the sink, and started to fill it with soapy water. I eagerly offered my help.

"Naw . . . you set this one out kid," he said pleasantly, "I'll get 'em this morning."

I hung around feeling stupid and useless for a few minutes, and then I sidled up to my friend Humbert and asked him a question in a small and quiet voice.

"Where's the toilet, Humbert?"

He looked at me startled, almost unbelieving, and with real concern in his eyes. "Out the front door to your right . . . around the building . . . first door you come to."

"Thank you," I offered, and I went to check it out.

It was there all right, just like Humbert said, a combination toilet, shower and laundry room all in one. A set of Dexter twin-tubs, a washing machine for clothes, almost like my mother's washing machine back home, sat in one corner with hoses and electrical cords sagging to the dirty, still-damp cement floor. The place smelled musty like a cellar, but there was a real porcelain toilet and a dirty bathroom sink and I was glad I wouldn't have to pee in the weeds anymore.

I arrived back on the cookhouse porch just as Joe and Humbert came out, putting on their hats, buttoning up their sleeves and getting ready for the day. I stood by eagerly, waiting for Humbert to tell me to go get my things so he could take me to the mountain.

Bitter Disappointment

I was standing by, waiting for orders, when a large, goofy-looking, yellow dog came crashing around the corner of the building. He bounced across the porch all hyper and slobbering and I distinctly heard Joe's teeth slam together in a death grip. The dragon growled a foul obscenity under his breath. The dog ricocheted off a chair and jammed his wet nose into Humbert's crotch. Humbert grabbed at himself and kicked at the dog almost playfully, way more tolerant than the situation required. He turned his back, still covering himself and muttered "Hello Brody," with an embarrassed giggle. The dog trotted to the other end of the porch and cocked a leg on the corner post. Sticky, yellow dog pee puddled on the cement. I looked up at Joe and his face was deep red and all the little veins in his neck showed through the wrinkles.

"Brody . . . Brody . . . come back here Brody," a high-pitched male voice called from the direction the dog had made his entrance. The man came blustering around the corner and I was shocked to see that it was the Colonel. He came across the porch with his arms stretched out, his elbows tucked in close to his ribs and his empty hands up in the air like a girl shooing chickens. He was all flustered and walking on his toes. The dog ignored him and ran off over the lawn, scattering the stupid peacocks.

I'd seen the man before, but always at a distance—or like last night, in the dark and when I was much distracted with other matters. This was the first time I had ever seen him up close and in the daylight. I was surprised at how skinny he was, and how effeminate his actions and his mannerisms were, even his voice. I had expected a warrior, Conan the Barbarian or Alexander the Great, and I was shocked and disappointed.

The Colonel shook his head with a sigh of resignation as the Airedale zoomed back around the house and out of sight, and then he walked over to where we were all standing. He put the fingers of both hands into his back pockets; I guessed it was because he didn't want to shake hands. He stood there looking down at the ground with his elbows extending out like thin, bony chicken wings.

He was dressed in a clean, starched, khaki outfit—a uniform without insignia. He wore long pants with a regulation crease and a long-sleeved shirt with epaulets and starched pockets. The cuffs on his shirtsleeves were buttoned tightly around his thin wrists. He wore polished black boots, slip-on

Wellington boots with rounded toes and thin, flat soles—not the kind of boots that a cowboy would wear.

"How are you men this morning?" he asked with a detached look that betrayed him. He really didn't care to know; he was fulfilling a duty as the Colonel and the boss.

Joe and Humbert and I all mumbled that we were doing fine, also fulfilling our obligation to be civil. We stood there in an awkward silence for a few moments, waiting for the big man to speak. He stood with his fingers in his back pockets and he looked at the ground and rocked back and forth from heel to toe. He wrinkled up his eyebrows like he was thinking heavily about something.

The silence was becoming strained when I felt a presence behind me. I turned . . . and there she was—Virginia Nutter. She stood proud in the morning light, a regal bearing with all the poise, dignity, and authority of the queen mother. I took my hat off.

I had never seen her before but I knew all about her. She was the daughter of old man Preston Nutter, the man who came to the canyon in the 1880s and carved out an empire. She was the son he never had and she inherited the largest privately owned cattle operation in the State of Utah. Her dad had controlled thousands of acres of ground and hundreds and hundreds of cattle. He rode a mule and he didn't allow dogs on his cattle drives—we all knew the stories. Old man Nutter died in the 1930s and this strong woman had kept his empire together. I felt honored to be in her presence. I had wanted to meet this famous woman for a long time.

She looked me square in the face and offered me her hand, proper and ladylike.

"How are you Tom?" she asked quietly.

"Very well . . . thank you," I stammered, taking her hand awkwardly.

"It's good to have you here . . . we can use your help," she said with a generous smile.

I was enraptured.

From that moment on, I would have died for her. I would have fought dragons, faced cannons, walked on water or given my body to the flames. That wonderful, older woman had treated me with true dignity and respect—like a man. She knew my name, she welcomed me to the outfit, and she offered me her hand.

I was charmed to be in her presence. She had a magnetic personality and I couldn't stop looking at her. She seemed to be almost as old as my grandmother. Her gray hair was cut short and she was thin. She was of average height, but the way she stood, with her back straight and her head held high, made her look tall. She was not a pretty woman, but her bearing made her attractive, even handsome. Her eyes shone with a quiet self-confidence that made lesser beings look away, awed to be in her presence.

Like her husband, she too was dressed in khaki. She wore khaki safari shorts that ended at her knees with big pockets on the outside, and she wore a short-sleeved safari shirt with epaulets on the shoulders like a soldier. She wore low-cut women's shoes with long stockings pulled up over her calves.

The Colonel cleared his throat and started to give orders. He was rocking back and forth and he was talking to the dirt in front of us. His fingers were still in his back pockets and his chicken wing elbows flapped for balance as he rocked back and forth. He was telling Joe and Humbert to go to the lower field and clean up some brush and trash along the edge of the fields.

He had barely stopped talking when Virginia quietly reminded him that the fence in the bull pasture needed fixing today so the cows could be moved before the end of the week. The Colonel looked at her and blinked a couple of times and then allowed that the fence in the bull pasture needed fixing

The Split Sky

right away and maybe that would be a good thing to do today. Joe and Humbert moved off to their assigned tasks and Virginia told me to come into the kitchen where we could talk.

We went into the cookhouse, Virginia, the Colonel and I, and we sat at the kitchen table on the hard metal chairs. Virginia got right to the point.

"Tom . . . we've decided to keep you here at the farm for the summer.

"It doesn't pay quite as much, and the work is probably even harder, but the food is better and the bunkhouse is better than any of the line shacks.

"We can give you four dollars a day here on the farm. That's one hundred and twenty five dollars a month, not quite what the cowboys make, but still pretty good.

"If you do us a good job this summer, we'll consider sending you to the cow camp next summer—if you still want to go."

My world came crashing down. My dreams, my hopes, my future—all out the window. I was stunned.

Was it because of the stupid bedroll? Was it because I was too small? Too baby-faced? Too inexperienced? All of those thoughts elbowed their way through my mind.

It didn't really matter . . . it all boiled down to the same thing. If I wanted to work on the ranch I was going to be a hay hand, stuck on the farm with Joe the dragon. The only alternative was, that I could walk. I could call my dad to come and get me and I could go home in defeat and disgrace before I even got started. The decision was mine.

The seconds ticked by as I thought it over.

I could go home and haul hay for Dal Wells again. Or, I could work for any number of hometown farmers this year. Most of them paid more than Virginia had just offered me, but the work might not be as steady. I could even join with some other boys and contract to haul hay for six cents a bale and probably make more money than working for a day-wage at the ranch.

And money wasn't the only issue. I'd been treated badly. My welcome to the outfit had left a lot to be desired. The Colonel had wounded my pride and Joe had scared me badly. If I stayed at the ranch, I had to face the cold wind of knowing that I would be stuck with the two of them for the rest of the summer. I was very apprehensive. I could forgive the Colonel, but I was afraid of Apache Joe.

I was tempted to bag it all and go home.

Virginia sat and looked at my face with hurt in her eyes. I could feel her trying to prompt me to make the right decision, silently urging me to accept her offer. The Colonel sat and looked out the screen door and drummed his fingers on the table, anxious to have this silly business over with so he could go outside and play with his dog.

I couldn't give it up. Working on the ranch had always been a dream of mine and I just couldn't let the dream die. It broke my heart to be demoted from cowboy to hay hand, but I knew that if I went home now they would never hire me back next year, and I might never have another chance to be the cowboy I saw in my dreams.

Pride was another obstacle in the path. I had told my friends and family goodbye and I had told them I would be at the ranch all summer. I just couldn't bring myself to go back without seeing it through. Deep down in the bottom of my heart, in that secret place where no one else can go, I knew that no matter what happened, no matter how bad it got, this was a mountain I had to climb.

I took a deep breath and let it out very slowly. I knew that when I answered, I was committing myself completely. I was laying my body and soul on the altar of my word.

It took a few minutes to gather the courage. I was going to drink the bitter cup of disappointment and accept the humiliation. I also completely understood that I was resigning myself to spending all of my long summer nights in the gloomy, hate-filled den of the dragon.

"Okay," I said, with a voice that choked.

"Good," Virginia said. "Are you ready to start right now?"

"Yes" I said, not trusting myself to say any more.

"Good," she said again, "let's get you lined out."

She took me out to the main road that ran through the ranch and pointed to a long fence line that paralleled the road. She told me that the ironweeds were unsightly and she wanted me to go get a shovel and cut those weeds. I was to cut them, rake them up and throw them into the pasture on the other side of the fence. She asked if I had a watch, and then she told me to come up to the cookhouse at noon for lunch. She then left me there by myself and returned to the big house, passing the Colonel who was playing ball with his dog on the front lawn.

THE WEEDS OF WRATH

I knew how to cut ironweeds; my dad's little farm was full of them. I got the shovel and made a feeble start. I was glad to be left alone for a while. I needed some time by myself. I needed time to think, to mourn, and to sort it all out.

I had told all of my friends and my family that I was going up on the mountain to be a cowboy for the summer. I wondered how they would all take the news when they found out that I was farming again. I could imagine them all giggling and gossiping about how I was too young or too small to be a cowboy—or just not good enough.

For a while I wallowed in self-pity, chipping at the weeds with a detached and half-hearted effort. I was buried deep in my inner thoughts and miseries, and then a car passed on the road, going down the canyon, filled with people I didn't know who waved and smiled politely. An obnoxious little boy squashed his nose against the glass of a back window and stared comically and cross-eyed as the car passed—mocking me!

In panic, I realized for the first time that I was on the main line between Price and Myton. Any of my friends or their families could show up on that dirt track at any minute and see me there, chopping weeds, when I should have been herding cows up on the mountain. Farming instead of cowboying was one thing, but to be stuck out there on the main road chopping weeds was something else again. Farming was a noble profession; chopping weeds was work for a kid and punishment for a grown man.

I faced the reality of my situation like David before Goliath. I had already made the final and irrevocable decision that I would stay at the ranch come hell or high water. I now came to grips with the fact that I had been given the humiliating job of cutting those ironweeds. I knew I would be stuck there by the road until they were all cut if it took me an hour or a week. And so . . . I decided I had better cut them fast so I could get away from the road where people could see me.

I tore into that weed patch with a fury. I began to sweat and the dirt and weeds began to fly. I bent down low so the shovel would be most effective, the blade coming in at a flat angle like a Viking battle-ax, cutting the weeds off at ground level without digging into the dirt, saving time and energy. I settled into a mechanical rhythm, chop-step, chop-step, chop-step.

I threw my full weight into the task and I worked my way up the fence line, killing weeds and working off my frustrations, humiliations and disappointments. I talked to myself under my breath and I let it all out, the hurt, the pain and the embarrassment. I took it all out on those ironweeds.

At noon I walked to the cookhouse for lunch covered with sweat and dirt. Joe had cooked fried potatoes and onions with

Spam and pork and beans. I ate hurriedly, greedily, eager to get back to the weed patch and kill some more of my disgusting, little green antagonists. Joe and Humbert lounged around in the shade for a while after lunch and smoked, but I was on a mission. I gulped down my food and went back to beat up on those ironweeds.

The afternoon was a blur of hot sun and sweat, the metallic clink of the shovel over the stones, clouds of flying weeds and dirt, sweat dripping off the end of my nose, sweat stinging my eyes, sweat soaking my shirt. I battled those little green heathens like a Templar knight, a holy Crusader, a soldier with a sacred cause. I mowed down the enemy host and then I scraped their mangled and disgusting little green bodies into piles and tossed them over the fence and into the pasture like the Boss Lady said.

I kept glancing up the canyon road, dreading the cloud of dust that might herald the approach of a car. My worst fear was that someone I knew would suddenly appear on that dirt road and stop to pass the time of day and ask me what I was doing there in the weed patch. I was not going to let that happen. I had to get the job finished; my reputation and my good name depended on it.

I refused to stop and rest, even for a minute. I pushed my sweating body on and on. Minutes rolled into hours and the hours were endless. Time didn't matter—nothing mattered but finishing that job. And then I came to the end of the fence line and the job was done. My mission had been accomplished.

Something else had happened too. Without realizing what I was doing, I had vented all of my anger, fear and frustrations. I'd been pounding little green weeds but it was the demons in my mind and soul that I was slaying. The ghosts of gnawing apprehension and painful humiliation had been purged. The pressure valve on the boiler of my emotions had been opened. I'd finally been able to strike out, to hit back, to cuss and flail and let it all out. I was cleansed—body and soul. I was also tired and damn glad to get away from the road where people could see me.

I looked back toward the ranch buildings and down the fence line. The ground was as clean and bare as the seashore, not a disgusting little green heathen in sight. I had conquered. I had also won my race with that phantom carload of gawking friends that I imagined to be just around the bend on the canyon road.

I walked back toward the ranch house, picking up rocks, twigs and leaves, anything that obstructed the smoothness of the bare ground. I wanted to leave the battlefield clean and orderly.

I walked back to the cookhouse and got a big drink of water. I looked at my watch; it was about four o'clock. I'd heard someone say that we were supposed to work until five-thirty, and if that was true, I still owed the boss lady an hour and a half.

I walked over to the big house. I couldn't understand why the guys called it the big house unless they were attempting a snide analogy about plantations, slaves and overseers. Virginia's house was quite small actually, not much bigger than the bunkhouse. It was a very modest structure of cinderblock, made just the same as the other buildings. It was made in a style that was in vogue the late 1940s and early 1950s. The Boss Lady didn't seem pretentious at all. Her home and the vehicles she drove were quite utilitarian—at least the ones I saw. The guys told me later that she and the Colonel kept a luxury apartment and a Lincoln Continental in Salt Lake City.

The big house.

I timidly knocked on the back door and Virginia came to the door with a puzzled look on her face.

"Do you have something else for me to do today?" I asked.

"I asked you to cut those weeds along the fence," she said suspiciously.

"I'm done," I said quietly.

"You're done?" she said incredulously.

"Yes ma'am . . . I've finished that job."

She reached back into the room and brought out a large-brimmed hat, the kind girls wear to do garden work, and she followed me to the fence line to inspect my claim that the job was done.

When we stepped out by the road where she could see the fence line she stopped cold. She stood there for a while with a quizzical, disbelieving look on her face, and then she looked over at me. My shirt was still wet and there were streaks of dirt on my face and dust on my hat and shoulders. My hair was still matted and damp. The wooden handle of the shovel I still held in my hands was polished like the shaft of a metal golf club. My soft leather gloves, new that morning, were black with sweat and weed stains.

She turned without saying anything and started back toward the house. I followed, waiting for orders. We walked back to her house and she told me to take the rest of the day off.

"You go sit in the shade someplace for a while," she said. "Joe and Humbert will be along about five-thirty for supper . . . you don't need to do any more today."

I thanked her and she went back into the house.

I walked to the bunkhouse and cut the hay string on my bedroll with my pocketknife. I wouldn't be rolling it up again for a while. The mass of blankets plopped open and covered the small army bed. It looked like I was going to be spending the whole summer right there. I might as well make it a home. I dug through my cardboard box and found a good book. I took my boots off and laid back on the bed, waiting for Joe the dragon to come home and cook me supper.

Chapter 3

Getting Acquainted

Trash Man

Over the next few days I was initiated into the rhythms of life on the ranch. It was up at six to do chores, feed and water the cows and horses and throw wheat for the stupid peacocks. We always had bummer calves to feed. Breakfast was served about a quarter to seven and we were ready for the hay fields by seven-thirty.

Joe and Humbert spent most of their time irrigating and cleaning ditches. I spent most of my first week cleaning up the yard, cutting weeds and patching fences near the corrals. We were to start cutting hay in a week or so. We ate lunch in the cookhouse at noon and went back to the job at one. At five-thirty we quit the fields and came back to the farmyard to do the afternoon chores. We ate supper around six. Joe did all of the cooking.

Today people eat breakfast, lunch and dinner. When I was a kid, we ate breakfast, dinner and supper. Lunch was something you put in a paper bag and took with you when you couldn't be home at noon for dinner.

Joe and I had an uneasy truce. I stayed away from him and he ignored me. I respected his private space and used the back door of the bunkhouse and he left me alone. We hadn't had to work together yet, and so this arrangement was working out for now. Humbert showed up in his truck every morning in time for breakfast and he left to go somewhere else every evening just after supper. I wondered what the deal was, but for now I kept my mouth shut and just watched what was going on.

On my third or fourth day of cleaning up the yard, the Colonel told me that he was going to go with me to haul trash. I had piled up a lot of old wire and tree limbs and hay twine and other odds and ends that needed to be hauled off. It was also time to empty a couple of fifty-five-gallon oil drums that served as burn-barrels for the house trash.

I shoveled the yard trash into the pickup truck and the Colonel drove me to a spot at the very end of the lower fields that served as a private, open-air dump. I shoveled the trash out of the truck while he watched and waited for me. We made two or three trips and then we stopped to get the burn-barrels.

The barrels were spilling over with household trash. They had been burned dozens of times and the contents were condensed down into a thick, black sod of broken glass and stinky goo. It had rained during the week and the condensed trash had soaked up water and the rusty barrels were damp and spilling over with a wet and sticky ooze. The rainwater significantly added weight to the barrels. The Colonel backed the truck up to the barrels and I dropped the tailgate. He got out and stood with his arms folded while I put on my gloves and sized up the situation.

I rocked one of the barrels back and forth to test the weight and search for a place to get a grip. The barrel was impossibly heavy and terribly unwieldy. There is just no good way to pick up a fifty-five-gallon barrel that is filled with wet trash. I tipped the barrel forward until the upper rim rested on the edge of the tailgate. That way, the tailgate would hold some of the weight as I lifted the barrel up. I then knelt down on one knee and put one arm around the lower part of the barrel, like hugging a fat girl while she's sitting down. I put my other hand on the very bottom, where the sharp and muddy edge of the barrel seam sits on the ground.

I braced myself, held my breath and lifted for all I was worth. I struggled, gasping and straining. The barrel was unbelievably heavy and she fought me for every inch. I wrestled with the fat girl and her dead weight threatened to crush me. I fought, groaned and lifted with every fiber in my young body, and the barrel slowly slid up and over the tailgate. The truck finally took the weight, and I staggered back gasping. I stood for a while with my hands on my knees; my head down like an Olympic runner who is about to pass out. I could see little blue spots everywhere and I couldn't draw in enough air to satisfy my surging lungs. My arms were weak and limp and my stomach felt like it was on fire. I had been bucked off a horse just a week before going out to the ranch and I had hit the saddle horn pretty hard. I still had a bruise and a sore spot low on my belly, and that spot was knotted like a charlie horse.

I rested for a while and regained my composure. At long last, my breathing returned to normal and I sized up the other barrel. She sat squat and solid, obstinate, daring me to try, challenging my manhood like her twin sister in the back of the truck had done.

I didn't want to wrestle anymore. I wasn't up to another round. The barrels were out of my weight class and I wanted to throw in the towel. When school had let out just a few days before, I was wrestling at one hundred and thirteen pounds. The wet barrels were probably twice my weight.

I went to the second barrel and tipped it like I had done the first. I put a hand on it, and then hesitated. I was painfully aware that I almost hadn't made it with the first barrel and my confidence was shaken. The muscles in my arms and back felt like they had been over-taxed already and my stomach still burned. I dreaded the effort it was going to take to heft the second sister. I looked over at the Colonel with an anxious and pleading look. He just stood there in his starched and pressed khaki uniform, cool and detached, his arms folded across his chest, patiently waiting for me to load the second barrel.

I squatted down a second time and hugged the smelly fat girl up close. I closed my eyes and shot for the moon. The barrel came off the launch pad and then just hung there in space, balanced against the tailgate. My muscles screamed and the little blue spots came dancing back. Try as I might, I just couldn't do it.

At first my mind overrode my body and I refused to let the barrel down, and then in horror, I realized that I couldn't—too much of me was under it. It just hung there, balanced on my arm, my leg, and the tailgate. My knees were flexed like Atlas when he lifted the weight of the world, but mine were shaking and I was in big trouble. I couldn't go up and I couldn't go down. With wild eyes and a panicked groan of desperation, I savagely appealed to the Colonel and he finally seemed to wake up to the seriousness of my distress. He stepped forward and grabbed the barrel with me, and between the two of us, we somehow managed to get it up and over the tailgate.

I staggered away from the truck and almost went down. With the crushing weight lifted from me I felt like my body was filled with helium and I was just going to float away. My back and my legs throbbed like a toothache and my stomach was on fire. My arms were so stressed they were numb. I couldn't raise my hands above my shoulders. I was looking out at the world with tunnel vision, an inky blackness framed everything and my eyes wouldn't focus. I gulped at the air in great sobbing gasps, trying to restore enough oxygen to remain conscious. My whole system was in such distress that I couldn't remain still; I walked around in a tight little circle, gasping and repeatedly putting my head down low by my knees in an effort to stave off the blackness.

The Colonel was also in distress, but his distress was

different than mine. He had gotten his hands dirty—and his uniform. He stood with his arms held out away from the rest of him like a surgeon on his way to the operating table. He kept looking at the sooty, stinky stains on his hands like he couldn't believe it. He left me there, doubled over and gasping for air, and he walked across the yard to the big house with those hands out in front of him like they belonged to someone else. He tried to open the gate with his elbows.

The Colonel didn't come back to finish our job for quite a while, and when he did he had on a new uniform that was all clean and crisp and regulation. He had scoured his body as well, and he had regained his composure.

I had a hard time respecting the man after that day. He had asked me to do something that was beyond my physical capabilities—and then he stood by and watched as I died on that hill for him.

That next fall, after leaving the ranch, I went back to wrestling practice and had to drop out because of pains in my groin. I was diagnosed with a hernia and underwent surgery to repair the damage. Utah State Industrial Insurance paid the bill and the cost was charged against the Preston Nutter Corporation.

I had wrestled the two fat girls into the back of the truck, but they took me down and pinned me in the end. I had to give up wrestling in High School and it took me almost six months to get completely back on my feet. The doctor told me that with all of the heavy lifting I had done over the summer, I was lucky the hernia hadn't strangulated and killed me.

I've sometimes wondered about the man who stood by with folded arms and watched me break my guts for him. Was he stupid, indifferent, or cruel? The core of his personality must be hidden behind one of those three doors. I only knew him for a short time, but I think we can eliminate door number three. I don't think he was cruel. I do have a hard time choosing between the other two possibilities. I suspect the essence of the man was a blending of the two.

I believe there was a stupidity about him that was born from living a sheltered life. I don't think he had ever carried the burdens of the day, be it a trash barrel or a bayonet, and without that frame of reference he could find no empathy for those who did. I also think he was guilty of a certain indifference toward working people that came from always looking down from a perch among the wealthy and privileged. I think he came from a world where working people were servants and pawns and they weren't supposed to feel pain and emotion in the same way he did.

My philosophizing about the man may well be a puffing engine on the wrong set of tracks, for I know next to nothing about his rearing, background or pedigree. I can only judge him from what I saw and what I experienced. I am confident, however, that when I focus the spotlight of review on his manners, mannerisms, and actions—I've got him in the headlights.

Looking back with the perspective of many years in the saddle, I can see that most of the responsibility for what happened that day rests with me. I should have refused to do the task without some help. But I have an excuse for my actions and my excuse is better than the Colonel's. I was sixteen years old and in the first week of my first real job; and I was a stupid kid—and trusting. I was trying to be a good soldier and do what was asked of me. I think the Colonel demonstrated a calloused indifference toward my welfare, and he took advantage of my youth, my naiveté and my willingness to serve him. I met another Colonel like him a few years later, in Vietnam.

The Road To Understanding

Sometime toward the end of that first week, just after breakfast, Virginia came over to the cookhouse to tell Humbert that she had received a report that there were half-a-dozen cows in the Sand Wash area that might belong to the outfit. Nutter's weren't supposed to have any cows in Sand Wash and she wanted him to go and check it out. I was envious. From some of my older, teen-aged cowboy friends who had worked for the outfit, I knew where Sand Wash was, even though I'd never been there. I knew it was near the confluence of Nine Mile Creek and the Green River, and it was a long way from the farm by rough road.

I was astonished when Virginia turned to me and asked if I wanted to go with him. Did I want to go with him? I would have followed Humbert the whole way walking on my elbows in the gravel—that's how much I wanted to go with him.

"You bet," I squeaked, trying hard not to sound too eager.

"That's good," she said. "We start haying next week and it might be the only chance you get to see some of the ranch before we get real busy."

I must have lit up like a Christmas tree and wiggled like a hugged puppy because she was smiling when she left the cookhouse. Humbert was smiling too. Joe stirred his coffee and remained in a neutral corner. Nothing I did mattered to him.

From the cookhouse, Humbert appropriated a Spartan's lunch. He wrapped up half a loaf of bread, a chunk of sliced baloney, a jar of mayonnaise and a couple of apples. He filled a large canvas water bag from a hose on the lawn and hung it over the mirror of his truck.

"Lets get outta here," he giggled, and we were off.

I was free.

The ranch and all of its grown-up anxieties disappeared behind us. The cool morning air gushed in through the open window of the truck and washed over my face. I sat back and enjoyed the fact that Humbert was driving. I could relax and watch the canyon go by. I could look for Indian writings in the ledges and count deer on the side hills. I was on summer vacation.

We turned up Gate Canyon for a few miles and then took a narrow dirt track that split off to the right and into the badlands toward the river, going to a place I had seen only in my dreams.

A view of the lower canyon.

I was surprised at how barren the country was after we left Gate Canyon. We traveled for miles over a wasteland. There were very few trees and the sage and rabbit brush was short and stunted. It was dry country. On our right hand there were deep gashes in the earth where the high desert plateau dropped off onto Nine Mile Canyon. To our left was a barren, sorry excuse for mountain, a stark, steep, blue-gray wall of shale and clay. To the East, in the direction we were traveling and many miles away, I could make out the course of the Green River. All of the ridges and waterways of this barren country were sinking toward the East, to a great, long channel that I knew was called Desolation Canyon.

We had been traveling in silence for a long time when Humbert began to speak.

"They call this Cowboy Bench," he said.

"Why bench?" I asked.

" It's a flat place between the top of the canyon and another mountain," he explained. "Like steps on the porch . . . that's how the book cliffs are."

"Oh," I said, accepting the simplicity of it.

"This used to be a long trip in a buggy or on horseback," Humbert offered.

"I'll bet it was," I mused, looking out at the dusty ribbon of dirt road that stretched for miles and miles out ahead of us.

We drove on for a few more dusty miles and I slowly gathered the courage to ask him some questions.

"How come Joe's hair's so long?"

Humbert smiled and kept his gaze on the rough road.

"Joe hasn't been to town for over a year," he said finally. "I offered to cut his shaggy curls with a pair of scissors but the old (expletive deleted) wouldn't let me."

"Why hasn't he been to town for over a year?"

"Well . . . Joe drinks . . . and he gets into trouble when he goes to town."

"Oh," I said, beginning to comprehend.

"He used to cut meat for a living . . . and he had a family and everything." Humbert offered. "He's been out on the ranch for a long time."

"Oh," I said again, beginning to understand why Joe the

dragon was such a grumpy old salamander.

It started to make sense to me. The man was in exile. The ranch was a prison, a place for the dragon to hide, a place away from people and demon rum.

We traveled on for a while, thinking about Joe, and then I asked Humbert about himself.

"Do you go to town every night?" I asked

"Oh no," he giggled. "I've got my own place up the canyon . . . up in Argyle. I live at my own place and just work for Virginia. Sometimes I stay over at the ranch when we work late or have a lot going on."

"Is this your truck?"

"Yep . . . it's my truck. I use it and they make it up to me."

"Is the Colonel the boss or is Virginia the boss?" I asked.

Humbert laughed out loud.

"Well . . . " he said, " it does get sort of confusing sometimes, doesn't it? You just do what Virginia tells you and you'll do fine."

"Okay," I answered, grinning, "I'll remember that."

"I was supposed to go to the cow camp," I said, hoping for sympathy and a friend to confide in.

"I know," Humbert said quietly, "but you're better off at the farm." He said it with a strong tone of adult conviction, like my dad would have said it.

"Why?" I asked, feeling that he had turned on me; not sympathizing like I had expected.

"Eldon's up there again this year," Humbert said, "and he'd be a real (strong expletive deleted) to work for, especially for a young guy like you."

"He couldn't be worse than Joe?" I insisted.

Humbert gave me a long look, even though he was driving, and then he said, "Don't be too damn sure."

We drove on in silence for a while and I began to feel sorry for myself again. I wanted to be a cowboy more than anything in the world. I wanted to see the line shack at Sand Wash with a packhorse and camp outfit, not as a tourist on my way back to a damn hay field. I knew I could be a good cowboy too; I had all the right stuff, even a genetic predisposition.

A Cowgirl Named Goldie

My Grandmother was a cowgirl. Her name was Goldia Celestia Bromley. She was born in Arizona in 1897 and immigrated to Utah as a child. The family called her Goldie. Her father was a horse trader.

Grandma grew up on a horse. As a young girl she was an important part of her father's horse-trading business. She rode the new ones to see what they had and what they would do. If a new horse would buck, it was Goldie who found out. If a new horse could run, it was Goldie who raced it. If a new horse had a tendency to kick, bite, or strike, it was Goldie's job to find out.

Goldie's father often used his young daughter to good advantage when selling horses. He would have her ride a horse before and during a sale to impress the prospective buyers. Everyone knew that if a little girl could ride that horse, any man should be able to do so. She helped her father sell a lot of horses.

Goldie was married when she was fifteen, and she had six children before she was twenty-six. My father was her fifth child and her third son. Dad saw her ride only once, when he was about six years old, and it impressed him so much that he has told the story all of his adult life.

The year was 1927. Grandma Goldie's sister Lizzy was married to J.P. Christensen, and they owned a ranch in Argyle Canyon, a tributary of Nine Mile. My father and his family were visiting aunt Lizzy and Uncle Julius on the ranch, and Vernal Bromley, a younger brother to the two women, was there with a couple of young horses. He had a matched pair of colts from the same dam and only a year apart in age. He was riding one and leading the other. They were good-looking, sorrel (red) horses with similar markings and conformation. The family had gathered to admire the animals when the conversation turned to which of the two might be the best runner. Uncle Vernal opted that the one he was riding was the fastest, but Goldie offered to bet him that the other horse, the one he was leading was best. They argued, and she offered to race with him. He agreed.

Grandma was thirty years old and the mother of six. She hadn't been on a horse for years. Dad says she hitched up her skirts and swung up on the young sorrel bareback. She and Uncle Vernal rode the pair down the road about half-a-mile and then lined up to race back to the ranch house.

I can see my young and pretty Grandma in that race through my father's eyes. I have seen her many times from the way he tells the story. I can see her flying back to the ranch in a cloud of dust, riding without a saddle, leaning forward over the horse's neck and urging the animal to run faster. Her bare legs are wrapped tightly around the horse, showing pale beneath her billowing skirts. Her yellow hair is flying and her eyes shining. She is laughing, young, small and graceful, and is having a wonderful time. She beat Uncle Vernal by a length.

Dad said she surprised everyone when the race was over by telling Vernal that she actually thought the horse he was riding was the fastest, and if he wanted to race again she would show him. Vernal went for it. After all, he was going to be riding the winner of the first race, and in his mind, the contest had already been decided.

They changed horses. Vernal put his saddle on Goldie's mount and she again hitched her skirts and swung up on the one he'd been riding. They went back to the starting place and she beat him again, on the other horse. She squealed with delight and laughed and laughed and laughed. Vernal was humiliated by having his sister beat him twice on two different horses. She teased him for a while and then shared the secret with him.

"Look at you," she said. "You weigh almost two hundred pounds and you're using a fifty pound stock saddle. I don't weigh a hundred and ten pounds soaking wet and I'm not using a saddle at all. I can beat you every time, no matter what you're riding."

Grandma was a real cowgirl, and her love for horses was passed on to her sons.

Cowboys Close To Home

My dad and my uncles always had horses. One of the first memories I have of my father was when we were riding his horse. I remember he had me on the saddle in front of him, holding me tight. My stubby little legs were up and over the shoulders of the saddle and the saddle horn was almost as tall as I was. Dad was a cowboy, and he was a good-looking cowboy too. He always wore a nice western hat and drove a pickup truck, and we always had a couple of saddle horses in the corral.

Dad judged horses professionally for a few years. He traveled all over the state judging at stock shows, fairs and rodeos. Dad and my uncles were members of riding clubs and we spent many weekends as a family following horse events around the state.

I learned to ride young and I got pretty good at it. In 1960 dad was invited to participate in a centennial reenactment of the Pony Express. Various riding clubs from around the country were to carry a satchel of mail from St. Joseph Missouri to Sacramento California by horseback, using the exact trail that was used in 1860. The section of the route that our local boys drew was one of the most desolate—a stretch of desert on the Utah, Nevada border. Since he was working long hours for the sheriff's office, dad gave me the job of preparing his horse for the event.

My job was to exercise the horse and toughen him up. Like most jobs when you're a kid, I quickly became bored with the repetition of the task, and being thirteen and as lazy as a bird dog on the porch, I started to take the horse out without a saddle. It was easier that way, and faster too. There were no buckles and cinches or straps to mess with, and riding the horse bareback on those long four and five mile gallops out over the countryside was the sort of thing a kid could really enjoy.

That young horse and I both got toughened up that summer. I would leave the house early while it was still cool, and we would go for miles at a high lope. We went out through the clay hills south of Wellington and across the Miller Creek flats. I learned to ride by balance, not touching the horse with my hands, using my knees to guide the horse like an Indian. I practiced riding hard while holding my free hand away from the horse like a rodeo rider, sometimes with my hat in my hand to discourage any inclination to grab a handful of mane. I ran him. We jumped ditches and made big figure eights in the sagebrush and chased jackrabbits. I learned to ride well that summer, and like my Grandma, I didn't weigh a hundred pounds soaking wet and I could jump on and off that horse with the dexterity of a squirrel.

I loved to hunt arrowheads, and there was an expanse of cedar ridges a few miles Northeast of Wellington where I found some good ones. In the years before I had a driver's license, I would sometimes ride my horse out there and spend the day alone, wandering around in the junipers, looking for old Indian campsites. It was great fun, and for a thirteen or fourteen-year-old boy, it was like exploring with Lewis and Clark. There was new and unexplored country over every ridge.

I had friends who owned horses, and we sometimes went riding together. I admired guys who could ride well like Jesse Rich and Michael Riley, but the ones I admired most were the big boys, the older brothers of some of my friends, the seventeen and eighteen year old young bucks who had driver's licenses and who worked on real ranches during summer vacation. I couldn't wait to be big enough to do what they did.

My young buck heroes were Leon Rich, Arnold Adair, George Cook, and Smokey Clark, and others like them, including Dave Cave and Leon Curtis. Those handsome cowboys would come back to school in the fall with suntans and fancy new clothes and pockets full of money, and they would tell stories of weeks and months spent at cow camps on the mountain, ridin' and ropin' and exploring timbered canyons on horseback.

They rode in the local rodeos: bareback horses, sadddle-broncs and bulls. They dressed like peacocks in fancy western shirts and expensive felt hats that tilted just a little cocky to one side. They wore silver belt buckles, some inlaid with turquoise and some sporting real silver dollars as centerpieces. This group of cowboy cavaliers was from three to five years older than I was and I always strained hard to catch up. I wanted to be just like them. They were my heroes.

In the summer of 1960, when I was thirteen, Leon Rich and Arnold Adair were working in Nine Mile on a ranch owned by Dan Hays. David Rich, Leon's little brother and I, were the same age and we spent a lot of time together. I don't remember just how it all came about, but somehow we decided we were going to ride out to the ranch and spend a few days with the cowboys.

The Hay's ranch was near the mouth of Currant Canyon, just above Nutter's, and it was just a cat's whisker less than forty miles from Wellington, a good days journey for Custer's Seventh Cavalry when they were traveling light. The old horse-drawn freight wagons that used the same trail at the turn of the century used two full days to make the same distance. None of that bothered us. Practical matters like distance and logistics were grownup concerns; we were kids stuck in a daydream of romance and adventure. We were planning a fun-filled weekend and not an expedition. David borrowed a horse from his Uncle Art Rich, and we picked up his cousin Jesse in the bargain. Jesse was only eleven, but he was a good horseman.

We saddled up early in the morning and tied our sleeping bags and canteens on the saddles. Our mothers fixed us up with tuna sandwiches and Twinkies and we were off on a great adventure.

We started out, as kids will, overeager and anxious to put the miles behind us. It was cool and we felt great and we trotted and even loped the horses for short distances along the road. After a few miles, we got bored and started to leave the trail to chase jackrabbits and ride the horses along the bottom of Soldier Creek in the water. We took the horses four-wheelin' up sandy slopes and steep wash banks, making the poor animals work much harder than the journey required. We ate our lunch too soon and we emptied our canteens long before we were thirsty. We flipped branches and threw pinecones at each other and we laughed and clowned around and had a wonderful time.

We were on good horses and they covered the miles in spite of us. We reached the top of Whitmore in the early afternoon, out of water and out of lunch, the sun boring down on us mercilessly. We had been in the saddle for twenty miles now and we were growing tired. The journey was finally becoming a serious trek. We were hot and the saddles were beginning to chafe and we realized that we were only halfway to our destination. By now we were spending more time riding along quietly, and we ignored the rabbits and squirrels that sprinted across our path and challenged us to race. The horses had long since settled into the routine and they were walking strong; the fence posts clicking past at a good rate.

By the time we reached Minnie Maud Canyon we were scalding in the sun and we were very tired and dying of thirst. We joked about it. We sang all the words we knew of the song *Cool Water*, made famous by the Son's of the Pioneers. We teased each other that buzzards were circling overhead and following us, watching and waiting to pick at our sun-bleached bones. We tormented each other with tales of cold soda pop, frozen Popsicles and ice cream bars. We dreamed of ice cubes and snowballs and running through the sprinklers on the lawn. David even waxed poetic, suggesting that he was drier than a popcorn fart, and our squeals of laughter echoed from the canyon walls where the buzzards lurked and waited for us to die.

There was water all along this stretch of canyon, but we knew we were not supposed to drink from the creek or from the irrigation ditches. We watched as the horses drank in great gulps and then playfully snorted and blew bubbles in the ditch water. Watching the horses drink and splash in the water was torture. We knew there was a good spring near the road at the mouth of Sulphur Canyon, and we hurried along to get there.

We imagined ourselves to be Errol Flynn and the French Foreign Legion, Beau Geste and Gunga Dihn, comrades-in-arms crossing the desert sands, dying for water. We practiced sliding down the side of the saddle, almost falling off but never quite doing so, mimicking the thirsty pioneers we had seen in the John Wayne movies. We even made bets that old John Wayne would show up at any minute, come to save the day by leading us to the next water hole, and we hollered at him to get his attention, listening as the echo danced through the ledges. When John Wayne didn't show up to save us, we lay over the front of the saddles, arms drooping over the horse's neck and moaning, "water . . . water," with our eyeballs rolled back in our heads and our mouths open and our tongues hanging out. And then we would giggle and poke the horses to make them hurry along. The spring was still a mile or two away.

The spring came from a pipe, and the water was cold, clean and delicious. We drank our fill and then filled our straw hats with mossy water from the stock trough and had a water fight. We were conscientious little Boy Scouts, and we did have the good sense to refill our depleted canteens before starting out across the Sahara again.

It was late afternoon by the time we got to the mouth of Argyle Canyon. We were getting seriously tired now and the daydreaming, role-playing and clowning had stopped. The journey was getting to be a serious endeavor. Our little bums were saddle sore. It would be dark before too long, and we still had a few miles to go. We were very tired now, and we were starving.

There was an apple orchard in the canyon near an abandoned farmhouse and not far from our destination. We couldn't wait to get there. Our daydreams were filled with visions of apple pie, and big, red, delicious apples, cold to the touch and dripping with sugary juice. We could visualize the crunchy morsels languishing on shady branches, waiting patiently for us to pick them and gobble them all up. We were sure we could smell the apples from two or three miles away.

When we finally got to the orchard, our growling little tummies were bitterly disappointed. There were apples there all right, but they were small and greenish and wormy. They were tough-skinned little Jonathans, and they hid from us in a tangled jungle of untrimmed branches. The orchard was reverting back to mother nature; there was no man to prune and tend it and the apples were digressing and becoming as wild as the canyon. The few we managed to pick were as bitter as vinegar and as hard to chew as gourds.

We discovered a stash of rock salt near the orchard, and we had rock salt and green apples for lunch. It was awful. We chewed with the sound of a gravel crusher, puckering up like we were sucking lemons. I'm not sure if the rock salt added to, or detracted from, our green apple repast. We managed to cheat the worms out of only a few of Mother Eve's tempting morsels before we started out again.

It was getting very late now, the sun was going down and we were exhausted. We were becoming anxious that we might be caught in the canyon after dark. We spurred our tired horses to even greater efforts and we made one more long turn in the canyon road and found ourselves at the ranch. The Hay's place was just half-a-mile from where we had stopped to have our last meal of green apples and rock salt before perishing in the wilderness, and none of us had realized it.

We had been riding all day and had seen only a couple of cars, even though we were following the main road through the canyon. But just when we were approaching the gate to the ranch, a beat-up old pickup truck pulled up behind us. It was Art Rich, Jesse's dad. He had come to check on us. Art was a good man, and besides, he had a young son and two good horses in this contest. He was looking after his interests. He followed us into the yard of the ranch with his headlights on— we were there at last.

Dan Hayes and Leon and Arnold came out to greet us and we put our tired horses in the corral, pulled the saddles, rubbed them down and fed them baled hay and oats. They were happy. We then went into the ranch house and old Dan Hays treated us to fried potatoes with pork and beans, store-bought Wonderbread and whole milk. We ate like a litter of pups, growling and grinning and wolfing it all down. We were starved.

Art Rich went back to town after supper, satisfied that we were in good hands. We boys rolled our sleeping bags out on the floor of the ranch house and went to sleep early. It had been a long and adventurous day. General Custer would have been proud of the miles we had covered.

TRACKING GERONIMO

The next morning we were up very early. We took care of our horses and Dan Hays fixed us breakfast. The cowboys were going up on the mountain with packhorses to deliver salt and we were going to tag along. We saddled our mounts and watched, fascinated, while the pack frames and panniers were loaded on the packhorses and buckled down. And then we were off, our horses pointed uphill to the mountain.

We left the ranch house and rode into the mouth of a small, unnamed little side canyon, and there we picked up a faint trail that started up the ridge. It was little more than a game trail, a secret path known only to deer and cowboys and homesick old cows.

We were hardly away from the ranch house when Leon pulled up his horse and pointed to a beautiful Indian granary tucked back into the shelter of an overhanging ledge. The mudded walls looked like they had been made last week, and long cedar poles stuck out from the perfectly preserved willow and clay roof. It looked like a huge swallow nest, or a great clay beehive. It had clung tenaciously to that ledge for hundreds of years and was so sheltered from the elements that it had been perfectly preserved—a masterpiece of Fremont Indian architecture. Excitedly, I ask Leon if he had ever been in it. He smiled and said that he had, but he found nothing in it but prickly pear and a packrat nest.

We followed the trail up along the ridge. In places it became very narrow, almost dangerous, squeezed between the canyon wall and a steep side hill that dropped off for a hundred feet or more. We younger boys stayed behind, keeping away from the pack animals that the old hands were leading. The old hands were seventeen-year-old cowboys, as good as any from the 1880s. They were lean and tough and they knew what they were doing.

This was real cowboy stuff and I was excited. I rode along the steep canyon trail, tall in the saddle, admiring my shadow. I looked older in my shadow—a real cowboy and not a kid. I noticed that my stained and beat-up old cowboy hat looked new in the shadow, and I pretended that it was new. Everything was new: the smell of the pines, the secrets of the trail, being on the mountain with real cowboys, even the freedom to be there. I was experiencing the first blush of the apprehensive independence of early adolescence—the timid, first-testing of my wings.

My spurs jingled like Gene Autry's, and the horse's shoes clicked on the rocks in the trail. I watched my two teenage cowboy heroes and I followed their every move. I watched as they bent low over their saddles to duck branches. I watched as they picked their way through the boulders and the pines with the packhorses on long tethers. I followed reverently; doing everything just the way they did it, mimicking, learning, and studying to be a cowboy. I wanted to sing like a bird. The experience was like something out of the western movies and it was easy for me to wallow in the romance of it all. I pretended we were the U.S. Cavalry, out on patrol, searching for Geronimo and crossing the unexplored Sierra Madre's.

We topped out on the plateau, a large, flat area covered

with sage and grass. The area was sprinkled with pinion and juniper trees. Metal water troughs for livestock squatted low in the sagebrush while an antique windmill towered precariously overhead. The windmill squeaked a painful lament and sucked up a pitiful drizzle of water that dampened the bottom of the troughs. I was surprised to see a good dirt road near the windmill, and Leon explained that yes, we could have driven a pickup there if we really wanted to. Darn—so much for the unexplored Sierra Madres. Oh well, it was still an exciting adventure for a band of little boys.

The cowboys told us they had found some good arrowheads in the flats near the windmill, and so we younger boys opted to spend the day right there and try our luck. We were tired of riding. Our little bums were still saddle-sore from our forced march of the day before and hunting arrowheads sounded like a lot of fun. And so, while the cowboys rode off to deliver the salt, we who were tourists tied up our horses and spent the day trekking over the flats on foot, searching for arrowheads. It was good to walk for a few hours and work the kinks out of our blistered little backsides.

Old Geronimo had been there, all right. We found Injun sign all over the place. The flats were sprinkled with flint chips and we found a couple of pretty good arrow points and a handful of broken fragments. In our romantic little minds, there was only one way those arrow points could have gotten there—years ago the Indians must have fought a great battle there in those flats. I could imagine scores of painted savages coming at each other with tomahawks and spears, shooting arrows and leaping over the bushes and screeching outlandish war whoops. I just knew that the little white arrow point I held in my hand had embedded itself in some brave warrior's thigh and he had stoically pulled the shaft free and tossed it aside before rejoining the fight. I had seen the same thing happen in a cowboy movie and I couldn't think of a better reason for that little arrowhead to be lying there in the dirt. I turned the point over and over in the sunlight, searching for a telltale stain of blood, and I was disappointed when I couldn't find one.

The cowboys came back and picked us up again that afternoon, and we followed the same trail off the mountain and back to the ranch.

The third day we saddled up and left the ranch early on our trek back to town. We were older and wiser horse-travelers now, and we let the jackrabbits and squirrels run away unchallenged. We saved our strength, our horses and the tender hide on our saddle-sore little behinders. The horses knew they were heading for home and they stepped out smartly, chewing up the miles, one step at a time.

We didn't have a lunch this time, and fearing we might perish before our journey was done, we stopped at the apple orchard and filled a grain sack with emergency rations. We were just kids, and the bitter, sour apple experience of just a day before was already forgotten.

We mixed the green apples with large chunks of rock salt and I tied the sack on the back of my saddle. Dan Hays had fed us a good breakfast and so we weren't desperate enough to eat too many wormy morsels yet. We felt we were being good Boy Scouts by being prepared, and besides, if we didn't eat the apples, we could always throw them at each other.

We were eager to get home and so were our horses. So we trotted and even loped the nags for short stretches up the canyon. The apple sack was bouncing up and down on the back of my saddle, churning the wormy apples and rock salt into applesauce. The salty juice soaked through the bag and ran down the sides of my horse, the sour and salty juice foaming like soap. I didn't notice this until some time later when the bees and wasps started circling like sharks. I jettisoned the wet and sticky sack into the wash, but the bees followed me home anyway. I was lucky I wasn't stung. Dad had the sweetest smelling saddle at the rodeo grounds for the rest of the summer.

We hadn't gone very far up the canyon when Art Rich and his brother David Rich Sr. showed up in Dave's big Buick to follow us home. They took our sleeping bags and saddlebags and put them in the trunk of the car to lighten our load. They brought us cold soda pop from town and a lunch, candy, and encouragement. They orbited around us the whole trip. They would stay with us for a while and then stop to visit people they knew in the canyon and then catch up to us again. They seemed to enjoy the outing, and I thought they seemed to be just a little proud of our accomplishment. They were both old cowboys with a history in Nine Mile and they told some good stories about their exploits when they were kids.

Art Rich turned out to be one of my cowboy heroes too. I always knew he was a real cowboy, even though he made a living working in a coal mine like most of the men in our little town. He became my hero in 1965 when his son Jesse first started riding in the rodeos (the same Jesse who was on the Nine Mile trek with us). In '65, Jesse was sixteen and had signed up to ride a bareback horse in the Wellington rodeo. Jesse was thrown off, got the wind knocked out of him and his mouth full of dirt. Art met him behind the chutes and started to tell him what he had done wrong and how to do it better next time. Jesse was still hurting, embarrassed, impatient, and a rude little teen-aged brat (he got over it in later years) and he told his dad to leave him alone. He said, "Let's see you do it if you know so damn much."

Art was forty-five years old that summer, an old gummer by rodeo cowboy standards, but he was small and wiry, thin as a snake and tough as a truck tire. Art went right up to the announcer's stand and signed up.

The way I remember it, Art won the saddlebronc event, took third in the bareback (he had never ridden a bareback horse in a rodeo before), and he spurred both his boots off riding a bull. He would have won the bull riding too but they disqualified him for fanning the beast with his hat (the rules say you can't touch the animal with your free hand).

I've never heard the hometown crowd cheer like they did that night as old man Art Rich, smiling shyly and waving at the crowd, walked across that arena in his stocking feet to gather up his boots. Art walked on water after that, as far as I was concerned.

The trip home from Nine Mile was the same, almost forty miles in length, and we were tired and sore little cowboys when we finally got back to Wellington that evening.

We had other adventures on the horses in those days before we had driver's licenses, but we never did the Nine Mile Marathon again. Once was enough. I have infinite respect and empathy for those iron-bottomed Cavalry soldiers who really chased Geronimo into the Sierra Madres and who spent weeks and months in the saddle. I'm sure they had times when they felt the way I did some years later. Riding home from a long horse-excursion into the San Rafael Swell, I told a friend of mine, "It's no wonder I'm so thirsty, all the water in my body has gone to the blister on my butt."

SAND WASH HOTEL

Humbert and I followed the dusty road out on top of a long ridge and we could finally see the Green River. It was a muddy tan color. The Green River may be green in Wyoming, but in Utah it's the color of dirt.

The cows were in Sand Wash like Virginia said they would be, and Humbert stopped the truck and studied them for a while with a beat-up old pair of Navy field glasses. He pronounced that they belonged to someone else. He explained to me that the Nutter outfit branded with a pair of circles, one circle on the hip and one circle on the shoulder, on the same side of the cow. The brand was called the double ought, or simply the circle brand. The outfit branded their horses and some of their tack with a "63" brand—1863 being the year that old man Nutter came west to seek his fortune.

We continued our journey, and the road dropped off a steep little dugway into the bottom of Nine Mile Canyon, right near the confluence of the Green River and Nine Mile Creek. Old man Nutter had a cabin and a farm there in the olden days but the place was in ruins now. It had been abandoned many years before and we didn't go over to see it. We found an open gate in the drift fence and Humbert made a big circle near it, inspecting the ground for any tracks of cows that might have passed through. He didn't find any.

Humbert explained that the road crossed Nine Mile Creek and then went up the other side of the canyon to what was known as Horse Bench. On top of Horse Bench, it turned back toward the west, and by following this same road, it was possible to make a complete circle and return to the ranch without backtracking. And . . . if a person really wanted to, he could follow the Horse Bench road up and over Patmos Ridge, and drop down into the town of Sunnyside.

I was excited about making the circle and exploring the country on the other side of the canyon, but Humbert decided that we should backtrack and return by the same trail we had come in on. He was afraid the road ahead might be washed out, or there might be a rock in the road or something. I was bitterly disappointed. My timid tour guide was depriving me of half the trip and there was nothing I could do about it. He was my boss today and we were in his truck and my vote didn't count.

We backtracked up the little dugway and Humbert turned off on a sidetrack that took us to the Sand Wash Cow Camp. Sand Wash was not owned by the Nutter outfit and I think Humbert was just killing time and being a little nosy when we stopped in to check it out.

It was not what I had seen in my daydreams. There was an ancient and dilapidated old log cabin and the remains of a cottonwood pole corral. A trash pile of rusting tin cans and broken glass and ashes was just a few steps from the cabin door. There were no trees or grass or running water, just a good view of the Green River as it floated slowly past, gathering the courage to enter Desolation Canyon.

There were a few cottonwood trees standing along the river channel, gnarled and bent, bravely showing a little green in contrast to the dull brown and tan colors of the rocks and sand. It was a stark and depressing place. I began to understand why John Wesley Powell had named it Desolation.

The cabin squatted close to the river. There was sage and greasewood in the dooryard and the only other vegetation was the willow and tamarisk that crowded together and formed a thin strip of jungle along the riverbank. Sand Wash was aptly named. It was devoid of grass and trees and other vegetation. Its headwaters were somewhere in the blue-gray shale and clay of the Cowboy Bench, and any water it might have collected had sunk into the sand long before reaching the river. It was a habitat for lizards, snakes and starving coyotes. The cows we had seen were poor and wasted.

The log house contained a homemade, rough-cut-board table and an improvised plywood cupboard that sported a few bent-up pots and pans. Packrat poop and spider webs were everywhere. There were holes in the ceiling and big gaps in the log walls. It was obvious that the place would never turn a winter wind or even slow down a determined rain. Everything was covered with a thick blanket of gray dust and it didn't look like anyone had used the place for a long, long time.

Humbert went to the plywood cupboard and looked inside. He brooded and cussed a little, quietly, and to himself. He then told me that there was an old tradition among the cowboys. They always tried to leave a little food in their line shacks as a measure of hospitality, just in case someone wandered in who was in real need, like lost, stranded, or broke-down or something. He shook his head sadly and said that nowadays young people are real (strong expletives deleted) and they wouldn't allow the old traditions to continue.

"We can't even leave a sack of beans in one of these camps anymore without some panty-waisted juvenile delinquent from town stealing it or shooting holes in it. They even shoot and smash-up our washtubs and pans . . . people just aren't the same anymore."

He started to go on and on about the deficiencies of young people and how they didn't appreciate things the way his generation did. "By damn, if we ever get in another depression, that'll teach those (expletives deleted), lazy little (expletives deleted again) a thing or two. Maybe if they went hungry for a week or two they'd appreciate a sack of beans somebody left to help them out."

I fidgeted anxiously, taking the lecture very seriously, not sure if I was being included as one of those young juvenile delinquents, prone to destroying, and guilty of ingratitude—or if he was considering me to be one of the good guys and on his side. Unsure of where I stood in the eyes of my lay-preacher tour guide, I sneaked back outside at the first opportunity.

I was glad to have escaped the sermon about the sins of my generation, and I went over to investigate a rock I had seen when we pulled up in the truck. There was a smooth, flat piece of sandstone, about an inch thick and a couple of feet across, propped up against the side of the cabin that faced the road. There was a message engraved on it with a nail or some other crude instrument.

The message said:

> *Sand wash hotel and cafe*
> *If you stay you must pay*

The message made me smile. I could imagine some young and mischievous cowboy, bored out of his ever-loving mind by the isolation and stark surroundings of the place, laboring for an hour or more to scratch his little joke into the stone.

We lingered at the cabin for a while. Humbert acted like he didn't want to leave. He had a wistful, faraway look about him, a man remembering another time.

We walked over by the river, leaving boot tracks in the sandy beach, the only people tracks for miles and miles, and we drank in the smell of the wild and muddy water as the big river rolled past. Being a kid, I dutifully tossed a couple of sticks into the water and watched them float away, unmanned little boats going down Desolation Canyon to meet the mighty Colorado, Glen Canyon, and finally the rising waters of Lake Powell. The gates of the Glen Canyon Dam had been closed just a few months before, and already the lake was fifty miles long and rising at the rate of one to two feet each day.

Finally, we took the road back toward the ranch, heading into the afternoon sun, back toward Joe the dragon and the acres and acres of hay fields that were waiting to be harvested. Back to the bunkhouse and the lessons of the farm.

My summer vacation at the Sand Wash Hotel was over.

Chapter 4

The Job

Wire And Water

It was time to start putting up hay.

The Nutter Ranch ran a very extensive haying operation in the canyon near the ranch headquarters. The steep canyon walls confined the farm to a narrow strip of fertile land where the fields followed the twisting contours of the creek and the canyon. I don't know how many acres were under cultivation, but I know it was a lot. The fields stretched for four miles down the canyon. There were fields large and small and thin and wide. They were irregular in shape and contour, bending and twisting, hugging the canyon walls on one side and dropping off into the creek on the other.

A series of barbed wire fences, prickly steel barriers, marked the lines between the civilized fields and the wilderness of the natural canyon. The fences were supposed to be a means to control the movement of cattle, and they did a good job, but like most fences, they were also territorial boundaries. Men, like Coyotes, mark their territory. Coyotes put up *No Trespassing* signs by cocking a leg on a bush, men by stringing wire. A fence tells the whole world that a piece of ground is owned, controlled and dominated by someone. When a Coyote passes a scent marking on a bush, he knows he's in someone else's territory. A man has the same feeling when he climbs over the wire.

A man can usually tell if a fence was constructed to keep

cattle in, or trespassers out, by noting which side of the post the wire is stapled to. The wire is always put on the side where resistance is expected so when something pushes on the wire, the fence post will act as reinforcement. An old cow leaning on a fence can pop the staples if she can push at wire on the backside of the posts. She can then escape the confines of the fence by squeezing through the sagging strands. Cowhide is tough, and some old cows will work a fence for hours, looking for a weak spot, pushing against the wire and ignoring the sharp pokes of the barbs.

In the canyon, the fence posts stood in long lines like riot police enforcing the boundary line. Each post stood in its assigned place, guarding a ten or twelve foot expanse of territory. Each individual post was a marker, a monument to the will of a man. The posts had been strong young trees, severed from root and limb and planted in long, unnaturally straight lines to serve a new destiny; the scars of the woodsman's ax a cruel reminder of the taming. They were bleached from years in the sun and they faithfully held their ground through all weather and through the darkest of nights. Some embraced the calling and stood straight and proud in the wire harness. Others slouched, leaning at odd angles as if yearning, even reaching to be wild again.

The fields claimed the canyon bottom anyplace the ground was flat and could be cleared of brush and boulders. They were good fields, fertile and productive. Men from another generation had grubbed the brush and leveled the fields and cleared the briars and stones. The fields were clean and healthy, sculptured with irrigation furrows and well-maintained ditches and fences. The whole farm had a look of vitality and orderliness. It was a working farm that supported a working ranch.

In the rough spots between the fields, in the rocky and steep places, or where natural gullies from the side canyons precluded any chance of agriculture, the canyon reverted back to its natural state. In those wild places there were large boulders and gravelly alluvial fans from thousands of years of erosion down the canyon walls. The unconquered and uncivilized places were thick with greasewood, sage and thorn bushes.

The creek, or crick as it was called in the Utah pioneer vernacular, was the lifeline of the canyon. It was a vein, an artery of life-giving water that ran through the parched wilderness near John Wesley Powell's Desolation. The water created an oasis in the high desert. It was a long, green brushstroke on a canvas of brown and gray—a magnet to wildlife, farmers and ranchers. For centuries, Native American farmers had tapped its green water to raise corn, beans and squash, and since the mid-eighteen hundreds, farmers with European faces had raised grain and hay along its banks. The crick was not big but it was dependable, and it supported a large amount of agriculture.

As the stream made its way toward the Green River, each farmer it passed diverted a percentage of the flow over his fields. The canyon generously made up the loss by bringing in more water from the side canyons and from springs in the canyon bottom. Water was diverted and replaced and diverted and replaced numerous times, and in spite of the heavy irrigation, there was always water in the creek to join hands with the Green River.

Nine Mile Creek is not a typical high mountain stream like those seen on Western calendars and travel guides. It does not attract recreationists and sportsmen. There are no rapids to run and no fish to catch. It's a farmer's stream, more like a big ditch than a wild river. It flows quietly and unpretentiously, slowly twisting and turning in its deep channel. The banks are thick with willow, tamarisk and cottonwood. The water has a pale green cast to it, caused, I suspect, by the tint of the shale, limestone and clays that line the creek bed.

In pioneer days the canyon was badly overgrazed and the water eroded and cut down into the thick, gray dirt of the canyon bottom. In many places there were cut-banks exposed that were ten and twelve feet high, sometimes even higher. These vertical walls of dirt were continually caving into the channel and diverting the stream before being washed away. The channel was always changing. A small tribe of beavers tried to help by cutting down the willow and cottonwood and making dams to hold back the silt and erosion. Their efforts were commendable, but the high desert canyon had too few trees to help them make good, strong dams and their efforts are generally ineffective. Shallow, willow-woven beaver dams were quickly filled with silt and the stream found a new course around the obstruction.

In a land of little rainfall the only way for farmers to raise a crop is by bringing water to the fields. In the canyon, there were miles and miles of irrigation ditches that followed the contours of the fields and the canyon itself. Pioneer farmer-engineers dug most of them by hand or with the aid of horse-drawn equipment. Some were dynamited through the rocks and the high spots and diverted through flumes and culverts across the gullies and the low spots. They were constantly filling with silt and debris and they took a good deal of tending. Every spring for a hundred years the ditches had been cleaned by pulling a "V" shaped metal plow through the ditch with a horse or a tractor.

The beavers loved the ditches because they were small and easier to dam than the main creek. I spent more than one full day on the farm walking miles of ditch with a pitchfork, cleaning out the beaver dams. The dams not only inhibited the free flow of water to the fields, but they caused the ditches to spill over their banks and flood the fields, roads and stack yards. Sometimes the flow of uncontrolled water would cut nasty channels down the slopes below the ditches, creating the need for lengthy and costly ditch repairs. The beavers were trapped, shot and even poisoned when they became too much of a nuisance to the farm. This was done with the blessing of the Utah Fish and Game Department. No one bothered the beavers if they stayed in the creek and behaved themselves.

The Mechanics Of Making Hay

There was only one crop raised on the Nutter Farm and that was alfalfa hay. There were acres and acres and miles and miles and tons and tons of it. It was cut, raked, baled and stacked to feed cows and horses during the long winter months. At regular intervals, usually near each large field, there was a fenced and gated stack yard where the hay was stored. These stack yards were enclosed by high, deer-proof fences made from net wire and pine poles, sometimes with vertical slabs of pine laced to the outside with wire to help support the fence and discourage wildlife or cows from trying to reach through.

Some of the haystacks were huge, containing more than a hundred tons of hay. They were stacked in great, tight, rectangular blocks. The stacks were often fifteen or eighteen feet high, thirty feet wide and sixty or more feet long with the bales interlocked like brickwork to keep the stack from falling apart. The top four or five courses of bales tapered up to a point like the roof of a house where a single row of bales crowed the structure. From a distance the huge stacks looked like large barns or warehouses.

Every bale was placed by hand. Every bale—every ton of hay—was handled by someone as many as four times before it was put to bed in the stack. It was backbreaking work. A ton in the stack was three or four tons lifted and moved by muscle, sweat and sinew. I was too young to be trusted with expensive machinery and my job was to provide the muscle, sweat and sinew.

I knew what was coming. I was already an old hand at hauling hay. The year before, when I was fifteen, I had worked

The Split Sky

Tom and Donald McCourt–Nutter Ranch, July 1963.

for Dal Wells who owned one of the best and biggest hay operations in Carbon and Emery Counties. It was with Dal Wells that I learned the art of stacking hay, the intricacies of jacking bales and the protocols of working with a hay crew. My early exposure to putting up hay was one of the reasons I wanted to be a cowboy. Working in the hay was dirty, thankless and exhausting work.

At the Nutter ranch, the haying operation began in the bottom fields; those that were the farthest down the canyon, in the lowest elevations where the hay tended to mature first. In the Utah hay business, hay doesn't ripen, it gets "ready to cut." Hay is ready to cut when it starts to make seed. Once the seedpods appear the hay has stopped growing. A field that is ready to cut is a field of deep green hay stalks, usually just a little above knee high (my knees), that have a dusting of blue seed blossoms along the tops.

The lower fields were harvested first, and then the haying operation progressed up the canyon, field by field until the upper boundary fence was reached. When we reached the neighbor's fence, the machinery was transferred back to the bottom fields and the process started all over again. The operation took several weeks to go from the bottom field to the top. As each field was cleared of it's precious produce, it was immediately flooded with water from the creek so the hay would start to grow again. The thirsty ground would soak up the water and the brown hay stubble would quickly turn green and vibrant, immediately beginning to grow into another crop. The operation was timed in such a way that the first field to be harvested would be ripe and ready to cut again when the last field was finished and ready to be watered. In this way, the haying operation lasted all summer without a break. We moved from field to field and from stack yard to stack yard. Each field was harvested three times between early June and late September. After the third cutting, each field was watered one last time so the hay would grow as much as possible for winter pasture.

Joe and Humbert started in the bottom field, Joe cutting the hay with a tractor-mounted cutter-bar and Humbert coming along behind him, raking it into long rows with a side-delivery rake.

A cutter-bar is an attachment that hooks to the tractor and is powered by the tractor's power-take-off unit (P.T.O.) which is a revolving shaft driven by the tractor engine that can be started and stopped with a clutch. Cutter-bars have almost become extinct since the mid-seventies with the introduction of hay conditioning machines that cut and rake the hay in one operation. The cutter-bar was a large folding blade, about ten or twelve feet long with pointed teeth like a comb. Riding in slots in the teeth was a cutting blade that went back and forth rapidly, cutting the hay stocks off near the ground. The severed stocks fell back over the cutter-bar and lay like a blanket on the ground, ready to be raked into long windrows where it could be baled. It was an effective machine but it was basic nineteenth century technology and the early cutter-bars were horse-driven affairs.

When the cutter-bar was not being used to cut hay, the cutting motion could be stopped and the blade raised into the air and locked in place. It would then ride with the tractor, through gates, on the roads, or wherever the tractor went, looking like the folded wing of an airplane on an aircraft carrier or like the great, serrated blade of some monstrous medieval weapon.

A side delivery rake folded the blanket of cut hay into long windrows. The rake was a machine towed by a tractor and powered by a gear-driven chain attached to one wheel. The rake was a series of vertical, revolving wheels about four feet high with teeth like heavy wire that pushed the hay into a neat row. It was necessary to rake the hay into long rows for bailing, and the windrows, as they were called, also helped in the curing process. Windrowing kept the hay from drying too fast and it helped to save the leaves, which are the most nutritious part of the hay.

It is in the curing process—knowing when to bale and when not to bale—that separates the real farmers from the wanna-be farmers. A good farmer knows just when to do it. If the hay is not cured enough and is baled too green, the bales will mould and rot in the stack. If the farmer waits too long and bales his hay too dry, most of the leaves will be lost in the bailing process and the bales will be dusty and filled with stems. When the farmer bales too dry, the leaves he looses will cost him tons if he's selling, and nutrition if he's feeding. Another serious drawback is that dry hay is dusty hay and it can be fatal to horses if they eat it for very long.

The length of time the hay is cured depends on the weather. If it is very hot and dry, with a little wind, it can be baled in a couple of days. If the weather is cool and cloudy it may take most of a week. The very worst thing that can happen in the curing process is for it to rain. Hay in the windrows will turn black and rot in the fields if it is rained on, rendering it almost useless for sale or for feed. And yet, even if it is rained on and ruined, it is still necessary to bale it and haul it to get it off the field so the next crop can grow and be harvested.

Farmers are a fidgety and anxious bunch when they have hay down and curing. They are tuned to every weather forecast and they pace nervously about, trying to wish away any clouds they see loitering on the horizon. Growing hay is a very labor intensive, risky and stressful occupation.

And so . . . there is an art to making hay. Some farmers master the art and some sell inferior hay year after year. People who buy hay, especially those who feed horses, learn quickly who the real farmers are.

Tending Water

When Joe and Humbert started cutting and raking hay in the lower fields, I inherited the job of irrigating in the upper fields. I wasn't trusted with the machinery and there wasn't any hay for me to haul yet. For a few days I took a shovel and a pickup truck and tended water.

Irrigating was something I had learned to do on my father's little farm and I enjoyed it. Irrigating from a ditch is much the same no matter where you do it. You divert water from the main ditch into the laterals at the top of the field and then into the furrows, making sure that each shallow scratch of a furrow gets it's fair share of water. It's then necessary to make sure that the water can flow free and unobstructed all the way to the bottom of the field. Often, especially if it's the first time water has gone down a newly plowed furrow, a person must walk each trickle of water the full length of the field to clear dirt clods and clumps of grass so the water will get to where it is supposed to go. There is an intensity of labor involved in watering high desert fields that is not appreciated by farmers who dry farm and who are blessed with ample rain.

It was hot in the canyon and the ground was dry and sometimes I could actually hear the water being absorbed into the ground with a sound like a dry sponge unfolding. There were faint gurgles and bubbling sounds as the water found its way down insect holes and cracks and fissures in the parched ground—a sound similar to the bubbling of a glass of Seven-Up. The clay and shale dirt of Eastern Utah soaks up wetter and dries harder than any soil I have ever seen. When wet, it can be like quicksand and will swallow a pickup truck to the axles in a single gulp. And when dry, it is like a cement pad that could be used for an Air Force runway. Hay and corn and other surface crops will grow fairly well in the unyielding soil, but potatoes and carrots often give up. In many places, even if the ground is deep-plowed each season, root crops will despair at trying to expand into the hard cement and they will try to grow on top of the ground. Potatoes and carrots turn out bent, twisted and contorted. I've had potatoes in my garden grow like ostriches with their heads down in the dirt and their brown and bare little bums sticking up into the air like a plumber without a belt. The one exception, in my experience, is sugar beets. Most farmers in my hometown could grow a fair crop of sugar beets year after year—back in the days when there was a market for them.

In spite of the unusual physical properties of the gray soil, it is fairly rich in minerals and nutrients and when given a little water and fertilizer it will grow a pretty decent crop. Farmers in the town of Green River who live on the sandy, alluvial flanks of the river and who enjoy a special relationship with the weather, grow the world's best watermelons. About sixty miles away, on my father's little place in Wellington, we couldn't grow melons at all and I wondered why. A cold watermelon is one of life's greatest pleasures. I asked a local farmer once why we couldn't grow melons and he told me the soil in Wellington was so rich, and the melons grew so fast, that the vines would drag the melons around on the ground and wear them out before they could ripen. I planted some melon seeds to check it out, but it never happened the way he said. My melons stayed put, and they were still small and green and unripe when old Jack Frost finished them off. I was disappointed, but I learned a lesson anyway. Never believe what some old farmer is telling you if he smiles too much while telling the tale. If gullibility was a virtue, I could have grown up to be a Saint.

As I irrigated in the canyon fields, the blackbirds came in troops to walk with the water, slurping up the tasty bugs that fled their hiding places as the water advanced. The birds loved it when we irrigated and they had family reunions and summer picnics at the edge of the advancing water. The birds would actually help in tending the water. Often, I didn't have to walk down into the field to see how far the water had gone. I could tell where it was by the thin line of blackbirds that frolicked and ran about, chuckling back and forth as they picked off the hapless insects.

Irrigating was the best job on the farm. In the middle of a big haying operation, tending water was like playing hookey from work. It was great, because when you were watering a field it was legal to stand for minutes at a time leaning on a shovel while you waited for the water to do something you wanted it to do, like soak up a new ditch, or push its way through the grass far enough to reach the last set of furrows. Tending water wasn't near as much work as putting up hay and it was a good diversion from the bone-crunching routine.

During the summer I tended water only once in a while because there was always someone with more whiskers who wanted the job. I was always jealous and even angry when one of the old boys would duck out on the hay hauling during the hottest and most trying time of the day to go tend the water. Irrigating was an important and necessary part of the haying operation, but it also provided a great excuse for a lazy man to dodge some of the heavy work. I was quick to notice that in the mornings, when it was time to go to the fields, the irrigating always took one of my companions an hour or so to accomplish. Around noon, when it was scalding hot and the hay bales were getting heavy, it might take as much as an hour and a half. But in the evenings, when the day's work was done and supper was waiting, the job could be accomplished in thirty minutes.

One of the rewards of tending water was that we would often see wildlife. The canyon was full of wildlife: birds of all kinds, creepy crawly things, colorful bugs of every description and every type of mammal. It was not unusual to see a fox chasing grasshoppers at the bottom of the field, or a Red-tailed hawk working hard to carry a Cottontail to her nest high in the ledges. The Cottontails were fat and so were the Red-tails.

There were marmots—woodchucks or Rockchucks we called them, whistle pigs to some—always in the fields. They were fat, short-legged ground squirrels that looked like small beavers with bushy tails. They ate alfalfa shoots and did a lot of damage to the crops. Sometimes there were dozens of them in the fields and they would stampede like herds of miniature buffalo when we approached on the tractor. I've seen times when whole hillsides were crawling with them. They were scruffy and irreverent little beasts, and they would retreat to their sanctuaries in the rocks and shout insults and ground squirrel obscenities at us in the form of loud barks or chirps. They were arrogant little whistle pigs, and they claimed the fields as their own.

And then of course, there were always the deer. Deer are beautiful and graceful creatures and I always enjoyed seeing them. It was not uncommon in the summer to see an old doe with a matched pair of speckled fawns feeding along the edges of the field, staying close to cover. Sometimes, in the cool afternoon, the fat little fawns would run and jump and buck while Mom daintily picked at the clover and swished her stubby tail at the mosquitoes. Sometimes we would see young bucks with soft, velvety antlers, traveling in little bachelor groups like school chums. They always seemed to walk tall and proud in their new velvet antlers, stepping high like handsome young cowboys in new felt hats, reveling in their masculinity.

One particular late afternoon while I was tending water, I was privileged to see a grand old mule deer buck—the best one in the whole world—the fabled King of Kings. He was a deer the cowboys would have called the Big Mazook—a Honker—and he simply materialized from out of nowhere like a phantom. He walked out of the junipers and stood on the edge of a high cliff just a few hundred yards away. He was silhouetted against a beautiful late-afternoon sky, and his glorious crown, those magnificent antlers, were thick with velvet and shining in the light. He was the master of all he surveyed and he stood proudly, surveying his kingdom from the walls of his castle in the ledges. His image bred in me a hope and a dream that has led me, yet eluded me, through every deer season since. I've seen some good deer over the years, but I've never seen his equal. He was like a painting on velvet or glass—too big and too handsome to be real. He stood high on that promontory and watched me for a while, posing proudly while I etched his image into my memory, and then he turned and disappeared back into the junipers and I never saw him again.

KILLER BADGERS

I was tending water one afternoon when I noticed a commotion in the middle of the field. I couldn't tell for sure what was going on, but I could see dirt flying and I could tell that it was some kind of an animal doing something unusual. The field was short hay stubble and a full forty-acres. I couldn't figure it out, and so I walked toward the turmoil, curious yet cautious and with my shovel at port-arms, ready to defend myself.

As I got closer, I discovered that it was a badger trying to dig a ground squirrel out of a hole. The badger was a fine little excavator and he was making good progress. All I could see was his hind-end and stubby tail as he mumbled and grumbled and clawed at the ground, making the dirt fly. He was focused severely on his digging and on his fuzzy and entrenched afternoon meal. He was lost in his own little world, and completely unaware that the ground squirrel was not the only creature in the neighborhood being stalked.

I was excited. I decided right then and there that it would be great if I could go back to school in the fall and tell my buddies how I had slapped a badger on the butt with the flat blade of my shovel. Badgers were supposed to be mean and wicked little grizzly bears, and I would be a hero for sure if I could pull it off.

I had heard stories about how ferocious a badger could be, how they could whip any dog and how they would chomp down and then lock their jaws and hang on to the bitter end. I'd heard all the stories but I really didn't believe them. The few badgers I'd become acquainted with had always ran away from me as I expected they would. I was a tall, upright and intellectual beast with an opposing thumb and at the very top of the food chain. God had given me and my species dominion over all the animal kingdom and I expected every lesser creature to flee from me in panic.

I stood back and took the measure of the badger in the hole. I carefully sized him up against the yardstick of my limited experience. He didn't look very big. I'd seen Flemish rabbits bigger than him. He didn't look very menacing either, with his head in the hole and his stubby little tail popping back and forth like a windshield wiper as the dirt flew out from between his back legs. I was taller than he was, smarter and better looking too. I outweighed him by a multiple of at least eight. I factored up the odds and gave myself an eight to two advantage. I smiled and placed my bet.

The badger was working his little guts out trying to rustle up some supper. He was so absorbed with his menu that he hadn't noticed me tippy-toeing up on him. He was totally unaware that he was wearing the dark trunks and the bell for round one would sound in just a few seconds.

The Split Sky

I decided it would be poor sport to pot him with his head in the hole, so I decided to scare him and give him a head start and then butt him with the flat of the shovel while he was running away. I knew I might have to chase him for a ways, but I was a good runner and it sounded like great sport and I had it all mapped out. The badger had short, stubby little legs and I had him surrounded out in the middle of a forty-acre field with no place for him to hide. I was sure I could catch him and humiliate him good. I didn't want to kill him, or even hurt him. I intended to count coup like a Comanche and put a feather in my war bonnet. I chuckled wickedly as I tiptoed up to the badger's hole.

From a few steps away, I rushed right up and over that old badger and screamed like a gut-shot Godzilla—and the badger exploded from that hole like a hand grenade. I swear that badger came off the ground four feet high and right in my face. All I could see was gleaming teeth and blood-red gullet, clear down and past his electrified little tonsils. I was staring into the jaws of death and into the mouth of hell. He came up the shovel handle like a yo-yo and that fuzzy little fur ball was going to scatter my guts in the hay stubble. Those beady little eyes ripped into me like bullets and he was snapping and snorting and blowing snot and growling like a grizzly bear—a veritable blur of wild animal ferocity. I had scared him senseless all right, and I had just discovered that in the world of badgers, a good attack is the best defense.

The badger had me surrounded in the middle of a forty-acre field with no place for me to hide. I somehow managed to fend him off with the shovel, but he kept coming right back at me, trying to climb my leg and bite my nose off. I was jumping three feet in the air, trying to keep my feet and legs away from the blizzard of snapping teeth and the chainsaw wail of terror and outrage that escaped from his alligator-like throat. I kept backing up, somehow managing to keep parrying him with the shovel, avoiding the teeth, using the shovel for balance as I danced frantically to keep my feet and legs out of his cornchopper of a mouth. My body was in full adrenaline shock. There is nothing that will get your blood up like a vicious wild animal attack.

I kept backing up, defending with the shovel, and shouting back at him over his slobbering growls, "Hey... hey..." or "Git ... git..." or some other senseless thing—and finally, he shut down his assault and flattened out close to the ground, panting, but still hissing deep in his throat like a cornered alley cat. He was still threatening to slay me, but I was surprised to see that his dark little eyes were beginning to show fear—now that he had me ready for a diaper change.

I'm sure my eyes showed mindless panic. I wanted to run like the wind but I didn't dare turn my back on him. We were still in the middle of the field with no cover and no easy means of escape. I slowly moved backwards, cautiously, not wanting to provoke another attack by encouraging him with a too hasty retreat. I still held the shovel with a death-grip. I realized that through the whole attack I had never tried to hit him with the shovel, only to place the shovel between us to turn the attack. He had chomped down on the shovel several times, both the wooden handle and the metal blade, and had probably hurt his mouth some. I should have had that shovel gold-plated and hung on the wall; it had saved my thin skin. I don't want to even think about what the outcome might have been if not for my grubby little fingers around that shovel handle.

The badger began to back up too, very slowly and still facing me. We both retreated cautiously, crouching, posturing, each of us fully expecting the other to attack. We continued to back up until there was a respectable stretch of neutral ground between us ... and then we both turned-tail and retreated to our respective corners. I was glad there were no other members of my dominant species present to witness the little drama. I felt pretty stupid.

The referees and ringside judges in the animal kingdom might have called it a draw—I didn't get my nose chewed off and the badger didn't get his little bum whacked with the flat of my shovel. In all fairness, I think the badger won on points; he got in the most jabs. I might not have scored as many points, but I put on a great performance just the same. I'm sure that Mohammad Ali, on his best day, couldn't have kept up with my bobbing and weaving and fancy footwork.

When it was all over, when I started to shake from the adrenaline rush, and when I had time to and think about it for a while, I became euphoric. I was caught up in the sheer joy of being alive and in the excitement of having survived a close call. I counted my fingers and toes and wiggled my un-chewed little nose and I rejoiced.

The incident with the Badger reinforced for me an old Western adage that says: "A good scare is worth a lot more than good advice." I'm here to tell you it's true. I had heard stories about what vicious little tigers badgers could be, but I never dreamed it was so true until that close encounter. Any badger I meet nowadays gets a polite tip of my hat and all the space he wants.

My Cheyenne war bonnet is still a feather short.

Chapter 5

The Situation

A Man's Job

It didn't take us long to hit our stride with the haying operation. Everyone had a part to play: Virginia was management, the Colonel was the overseer, Joe and Humbert were operators, Brody was the boss man's pampered kid, I was labor.

Joe did most of the cutting and the baling. Humbert raked the hay and took care of the odd jobs and irrigated. I hauled and stacked hay full time. Joe and Humbert helped with the hauling and stacking as best they could, but we always seemed to be short handed.

There was another man who worked on the farm and his name was Willis Hammerschmid. Like Humbert, he owned his own place further up the canyon and worked for day-wages at the ranch. He wasn't there all the time, but he was a good farmer and a good worker.

Just a few days into it, Virginia hired a young fellow from the Uintah Basin to help me haul hay. He was seventeen and bigger than me, stronger too, but after a day and a half in the fields he was on the phone to his dad to come and get him. He wasn't there long enough for me to remember his name. Later in the summer, when we got behind with the second crop, Virginia hired a four-man hay crew to help us for about a week while we caught up. They were all young guys from the basin and they stuck together pretty tight; I never really got acquainted with any of them.

Joe the dragon treated the new hands with the same contempt that he showed to me, and I learned something from that. I began to understand that his disdain for young farm hands was universal and I shouldn't take it personal. The man was consistent—he hated everybody. And in a strange way I drew comfort from that.

Hauling hay by hand is grueling work. We always tried to be as efficient and labor saving as we could, but with the equipment we had there was only one way to get it done and that was to pick the bales up and move 'em. It sounds simple enough, but there is method in the madness. Believe it or not, there is a right way and a wrong way to haul hay. Some people haul hay the wrong way all the time and still get the job done, but if you're going to move a lot of hay, it's best to do it in a labor-saving way as efficiently as possible.

When the hay was baled, the bales fell from the baler chute and landed on the ground in long, straight rows as the baler went down the field. A field that has just been baled will look to a novice like the bales have been dropped from the belly of a plane and scattered all over. If you look closely, however, you will see that they are actually in a series of long, straight lines.

When we hauled hay we tried to position the hay wagon as evenly as possible between two rows of bales so we could load the wagon from both sides. Doing this made us carry the bales farther than if we did only one row at a time. But cleaning up two rows with one pass always seemed to make the bales disappear faster and there was less travel time in the field. In an ideal situation, it takes four people to load from the ground efficiently: one to drive the tractor and keep the wagon moving, one to shag the bales on each side of the wagon (that makes three), and one man on the wagon to stack the bales being thrown to him by the men on the ground.

We were always short handed. There were other jobs to be

done besides hauling hay and it was a rare thing for us to have four men available. It seems the best we ever had was three of us. We could do just fine with three—if one of the three was Willis. He was a good man, Gary Cooper in work boots, and I had to run to keep up with him. He always stepped out front, took charge, and never looked back. He was a big man, all business, and he could make hay bales fly. He hauled hay the way I chopped ironweeds. I was awed by his strength and by his laser-guided work ethic, and I always felt like a puppy when I followed him around the fields. If I didn't run to keep up, he would do his job and my job too, which embarrassed me greatly and almost worked me to death. I was glad that I didn't have to work with Willis very often—it was hard on me.

It was different working with Joe and Humbert. Joe would always drive the tractor and Humbert would stack on the wagon while I humped bales for both sides. Sometimes there were just two of us, and when that happened, one of the men drove the tractor and I humped bales from both sides of the wagon and then jumped on the wagon to stack them and then jumped off to throw new ones on the wagon again.

When Humbert was with me, he would usually park the tractor at regular intervals and come back to help me stack. When Joe was with me, sometimes he would help me stack on the wagon and sometimes he just sat on the tractor and waited for me to catch up. No matter which of them was with me, I could count on being the bale humper. I was the kid and I didn't rate a turn driving the tractor—ever. Somehow, I accepted this as normal. I knew it wasn't fair. I knew I was being taken advantage of and maybe even abused, but it seemed to be the natural order of things. The young guy was supposed to do the dirty work and work harder than the old guys.

There is a severe pecking order in fraternal organizations

like work crews, and the new blood is always at the bottom of the pile. It seems that a group of men will almost always gang up on the new guy, or the young guy, and expect him to do the dirty work. The old hands seem to feel that because of seniority they have been bumped up a notch when a new man is assigned to the crew. The new guy is expected to eat dirt until someone newer than him comes along. This can go on for weeks or even years until the new guy gets tired of it all and flexes his muscles and growls and makes himself a place around the dog dish.

I was experiencing this social cannibalism for the first time and I was ill prepared to deal with it. I was sixteen and dumb as a sheep. I wanted so very much to be accepted as a man and an equal, and I thought I could accomplish that goal by sacrificing myself on the altar of hard work and selflessness. I not only accepted the rough and dirty jobs, I volunteered for them, secretly hoping that my efforts would be seen as noble gestures of self-sacrifice and manliness. The older men loved it, and they took full advantage of my innocence.

I was vulnerable in another way too. I had been taught to respect and obey older men, and I was polite and respectful to a fault, amazed, shocked and hurt to be treated so shabbily in return. It took me a long time to learn that in the wolf pack, any act of civility is seen as a sign of weakness and submission. It took a long time for me to figure it all out and claim my spot around the dog dish.

Fairly often I ended up hauling hay by myself, which I really didn't mind. When I worked alone there was no one to give me orders and I could be like Frank Sinatra and do it my way. I would drive the tractor and hay wagon between two rows of bales and park it. I would then leave the tractor running while I gathered up all the bales I could carry to the wagon, some from fifteen or twenty yards away. I would throw the bales up on the wagon and then jump up to stack them. I then got back on the tractor and moved it up the field and did it all over again until the wagon was full.

The size and weight of the bales plays a big part in what is possible and what is not when it comes to hauling hay by yourself. I was lucky that the hay bailer we were using was a string tied bailer set to make bales that weighed from fifty to sixty pounds. I could handle these, and by the end of the summer I could throw them high over my head and make it look easy. There were bailers out there on other farms that tied with wire and made bales that weighed eighty to one hundred pounds—man killers that were so tight and heavy they could only be handled with a steel hay hook. I was grateful we weren't using one of those.

Most people now use mechanical haulers and stackers and they don't have that personal relationship with each bale of hay that we used to have. There was a time when each individual bale required the laying on of hands. The bales lounged in the field, fat and lazy, waiting to be handled and fondled and carried like babies. Each expecting to feel the touch of the Master's hand three of four times before being put to bed in the stack.

Each bale had a unique physique and personality, some were heavier than others, some dustier, some wetter and some were odd colored. Some were distinguished by bits of willow or gumweed or dead rodents protruding. Some were mostly grass, others pure alfalfa, some a unique blending of the two. Each was different. It was possible to recognize individual bales in the different stages of the process.

When you heft each bale in triplicate, you develop a keen, personal relationship that is lost to a fellow sitting on the seat of a bale wagon. I would pick up a bale in the field and notice that it contained a small snake, compacted tightly, and I would recognize it and say hello again when I stacked it on the wagon, and then, an hour later, I would see it again and say goodbye as I laid it to rest in the haystack and buried it under tons of other bales. Like a good Shepherd, I knew my bales and my bales knew me.

Hauling hay by hand is a dying art. A farmhand who knew how to move and stack hay was a valuable asset when I was a kid. Hay had to be moved quickly to make way for a second or third crop, and haystacks had to be built with care and skill.

The haystack must be prepared from its foundation the way a carpenter builds a good house. Without a good foundation a haystack will fall down, and a tall and leaning stack is dangerous to work around. When I was a young boy and lived next to the Petersen Dairy Farm, the owner's brother was seriously injured when he was caught between the haystack and the stack yard fence by an avalanche of cascading bales.

In order to make a good stack, the first course of bales has the importance of a cement foundation. A typical hay bale is about thirteen inches high, eighteen inches wide and three and a half feet long. To build a foundation for the stack, the first row of bales is placed on edge with the thin, thirteen-inch side on the ground. This makes the bottom row thicker than those above it, and it contains almost half again as many bales as any other row in the stack. The bales of this bottom row are pushed together very tightly so the whole bottom course makes a solid base without any gaps or holes. This is done for stability and to give the rest of the stack a cushion from the ground moisture. A farmer knows that the bottom course of bales is likely to be ruined because they will wick moisture from the ground. The damp and dirty bales from the bottom of a stack can be fed to cows but they will never sell for much.

The bales above the bottom layer are laid flat and tied-in by alternating the direction the different courses of bales are laid.

It's like building a brick monument. As the stack increases in height it is built in steps, with each layer of bales forming a step. A stack in progress may be one bale high at one end and twelve or fifteen bales high on the other end. In this manner, a man can walk a bale up the stack using the alternating courses of bales as steps. It was not unusual for us to walk a sixty-pound bale up ten or twelve steps in order to place it on top of the stack. When there were three or four of us, we did this like a bucket brigade, each man passing the bale to the man above him. This was not possible when I worked alone, and many times I would walk a bale up a full dozen steps and then return to the wagon to get another.

We had a gasoline-powered mechanical stacker, a conveyor that could be used to send bales to the top of the stack, but we didn't use it very often. It was more trouble than it was worth most of the time. It broke down a lot and the chain had a bad habit of jumping the sprocket. The stacker worked okay if there were at least three people to run it—and one of them was a mechanic.

When a person wrestles hay bales for a living, one of the most important things to know is how to dress for work. Hauling hay is not a time to try to impress anyone with your fancy duds. The first rule is never wear anything that means anything to you. The second rule is never, ever wear anything that leaves big chunks of your tender hide exposed. You should wear old stuff that won't make you cry when it gets stained and torn, and you should wear clothing that covers you up. You have to think armor—comfort will come when the work is all done.

Good leather boots are an absolute must. Dry hay stubble will pierce a canvas or rubber shoe and a low-cut shoe will fill your socks with stickers. The hay stubble will also chew your ankles until they bleed. We always wore good boots with our

Levis down over the tops to keep the hay leaves, stickers, dirt and bugs out. I've always been entertained by wanna-be cowboys who wear their pants tucked into the tops of their fancy western boots like Roy Rogers. Anyone who spends more than a weekend at a dude ranch will discover that when the tops of those high boots are exposed to the elements they become trashcans. They collect every sticker, briar, cocklebur, dirt clod, weed seed and insect on the trail, and all of that trash is carried right to the bottom of your boot by gravity. I understand that it's a real bummer to spend a lot of money on a pair of fancy western boots and then hide them beneath your long pants, but that's what the real cowboys—and humble farmers do.

Another necessary item a well-dressed hay hauler wears is long pants, tough long pants, made of denim or canvas—Levi Strauss got it right. When humping bales, you often use your legs or knees for leverage and shorts are simply out of the question. Hay bales are rough, stickery things and they will draw blood from your dimpled knees in a hurry. Some hay haulers even wore short, leather chaps over their long pants to protect their legs. I never did and it seemed that I always had cuts, scratches and abrasions on my knees and legs in spite of my Levis.

For the same reasons listed above, it was necessary to wear a long sleeved shirt buttoned at the wrists. If you wear short sleeves, or roll your sleeves up, your arms are scraped and bloody in no time at all. It's best if you wear a shirt of heavy material like denim. Even then, like my legs, I always had cuts, contusions and abrasions on my lower arms.

A person must also wear a hat. We were in the broiling sun all day and we all wore western straw hats with wide brims. Wide brimmed hats provide the best shelter from the sun. We tried to buy hats with open weaving at the top to allow for some air circulation, and we bought white or tan colors that reflected the sun and would not absorb heat like a black or a brown one. No one of my generation would think to wear a baseball cap to haul hay all day. We considered a baseball cap to be inadequate shelter. A wide brim helped keep the hay leaves and dust away from your face and from going down your neck, especially when you had to throw or hand a bale up and over your head. Another drawback to a baseball cap was that after a few hours in the sun, your ears would look like hot dogs ready for the mustard. We didn't have sunscreen lotion.

You just can't haul hay without a pair of good gloves. We wore good leather gloves or farmer's gloves that were leather in the palms and heavy cotton on the backs with stiff cuffs that extended up our forearms. Gloves wear out quickly in the hay fields and it seemed like I always had a hole or two in the fingers of my gloves. There was always one lonesome little finger sticking out there all by himself, suffering the slings and arrows of cruel misfortune, a tender spot that made me careful to position my fingers just right before I lifted a bale from the ground.

Hauling hay is dusty and dirty work and we usually kept our shirts buttoned up tight in spite of the heat. Sometimes we even tied a neckerchief around our necks to try to keep the dust and hay leaves from getting into our clothes. It never worked, and at the end of the day my sweaty little body would be covered with hay leaves and stickers that were glued to my skin by my own dried sweat. They seemed to congregate best in those areas where my belt held my pants tight, or around the tops of my socks.

It's almost impossible to wear glasses while hauling hay. Every time you stoop over, the sweat from your forehead drops down on the lenses, blurring them and giving the ever-present dust something to stick to. Even without sweat stains on them, the lenses are quickly coated with fine dust, rendering them almost useless. This is especially true for dark glasses. When wearing dark glasses you walk around like you're in a fog as the lenses collect dust and the light slowly dims, and when you finally reach up and take them off, the brightness slaps you like a glove and your eyes slam shut and you see purple spots for a minute or two. A person who wears glasses is always stopping to clean them and in the process of constantly handling them, they often become scratched, bent, or broken. People who wear prescription glasses and haul hay soon learned to leave them in the pickup truck and come to the field blind; it's easier and sometimes much less expensive than being able to see.

And so . . . all season, during the hottest and brightest of the summer days, during those times when the sun reflected off the canyon walls, the rocks and the bare ground like they were sheets of tin, we squinted into the glare like snow-blinded Eskimos. Sunglasses were not an option.

Being out in the hot sun all day and working hard while dressed in heavy, protective clothing, we were always good candidates for heat stroke. We drank copious amounts of water, usually from thick, canvas water bags that cooled the water by slow evaporation. I learned early in my hay-hauling career to keep and protect my own water bag. Some of the old-timers chewed tobacco while they worked—most farmers were rabidly intolerant about hands who smoked while sitting on a hundred tons of dry and precious hay—and very early on I developed a red-hot phobia about drinking from a common water bag with some old geezer with tobacco slobbers all over his teeth, mouth and whiskers. Call me prissy.

Dust was the real curse of the hay fields. It was always unbearably hot and our shirts and pants were always wet with sweat. The wetness trapped the fine dust that filled the air as the bales were being slammed around, and by noon we always had a fine coating of pale green, mossy, mud-dust stuck to our sweaty clothes. We breathed in the fine dust by the quart, and when it got real bad, we put bandannas over our mouths and noses like wild-west outlaws as we tried to filter out some of the big stuff. We were always coughing up green hay dust and it seemed that I could never get it all out of my nose and ears. The dust was especially hard on our eyes. They were always red and felt like they were full of sand. In the mornings when I washed my face, the corners of my eyes would be full of fine hay leaf particles that had washed from my eyeballs during the night.

And then . . . if the dust, heat, and hard work were not enough vexation, there was always the vermin that stalked us through the fields, the snakes, mosquitoes, and the biting flies that made our lives miserable.

VERMIN

The mosquitoes were always there. They lived down by the crick where it was damp and cool and shady. Mosquitoes are smarter than people and they shade-up during the heat of the day. They sallied forth in the mornings and evenings when it was cool, and they would attack us in clouds. There were times when I could stand very still and hear the whine of thousands of little mosquito engines like the hum of a power transmission line. The mosquitoes came at us like the Chinese army—in disorganized mobs, no attack plan and no coordination, just waves of brave little blood-sucking bugs, swirling, humming and biting. They always seemed oblivious to the fact that we might defend ourselves. A little mosquito warrior would dig in and then just sit there defiantly and wait for the big slap to send him to the happy hunting grounds. Mosquitoes might not be smarter than people after all.

We were always wearing thick, protective clothing but the little buggers would land on our backs, arms and shoulders by the dozens and try to find a place to get the stinger through the shirt. Too often they succeeded and at shower time I always had red welts on my back and arms.

In the middle of the day, when it got hot and Mr. Sun singed their tiny little wings, most of the mosquitoes went home to cool their heels, but they always left a few scouts out to spy on us and keep track of where we were and what we were up to. The little mosquito scouts were opportunists and they never missed a chance to swoop down and get you when you least expected it.

One day I was ambushed while balancing a sixty-pound bale against my belt buckle and still fifteen giant steps from the hay wagon. An especially adroit little mosquito warrior scout swooped in from out of nowhere and dug in between my nose and upper lip. This put me in a tight spot. I didn't want to put the heavy bale down and pick it up again, and both of my hands were busily wrapped around hay twine and fully engaged. I tried to duck my head and wipe the mosquito off against my shoulder—but I couldn't reach. I walked very fast, balancing the bale against my leg, and I tried to stick my bottom lip out and blow the little creep off with a jet of hot air. Too late, he was well attached; he had the drill pipe down and was going for the mother lode. I tried to use my tongue to lick him off my lip like an old cow. Sorry, too short. Finally, I ran the last couple of steps and threw the bale at the wagon. My lip was burning like it was in a vice and my eyes were watering. I smashed his disgusting little body all over my face with the back of a wet glove. Vengeance was mine and I reveled in the victory, but my lip swelled up like I had taken a left-hook to the kisser.

That brave little mosquito's friends from the Mosquito Kamikaze Squadron must have been watching from a distance and reported his successful mission to Biting Bug Headquarters. That little creep probably got the Mosquito

Medal Of Honor. His whole nation turned out that evening to hum his National Anthem and check out my swollen lip.

Not so numerous as the mosquitoes, but heavier armed and infinitely better tacticians, are the horseflies and the deerflies—they are cousins, you know. Horseflies are big and gray and obnoxious. Deerflies are small and brown and sneaky. A horsefly comes at you like a C-130 gunship, circling slowly out of range, his big engines droning, sizing you up and waiting for that perfect moment to make his gun-pass. You can see him out there and you can hear him, but you never know if he's on a recon mission or if he's waiting for clearance from headquarters to make that strafing run and take you out. If you stop what you're doing to watch him, he'll stay out of range and circle for minutes on end, content just to pin you down and keep you from doing any productive work. If you ignore him and go about your business, he'll dive in from up-sun and drop a 500-pounder on the back of your neck. Horseflies have teeth as big as a badger.

Deer flies are more like Apache helicopters; they use stealth, terrain and treachery to cover their attack. They are smaller and much quieter than horseflies but they are just as deadly. They sneak up on you. You don't hear his engine and you don't see him coming. You are heavily involved in the business at hand when you get a sharp, stinging sensation on your cheek, just below your ear. You reflexively slap at it because it hurts like hell, and down falls a brown-speckled Deerfly, his cellophane wings all bent up and his disgustingly fuzzy little legs doing the dying chicken in the air. He leaves a bomb crater on your face and the wound swells up, turns red, and is surprisingly numb for several minutes. Pound for pound, I think Deerfly venom is probably more potent than a snakebite. Deerfly bites on my tender hide always swelled up, festered, turned a nasty red and itched for two or three days.

The third type of biting fly is the common gnat. They are the stealth fighters of the desert sky. Gnats are itsy-bitsy little black flies and they are invisible in the air and make very little noise. They have a thing about ears. They attach themselves inside your ears and chew like little Bulldogs. They will bite in other places, but a tender ear is always the primary target. They were especially bad during the month of June and my ears were always sore and rubbed raw.

If a disgusting little gnat can't find his way into the inner sanctum of your ear, he will sometimes try to disable you in other ways. I don't know if gnats are terminally stupid or if they fly into your mouth with a purpose, but it was not all that unusual to inhale one of the little buggers and spend the next few minutes gagging and choking and trying to spit him back up while he wrapped his tiny little arms and legs around your tonsils and hung on for dear life. Sometimes one of the brain-dead little beasts would fly right into an eye and really lay a person up for a while. Even a tiny fly in your eye feels like an Irish wolfhound.

It's amazing, but when you have a fly in your eye nothing else in the whole world seems to matter. Your goals, plans and future are all put on hold. Your whole perspective about life and living is immediately altered. It suddenly doesn't matter if you don't finish the field this evening, or if you are late for supper. All your priorities have changed. You're obliged to join the ranks of the walking wounded until you dig your dirty handkerchief out of a dirty pocket and use it to scrape the disgusting little intruder from your raw and blood-shot eyeball—all the while exhorting the Great Spirit in the sky to curse his damnable soul, his forbearers, his fuzzy little friends and his progeny forever. The eye will be red and sore, gritty and swollen for a day or two.

Mosquitoes, gnats and biting flies serve no redeeming purpose in nature and we must accept them for what they are—a punishment from God.

And then there are the politicians, lawyers and used car salesmen of the canyon—those ever present snakes. Nine Mile is full of snakes. I found water snakes in the fields, blue racers out in the sage bushes, blow snakes around the corrals and ranch buildings and rattlers in the ledges and under the hay bales. Most of them were harmless, hunting mice and lizards and other small and deserving creatures. It was the rattlers that I feared and dreaded.

The rattlers would lay in ambush, much like an enemy sniper. In the back of my mind I always knew they were out there someplace, watching and waiting, biding their time. It seemed they always got you when you least expected it, when you were very busy and a damn snake was the last thing on your mind—when you were distracted and totally unprepared for the confrontation.

There is something magic about hearing that dry, muffled rattle as you pick up a heavy hay bale. The sound will set you free. You go into shock. The adrenaline hits the top of the adrenaline meter in one millionth of a second flat and rings the bell. You try to get your feet, legs, hands and body away from the bale—all at the same time. In one motion you throw the bale down and jump like a cat on his way into the swimming pool—spread-eagled and with your air brakes on. You make a one-eighty turn in mid-air and come crashing down in a hard three-point landing, a foot, a knee and one gloved hand, and then you run three or four steps on whatever parts of your body are touching the ground. You then gather your wits and your extremities about you while your breath catches up. You take inventory, there in the hay stubble, and when you decide that you're not snake-bit after all, you shudder convulsively and grab a shovel from the tractor and go after him. I always felt it was my civic duty to kill every rattler that crossed my path, and I got several of them.

And so . . . hauling hay by hand the way we did it at the ranch was exhausting and slave-galley type work, but it made muscles and it built character. For a kid like me without any real job skills it was an opportunity to have a job and to earn some money and I was happy to have the opportunity.

The first ten days or so were very hard on me. I would come dragging in for supper too tired to hold my fork. My arms would be so numb that I could hardly lift them to wash my face. I would come in from the field, help with the chores, take a cool shower, change clothes, eat, and then go to bed. It was still daylight and the world was still active, but I was dead. I would sink into that big, fluffy bedroll and I would be unconscious before my head hit the pillow. I would sleep without moving until Joe the dragon yelled at me the next morning.

It took the first two weeks to get toughened up and I expected it to happen that way. I had known what to expect. When I told Virginia that I would stay, I had knowingly resigned myself to a summer at hard labor.

Unfortunately, there was a price to pay that was unexpected. After a long day of heavy work I was experiencing pain in my lower abdomen and an aching throb down my right leg. There was a soft bump of tender skin just above my groin on the right side of my stomach that hurt like a toothache at night, and the only way to relieve the pain was to lie flat on my back and extend my legs for a while. I suspected what it was, but with a youthful optimism, I hoped that if I ignored it, it would go away. It never did.

God Among The Junipers

There was another, unexpected side to the job that ate at me; I felt very much alone. I was the only young person on the farm and the older people treated me with an indifference that bordered on contempt. I had no one to talk to. Virginia and the Colonel came by every morning and lined us out, and then they retreated to the big house and we might not see them again until the following morning. Joe ignored me with the resolve of a preacher walking past a porno magazine rack. He spent his evenings reading his newspaper and smoking his cigars. If he talked at all he talked to Humbert. Humbert was always polite to me, but polite from a distance, and he usually left to go back to his own place right after supper, anyway. Willis was the same way . . . and so I was alone.

I had a lot of time to spend with my own thoughts and feelings and it was easy to get homesick. I fought the sickness gallantly. We finished supper by about six-thirty and I had almost four hours to kill before lights-out and bedtime. I had brought two or three good books to read and I traveled through them very quickly. Joe had a treasury of old newspapers, *Readers' Digests* and some other magazines, but I was too timid to ask for a chance to look at them, and he never offered. For something to do, I started taking afternoon walks. It was early summer, so the days were growing long. It didn't get dark until after ten o'clock. I would walk away from the ranch buildings and climb up in the ledges and look for arrowheads. My first few trips were timorous excursions and very close to the ranch house, but as I got a feel for it, I started to go farther and farther each afternoon.

It was great to be up in the ledges by myself. It was quiet and the pressures and anxieties of the day could be left in the canyon below. Up in the ledges, in the cool of the afternoon, I was master of my own vessel. I was free. To my complete delight I had discovered a place to retreat to—a sanctuary—a place that was mine alone.

I was struggling with a great deal of inner turmoil. I was in my mid-teen years and suffering the pains and anxieties of trying to figure out who I was and what I wanted to become. My current situation, being in exile, the little coyote in the wolf pack, scorned, used, and taken advantage of, wasn't helping much. My self-confidence and self-esteem were taking a hard hit. I was a little fish that had been transplanted from the quiet family pool into shark-infested waters and I was bloodied. I was also very humble. When I was alone in the ledges, when I had time to think and reflect on it, I felt so very vulnerable, so weak and utterly dependent. I carried the burdens of my age and circumstance like a great weight. I needed help.

I pondered what to do for a while, toying with an idea, wanting to reach out but feeling timid and embarrassed; but finally, there in the ledges and among the cedar trees, I took the advice my maternal grandmother had always offered me, and I gave my burden to God.

I had always believed in God. I'd been taught as a child that he was there, and I had never seriously doubted his existence. In my home and family, God was as real as the wind and the rain, but we took him for granted. God was like a kind and benevolent neighbor, someone who wasn't around all the time, but someone you could call on when you needed help. I'd been told that he would answer my prayers if I prayed with faith, but like most young people, I'd never gotten to know him because I had never really needed him. I had never prayed in earnest.

Now, in my loneliness and pain, I sought out my good neighbor, and I timidly called to him over the back fence. I knelt in the dirt among the cedar trees and poured out my frustrations, fears, anxieties and concerns. I asked God to help me, and I offered him my bruised and fearful heart. I spoke to him as if he were a man standing near me.

What Grandma had told me was true. I felt the weight of my burdens lightened immediately. It was like the sun had come out from behind the clouds. God took me by the hand, dusted me off, gave me a big hug and patted me on the back. The world was never quite the same again.

God works in mysterious ways, and he allowed me to have a very personal relationship with him when I needed someone to stand by me. I began to speak with him often, man to man, and while he never answered me directly, I could always feel his hand on my shoulder. I knew that I was safe, no matter what happened. I knew he was standing by to help me over the hurdles and through the rough spots. I didn't feel alone anymore.

I found that having someone to talk to made me feel better, and there was another bonus. I was better able to face my fears and put things in perspective when I made the effort to formulate and verbalize just what my fears and anxieties were. To drag those demons out of the shadows and view them objectively and in the light of day made me see them for what they really were, and they were not so big and overpowering after all.

I felt better when I said my prayers, and I started to pray every night as I went to bed, quietly and in my bed, not wanting to provoke the ridicule and contempt of the dragon by kneeling and making a spectacle. God understood. And sometimes, when I was alone and had the opportunity, I knelt by the side of the haystack and said a quick prayer again. And then of course, when things got bad, I retreated to my sanctuary in the junipers and had a long talk with my special friend who didn't answer with words.

I was surprised at how quickly I gained strength and felt better. My outlook and my attitude changed overnight. I felt comfort, peace and strength. I was calm and self-confident. I became quietly resolved that I really could take whatever came my way. I was not alone anymore. I had a secret friend who watched out for me.

As my mental outlook changed, so did my physical self. Over the next few weeks I became stronger and more able to endure the burdens of the day. Slowly, I began to feel better every night, less tired and more hungry. My muscles grew hard and my back grew strong. I started to gain weight. The pain in my groin and leg was manageable. I learned to live with it.

As the first weeks passed, I began to be aware of an interesting thing. I noticed that I could stay with the hard physical work longer, and do it every bit as well as the old geezers who smoked all the time—Joe and Humbert. I began to realize that I actually had more endurance, if not more strength, than the men around me. To my complete satisfaction I found I could beat them at something. And so I began to push in that direction, making a show of my endurance, not saying anything but making them notice that I picked up more bales, or stacked higher, or stayed with it longer, or took fewer breaks. For the first time in my life I was measuring myself against grown men, and I was delighted to find that I wasn't doing too badly.

It was purely a male-ego thing, but as I experienced my first small successes, I became more and more like a young Bighorn Sheep. I began to push. Pushing with my head down—making the old rams give just a little ground. I was not ready for full combat yet, not ready to look my adversary in the eye, but I was trying my horns. As I flexed my new muscles and tasted the first fruits of sweet success, I actually began to enjoy the challenge—this test of my manhood.

Chapter 6

The Players

The Players

I slowly came to realize that Joe hadn't singled me out as a target for his bluff and bluster, he barked and growled at everyone. I just happened to be the youngest and weakest target around at the time. Joe was miserable, and like an old lion with a thorn in his paw, he growled and scowled and tried to be sure everyone around him was miserable too. I've heard it said that happiness isn't complete until it's shared, and Joe was proving that misery has the same qualities. He tried to sprinkle a little of his misery on everyone he met.

Joe was a fugitive. He'd given up a good life for an illicit love affair with old lady liquor and she was a jealous and demanding lover. He was living on the ranch so he could hide from her. The isolation of the canyon was a way to insulate himself from the temptations and consequences of his passion for strong drink. The only way he could have any kind of life was to stay away from town. Virginia and the Colonel were well aware of his background and his weakness, but they tolerated him. I think it was an act of compassion on Virginia's part, made easier by the fact that Joe was a pretty good farm hand. Joe also got a leg up because it was very difficult to keep full-time farm hands who were single men and willing to work for months on end without running off to town every few days. It was also hard to find someone willing to stay year after year and work the fields for five dollars a day and fried potatoes.

I've decided that when Joe was vicious and mean to me at the start he was protecting his territory. He was a full-time resident of the ranch while kids like me were transients—there for a few weeks and then gone. Joe was doing what an old dog on the porch will do when the master brings home a new and untrained pup. He would snap and growl and intimidate as much as he could to protect his rug and his dog dish. He set some rules and he defended his little corner of the bunkhouse. That cluttered corner of the bunkhouse was Joe's whole world. It was all he had to show for a life of work and worry and it was precious to him, humble as it might be.

Joe was on the fast track to self-destruction. He stayed away from alcohol as much as he could, but when it was available he drank himself unconscious. He loved whiskey. The summer I was there he got falling-down sick, and obnoxiously drunk three or four times and it was always a mystery as to where he got the booze. The ranch was fifty miles from the nearest liquor store and it was obvious that someone was buying it for him and bringing it to the ranch. Joe didn't have the self-control to keep a stash hidden anywhere. It was difficult to figure out who was buying for him because the ranch sat squarely on the main road to Myton and anyone could have passed him a bottle while he was out working.

The first time I saw him drunk it took me a while to understand what was wrong with him because I'd never worked around anyone drunk before. Joe had been cutting hay while I was hauling hay and I met him at the corral at five-thirty in the afternoon to do the chores. He was bleary-eyed and slurring his words and staggering when he walked. I was alarmed, wondering if he was having a stroke or a heart attack. I told him to go sit down and I would do the chores, but he only slobbered and waved his hand at me and mumbled some tongue-tied gibberish that I couldn't understand. I thought about running over to the big house and getting the Boss Lady, but I didn't. I just tried to hurry with the chores so we could be done and go back to the bunkhouse where he could lie down.

It had rained that week, just enough to make the ground muddy, and we were in the corral making some old cows stand still to let a batch of bummer calves feed when Joe went down. I saw him fall, and I've never seen anything like it. He was standing there with a shovel handle in his hand, holding an old cow in a corner while a calf stole it's dinner, and he stuck out his elbow as if to lean on the cow. The trouble was, he was a full eight feet away from the cow—about the length of a common two by four. He raised his elbow and leaned toward the cow, and in slow motion he just tipped over and fell full-length into the mud and wet cow manure without catching himself. He hit the ground hard enough to make a good splash. It knocked the wind out of him and he was covered with the vile, green and odious ooze the cows were walking in. I ran to him and helped him up and walked him to the bunkhouse. I could smell the booze on him then and even a baby-faced Mormon boy like me could figure out what the problem was.

I tried to help him out of his soiled clothes, but he became exceedingly belligerent and pushed me away and growled and coughed and then threw up. Luckily, Humbert showed up at about that time and took care of him. I went back to the corral and was happy to have chores to do that give me an excuse to get away from him.

Another time Joe got drunk he was cutting hay in the field by the ranch house and it looked like he had taken his whiskey bottle with him on the tractor and had just driven around all afternoon drinking. He had the cutter-bar down and cutting, and the swaths he cut just wandered around the field aimlessly. I'm surprised that no one noticed what was happening while he was doing it. When we came in to do the chores that afternoon,

Joe was passed out on the tractor seat, lying across the steering wheel like he was dead, his arms hanging down and his face all mushed up and distorted by the steering wheel. The field was a real mess. There were wide swaths of hay still standing in the field and it was easy to see where he had driven the tractor and cutter-bar into the fence, along the ditch banks and through the willows and weeds. It was truly remarkable that he hadn't ruined some expensive equipment and killed himself in the process. Humbert had to take the tractor and cutter-bar back into the field the next morning and clean things up before we could rake and bail the hay.

When Joe got drunk like that, it usually took him a day or two to recover and then he would be back to his normal, grumpy self, cutting hay and scowling all the time. We never did—at least I never did—figure out where he got the bottle when he went on one of his drunks.

I was a young observer, seeing and understanding for the first time some of the pain and ruin people bring upon themselves. And even then I was conscious of the way we all reacted differently when presented with such unpleasantness. When Joe got drunk and sick, Virginia seemed distressed and concerned, but she fretted from a distance. The Colonel was annoyed and angry, but again, from a distance. I never saw the Colonel ever confront Joe directly about his unseemly behavior, even though he complained bitterly to the rest of us. Willis simply ignored old Joe when he fell off the wagon. I stood back and played the part of innocent bystander. Humbert stepped in and assumed the role of Florence Nightingale.

In retrospect, it was like watching a *National Geographic* special about elephants. One old elephant has made a bad choice and is stuck in the mud at the watering hole. The other elephants all gather around while the stricken elephant struggles. Most of the other elephants stand around and stare, a few of them run around with their tails and trunks in the air, all excited and trumpeting the alarm, and one gets down on his knees in the mud and extends his trunk in an effort to help.

I understand now, that like the elephants, we were each presented with an opportunity to make a decision about what our reaction was going to be. Even on a remote ranch in Eastern Utah, each one of us could not escape our obligation to make the moral judgments that would ultimately define who we are.

We all knew that Joe was killing himself. He tried to go out with a bang by stopping his heart with alcohol. But as that option failed him time and again, he worked on committing a slower, but just as sure suicide with tobacco.

I've never seen a man smoke the way he did. Joe smoked cigars by the boxful. Whenever the Colonel or Humbert went to town, Joe would have them bring him a couple dozen boxes of cigars and they would last him for only a few weeks. Joe lit his first cigar as he got out of bed in the morning and he smoked continuously all day long. He had a cigar after breakfast and then he would fill both of his shirt pockets with cigars as he went to the fields. He would come in at noon dying for a smoke and he would have one and sometimes two cigars with his lunch. He would fill his pockets again before going back to the fields for the afternoon. In the evenings, he sat and read his newspaper and smoked one cigar after another until he went to bed at ten. One of the cowboys told me that old Joe couldn't afford to go to town more than once a year because he made five dollars a day and spent three dollars a day on his cigar habit. That analysis was probably true.

Joe chain-smoked cigars the way other addicts smoked cigarettes. He sucked 'em down deep, inhaling every breath as if trying to purge his system of oxygen. He made love to his cigars, tenderly patting those in his shirt pockets to be sure they were still there while chewing and smacking on the one in his mouth as the brown smoke swirled around his face. He would suck on a cigar with such enthusiasm that he could finish one in just a few minutes when he really put his mind to it. I joked to Humbert that Joe was our mosquito abatement man because the bugs seemed to flee whenever he lit up. The ashtray bucket by his bed was a smoldering smudge pot that tormented anything that drew breath, and the bunkhouse was always a mosquito free zone. Maybe mosquitoes are smarter than people after all.

Joe's passion for tobacco came with a steep price tag. He always emitted a gurgling, phlegmy sound when he breathed deeply, and he coughed a lot, sometimes to the point of throwing up. He had to know how harmful the habit was, but he didn't care. Cigars were his friends and he was loyal to them like nothing else in his life.

Joe had a sheep that he overindulged in the same ways he was ruining his own health. The sheep was named Tommy and he was a black-faced wether, a castrated buck sheep, the kind usually made into lamb chops. I don't know how Joe had come to have the only sheep on the big cattle ranch, but he kept him as a pet. Tommy lived in the stack yard near the ranch house and he was so fat he could hardly walk. Twice a day Joe gave him grain from the company granary. It was hot, high-calorie grain that was reserved for working saddle horses and bummer calves. Tommy loved the stuff and Joe would giggle and urge him on as he smacked and slobbered and ate the grain from a special pan that Joe held in his hands. Joe would also feed Tommy cigars. He had actually taught the sheep to eat cigars and Tommy seemed to like them. Joe would show off for company by having his sheep eat a cigar, and then he would laugh and laugh when people seemed incredulous.

Joe wouldn't let anyone else take care of his sheep. Like the corner of the bunkhouse, Tommy belonged to Joe, and Joe was a jealous master. Joe showered affection on his sheep in a way he couldn't or wouldn't show affection toward people. He talked baby talk to him and he would rub his ears and put his arm around his neck and hug him. Sometimes on Sundays, when we had our one day of the week off, Joe would brush Tommy and clean him all up. The sheep was a beautiful creature, the kind you see in stock shows, but he was grossly overweight and his wool was too long and he needed shearing. The sheep suffered greatly in the heat. Joe was loving his sheep to death.

Humbert was a good man. He had no ambitions beyond being a cowboy and a farmer in Nine Mile Canyon. In conjunction with his brothers, who had good jobs in town, Humbert owned a small ranch in the canyon and he lived there full-time. Humbert was a bachelor, and there were rumors that he was living out a self-imposed exile in the canyon after a failed relationship with a young lady many years before.

Humbert worked for Virginia as a way to make the few dollars a month he needed for the basics of life. Even in those days, owning your own farm and working for yourself didn't pay. A man had to love working his own place because it took everything he had away from him: time, money, patience and good mental health. A farm drained a man and he had to work for someone else just to be able to eat. Things are still that way today.

Humbert understood the operation very well and he was a valuable farm hand. He was quiet and shy by nature, and good to the bone. He took care of old Joe, helping him through his drunk and sick days when no one else would; running errands for him in town and cleaning up after him when he trashed the place. They sometimes fought like junkyard dogs, but Humbert was always there when old Joe needed someone to talk to or someone to cuss at.

Humbert was always good to me and I appreciated it. He was the kind of older man I had been taught to honor and respect. He had many of the Boy Scout virtues I had been taught were the measure of a good man. He did most of the irrigating on the farm and he was the one sent to town on errands because he had his own transportation.

Joe and Humbert reminded me of Laurel and Hardy. Humbert was thin and frail and soft-spoken, the perfect straight man for Joe's bluff and bluster. Joe would paint the air blue with vile obscenities while Humbert would giggle and duck his head and blush. Joe was dramatic and theatrical in his conversations, waving his arms and gesturing with his hands—and sometimes his finger. Humbert was quiet and reserved, sitting with his arms and legs all tucked in close to his body, smiling. Their personalities clashed, and yet they balanced each other like partners in a good stage routine. They were entertaining dinner guests, and I watched in fascination the interplay between these two refugees from the mainstream of human society.

There was always an irreverent banter between them, a gruff play on words that made an outsider like me wince. It was like what I've heard said about cats—by just listening to them, you can never be sure if they're fighting or making love. Joe and Humbert were like that.

They called each other vile and demeaning names as a matter of routine. They chided and criticized and pecked at each other . . . and it was all a game. It took me a while to realize that this was truly a form of peacekeeping social behavior. Those two old castaways had to live in close proximity without the ties of normal family bonding. Their relationship was not based on love and tolerance and commitment to one another, and they got on each other's nerves. The way to get along and not have constant conflict was always tell the other guy what you thought, but do it with humor and creative language so the other guy got the message without taking offense. The pattern had to be maintained by both parties and it had to be consistent.

A typical situation and exchange of communication would go something like this: at the dinner table, Humbert removes a boot to get a sticker out of his sock, and it feels so good to take his boot off after a long day in the fields that he takes both boots off and sets them alongside his chair. This annoys Joe.

Joe growls: "Good Lord, you stinky (expletive deleted), put yer damn boots back on before the paint peels off the walls."

Humbert answers, as he puts his boots back on: "Oh drop dead you old (creative expletive deleted). The paint in here is so covered with soot from those damn cigars you couldn't peel it off with a scoop shovel."

Joe: " I've smelled sun-ripened sheep guts that smell better than your damn feet."

Humbert, with a smile: "Isn't that what you cooked for supper tonight?"

This type of exchange often went by without a smile or a laugh from either party, which was part of the game. Once in a while, one of them would nod or wink at me when they got in a particularly witty or gruesome jab. Sometimes of course, the retorts were so good or so humorous that everyone would laugh out loud. This kind of interplay nearly always broke the tension and resolved any pending strife. It was social survival in its purest and simplest form. I learned to play the game with them and it served me well in the years to come.

In early July, the two of them, in an unusual mood of self-pity and deservedness, decided that it was time to take Joe to town and get his hair cut since he had been locked up on the ranch for over a year. Timidly, they approached the boss lady with their proposal, and Humbert, like a good older brother, promised to stay with Joe and take good care of him. They each drew a wad of back pay, climbed into Humbert's truck, and escaped into the wild blue yonder.

They came back a day later than they said they would, both of them sick, drunk, and hung-over. Joe was a complete stranger. His hair was cut and he looked almost normal; not at all the wild man I had become accustomed to, even though he still had a three-day stubble of gray beard poking from his chin that strangely complemented his raw and blood-shot eyes. The back of his neck and around his ears was ridiculously white where the long hair had been removed, and Humbert said the barber had worn out two sets of clippers just finding Joe's ears. Humbert giggled that the barber had told Joe that he should charge him for five haircuts, and the barber said that he figured there were at least three pounds of cockleburs buried in Joe's tangled locks. Some other guy in the barbershop said they should have stopped by Crazy Jim's sheep camp and run old Joe through the dipping vats and the shearing corral with the woolies.

Joe sneered at Humbert's playful banter but took it all in good humor. He was still delightfully drunk and unusually complacent. He had the self-satisfied smirk of one who knows where a treasure trove of alcohol is hidden. The two world-travelers had sacks and boxes of new clothes and new boots and books and snack foods, and Joe had more cigars than he could carry into the bunkhouse in one trip.

Later that same afternoon, Humbert left in a hurry to go back to town and Joe said they had forgotten something. Humbert came back later that night and the two of them sat and drank coffee and nursed their hangovers and were all sad and melancholy. I found out that one of the things Joe had done in town was to buy himself a new western hat. It was not a run-of-the-mill western hat, but an expensive Resistol hat that cost him thirty-five dollars . . . a whole week's pay. They said it was a beautiful hat, silver-belly gray in color, and even Joe looked good in it. Unfortunately, while in a drunken stupor, Joe had left it hanging on a coat-rack in the whorehouse in Helper, and when Humbert went back to get it for him that next afternoon, it was gone. Joe had worn his expensive new hat from the Price Trading Company to the house-of-ill-repute and then it was gone forever. Oh well . . . easy come and easy go, as the two of them always joked.

Joe lay drunk for a solid week after he and Humbert came back from town. We all knew he had a stash of whiskey someplace and the Colonel tried in vain to find it. He looked all through the bunkhouse, including my things, which annoyed me greatly. At long last, Joe must have run out of whiskey because he sobered up and was sick for a few days and then went back to the fields. It was easy to see why his trips to town were so infrequent; the man was irresponsible and had absolutely no self-control.

Willis came from a family with deep roots in the Nine Mile country. He had recently bought a ranch in the canyon, the old Housekeeper place, and like Humbert, his ranch was bleeding him white and he needed some money to eat. Also like Humbert, he showed up in the mornings and went back to his own place in the evenings. He didn't work with us all the time.

Willis was a large man and very strong. He was quiet and soft-spoken and he worked hard. He was the one old boy I couldn't keep up with. Willis could pick up a bale in each hand and throw them high on the wagon. I don't know if he ever knew it, but I almost killed myself trying to match him bale for bale. I finally had to give it up and accept the fact that God didn't create all men equal after all. I did what I could, but Willis always got more work done in a day than I could, and sometimes a lot more.

Willis wore an English pith helmet when he worked out in the sun—the kind Egyptian archaeologists and British explorers wore in the movies. Anyone but Willis might have been teased about that hat, but no one ever said a word to Willis about it. He had been a combat Marine in the Pacific during World War II and he reminded me of Clint Walker, the cowboy movie star. He had the size and rugged good looks to be my idea of what a real Colonel should look like, and I admired the man for his strength and quiet temperament.

Like Humbert, he was good to the bone and he always treated me with courtesy and respect. I always thought he was ten or fifteen years younger than Joe and Humbert, but I found out in later years that he wasn't; he just looked younger and acted younger and he didn't smoke and chew. He could work harder, faster, smarter and better than the whole hay crew put together, and I'm sure he was Virginia Nutter's all-time top hand.

Another person Virginia hired that summer was my cousin Donald. Donald and I are the same age and Donald is one of the strongest people I've ever known. Donald had polio when he was a child, and when he came to the ranch that summer he was just a few short years out of leg braces. It was an awful gutsy thing for Donald to even think of hauling hay all summer, but Donald was like that. He was determined to be just one of the guys, and he refused to be handicapped.

Donald worked as hard as any of us, but it cost him more. He was humping hay bales with a demon on his back and the devil drained him of strength and sleep. He worked hard and he never complained, but in the mornings he pulled his boots on with a wince and with his teeth clenched tightly. And sometimes in the mornings it was a full hour or more before he could stand up straight. He helped us do morning chores with the posture of an old man, limping and bent over. He never mentioned it, but I saw him taking more and more of his pain medication each day he was there.

For a while he kept up by sheer force of will, but he was paying a price that none of the rest of us could feel or understand. He stayed with it until he used up all of his reserves of strength and determination, and then his iron resolve was betrayed by a body that just couldn't respond. I felt terrible when he had to leave after just a short time, and I wish we could have spent that summer together. I enjoyed his company, and I'm sure his razor sharp wit, world-class sense of humor and Black Belt in sarcasm would have given old Joe and Humbert a run for their money.

I've always admired Donald, and I've never forgotten that I saw him fight a good fight that summer. Donald went on to work in the coal mines just a few years later and he raised a family working underground at one of the toughest, dirtiest and most dangerous jobs in the world. There are men who brag and men who swagger, but the real men are those who quietly slay the dragons in their path and get on with the business of living. Donald, I salute you.

There was a man writing a centennial history of the ranch that summer and his name was John. I never got to know him very well, but some of the old hands told me later that he was a pretty good guy. He was a young man, and a foreigner from a strange land. He dressed funny and he had strange customs and strange manners and he was sure to tell everyone he met that he was from California. It was like he was excusing himself. He seemed to be embarrassed to have people know that he was even visiting in Utah. He lived in the guest cottage near the big house for a few weeks and took his meals and his intellectual discussions with the owners of the plantation. His work was never published. I'm not sure why.

To me, John always seemed a little apprehensive and uncomfortable when he ventured too near the slave quarters where Joe the dragon and I lived. I thought it was kind of funny, and sometimes when he came over to the cookhouse I smiled and bit my lip when Joe or Humbert would pull up a chair right next to him. I would watch him quietly squirm, and then casually get up and move farther away, trying to be cool and nonchalant, smiling and pleasant, but with his ears flattened out like a cat in the sprinklers.

He was a true son of the surf and sand, the kind of guy who would always pause to admire his reflection and comb his hair when he passed a window—in true California beach boy style. He was a good-looking surfer boy and he seemed to be thoroughly enjoying himself at the ranch—in spite of the stain on his reputation for having to spend the summer in Utah. He was always true to the traditions and sentiments of his homeland, a quiet ambassador from the left-coast, a cultural missionary out to Californicate the wilds of Eastern Utah. He seemed to get along well with the Colonel, and sometimes the Boss Man even let him throw the ball for Brody, which was an honor seldom bestowed.

I was always a little leery of John because he wore searsucker shirts with sleeveless sweaters, sissy britches (slacks) and sandals around the ranch. I was just a kid, but I figured that anyone who dressed like that in Nine Mile in the summer must have only one oar in the water. I've been very cautious about people from California (the land of fruits and nuts) ever since.

1963 was the centennial year for the Preston Nutter Corporation and Virginia was doing all she could to properly commemorate her father's accomplishments. She had a '63 seal affixed to the company letterhead and she had John the writer from California staying at the ranch to write a history of her father and the ranch. She seemed to be very conscious of her role as successor to a great man and the caretaker of his empire. Under her management the ranch had prospered and her father would have been proud.

Virginia was a strong woman; she was educated and intelligent. She was also a good person. As the boss lady, she was always good to me and I would break my back to coax a smile or a nod of approval from her. I never did talk to her much, but she treated me with respect, and I worked so hard for her that I was never embarrassed to look her in the eye. She would smile at me knowingly, acknowledging a job well done, and she seemed to be charmed by the resolve of the little buck sheep that pushed at the old goats with his shiny new horns. She admired spirit and determination; I could see it in her eyes. One day Humbert whispered that she wanted to adopt me, and his remark embarrassed me. I tried not to show off quite so much when she was around after that.

Virginia impressed me greatly. She was Barbara Stanwyck in *The Big Valley* TV series, the charming, steely-eyed Boss Lady in skirts who runs the ranch and hires and fires all the cowboys. She was a strong woman, capable and competent—a leader of men.

She was the undisputed boss of the ranch, but she bowed to tradition and the expectations of her society at the time. She kept the reins of power in her own capable hands while respectfully allowing her husband to step out front to speak for the corporation. The Colonel did most of the talking in public meetings and his name was affixed to the official correspondence, but anyone working closely with the outfit had no illusions about who really made all the day-to-day decisions. As farmhands who worked very closely with them, we experienced this every day. The Colonel and Virginia would come to the cookhouse every morning to line us out and get the daily report. Virginia would stand back discretely and let her man talk all he wanted to, and when he was through, she would step forward quietly and give us our real and final orders for the day.

It wasn't that the Colonel was completely incompetent; it's just that Virginia was in her element. She had grown up on the ranch and it was in her blood. She knew instinctively what needed to be done. Old man Preston Nutter lived on, in her heart and in her veins, and he steered her through the obstacles.

The Colonel, on the other hand, was a fish out of water at the ranch. He had not been raised around livestock, hay fields and rattlesnakes in the yard. He put up a good false front, but he lacked experience and the background skills—and his heart just wasn't in it. He was an army brat, a world traveler and a reader of books. He dutifully wore the mantle of a Cattle Baron, but it never fit him well.

The bunkhouse rumor mill had it that since Virginia was Preston Nutter's daughter, surrogate son, heir apparent and future queen of his kingdom, she was duty bound to marry a man with a title. Doctor or judge would have been fine, but *Army Officer* had a special charm with a ring of manly authority to it. I was told that Virginia met the Colonel when she was working for the Red Cross in the early days of World War II. At that time, the Colonel was a young captain stationed at Fort Douglas in Salt Lake City. The Colonel's father was a general and post commander of Fort Douglas.

The Colonel had been a civilian for a long time when I knew him, but he still wore his military rank like a necktie. He always kept it out front where everyone could see and admire it. He even hid behind it. Being a colonel excused him from being a cowboy. It was okay if he didn't know how to rope a steer or castrate a calf; he had proven himself in another arena. He loved to have people call him *colonel* and everyone I knew did.

He was a man of some ability. He could write beautiful letters to the editors of the local newspapers and he could debate and win against BLM and Forest Service lawyers. I was told he could charm county commissioners and state revenue agents, and he was really in his element at the country club or the Hilton. He had friends in high places and he walked with the air of a man who is confident in who he is and where he's going.

I was disappointed when I first saw him up close because he was not at all the image of a warrior one imagines when the word *colonel* is bantered about. Colonels were supposed to be seven feet tall and three ax handles across the shoulders with steely gray eyes and a square, steel and concrete reinforced jaw line. This colonel was tall, but the requisite physical features of a military commander ended there. He was thin and frail. His movements always seem exaggerated, even awkward, and his mannerisms were calm and soft, bordering on effeminate—he was like Alan Alda's older brother. He was an introvert by nature and he reminded me of a typical college professor—always in a hurry, his arms swinging at his side, his head down and deep in thought, living inside himself, always unaware of his immediate surroundings.

He seemed to have an aversion to shaking hands—at least with those of us who worked in the trenches. When he approached a group of men he would reflexively stick his fingers in his back pockets. When he talked to his workers he always seemed to be a little stressed or embarrassed, even unsure of himself. He would stand there with his fingers in his back pockets, his elbows sticking out, and he would rock back and forth from the heel to the toe of his boots, nervously. He was always smiling and pleasant, but detached. Often his mouth would be saying something while his eyes and his mind were obviously somewhere else. He had a terrible time trying to make small talk with the troops and he didn't attempt it often.

He never worked with us. No matter how short handed we were, he never came to the rescue. I only saw the man get his hands dirty one time and that was during the little trash barrel incident, and then he acted like he'd been violated. He was forever the army officer—distant and reserved. He spent his time in the command bunker with his maps, charts, and official dispatches, safe from the summer sun and the mosquito kamikazes. Sometimes in a time of crisis he would show up dressed in his pressed khaki, and he would give us advice and oral support (yes—oral support), but I never saw him lift or carry anything. It's possible that he had a medical condition or an old war wound that I didn't know about, but there were times when I resented his apparent prissiness.

He was incurably absent minded. One morning he told me he wanted me to go with him to the bottom stack yard and fill the stock truck with hay to bring back to the farmyard. Dutifully, I climbed in with him and we headed down the canyon. He was driving of course. He was the master and I the humble boy servant, so I didn't initiate any conversation. And in his usual manner, he had nothing to say to me, and so we traveled on in silence.

We came to the stack yard and he drove right on past it and down the canyon. I supposed he had some other errand he wanted to perform, and so I said nothing and just sat back and watched the canyon go by. We went about eight miles down the canyon to where the road forks at the mouth of Cottonwood, and there at the fork in the road he slammed on the brakes like he was about to run over something in the road. I had to put my hand against the dashboard to keep from hitting the windshield. I looked over at him and he was blushing fluorescent red. He had a panicked look in his eyes like he had just come on stage without his pants. He didn't say a word; he just turned the truck around and started back up the canyon. I caught on then that he had been daydreaming and had simply missed his destination. I had to turn my head and look out the window and bite my lip to keep from smiling.

We traveled back up the canyon, retracing the extra eight miles, and when we got to the stack yard he went right on by it again. I couldn't believe it. I leaned forward and looked over at him with a raised eyebrow that should have tipped him off. He was focused severely on the road ahead, his eyebrows wrinkled up and both hands on the wheel, driving with a vengeance. He ignored me. I didn't think it was my place to question or ask, and so I sat back and supposed the big man had decided to do something different.

We buzzed on up the canyon until we came to the ranch yard where he slammed on the brakes and skidded in the gravel again. This time he was blushing deep red and his mouth was open like the wind had been knocked out of him. We sat there in the middle of the road for a moment, the truck engine running, the color slowly coming back to his face, and then he pulled the truck over by the grain shed and turned the key off. We sat there quietly for a minute and then he said, "Oh to hell with it . . . we don't need any damn hay anyway!" With that, he got out of the truck and hurried to the sanctuary of the big house, his head down, fists clenched tightly and his arms swinging wildly at his sides like he was mad.

That night at supper I told Joe and Humbert about my

adventure and I think it was the first time I had actually heard old Joe laugh. He made me tell the story two or three times. The old dragon was warming up to me.

Virginia and the Colonel always stayed just a little out-of-touch around the ranch hands, aloof, military officer style, preserving that vestige of mystery and unfamiliarity that gives people in authority an aura of power. What little time they spent with the hands was business related; there was very little "fraternizing" with the troops. We most often saw them at a distance. Virginia could often be seen through the window of her study as she sat at her desk and labored over the paper work of the empire. Most of the time we didn't see the Colonel at all unless he was out on the lawn playing with his dog.

The Colonel loved his Airedale Terrier, and Brody was spoiled like a pampered only child. The dog was groomed and clipped and perfumed. It's a shame he was never trained. The mutt lacked manners and he was an obnoxious crotch sniffer and indiscrete about where he used the sandbox. He would cock a leg anywhere at anytime on anything and even people had to be on guard. The Colonel doted over Brody like a new mother and kept him safely inside the big house at night and fed him cantaloupe and ice cream on the lawn during the day.

Brody had a malady common to little kids and dumb dogs—he thought everybody loved him (it's not necessarily true you know). He had a fatal, trusting stupidity about him and I truly expected that old Joe, who hated dog pee on the porch, would catch him in a dark alley late one night and send him to the big fire hydrant in the sky.

Old man Preston Nutter is said to have had some rules about dogs. He didn't like them around his cows. He is supposed to have said that they ran cows around too much and made them lose weight. Brody was granted an exemption from the century-old rule, probably because he was a fifty-pound lap dog and not much of a threat to livestock.

Brody was the Colonel's best friend: his companion, confidant, sidekick and soul mate. The two of them spent many long summer days tramping after a ball over the well-kept lawn, playing peek-a-boo in the lilac bushes and eating cantaloupe and ice cream in the shade of the porch.

Normally, we wouldn't have cared what he fed his dog, but it was a difficult thing, especially for a kid like me, to come to the cookhouse at noon after spending the morning jacking hay bales in one hundred degree heat and see the dog eating ice cream and cantaloupe in the shade while we went in to fried potatoes and canned vegetables. I could never understand why the Colonel wasn't more discrete. One of the basic rules of leadership pounded into Army officers is to never trade the respect of your men for the pleasures of petty self-indulgences. The Colonel must have missed that lesson.

We ate pretty well at the ranch, we got three squares a day, but there were never any luxuries: mostly canned goods, eggs, store-bought bread and lots of potatoes and onions. We never had ice cream—not once.

One day the Colonel came back from a grocery run to town and he brought over to us a very large Green River watermelon. Green River melons are the best in the world and Humbert and I danced a Virginia reel around the kitchen table we were so happy to have it. We put the treasure in the refrigerator to get it cold, planning to eat it that evening when the work was done and we could really enjoy it. To have a cold watermelon was like winning the lottery for us.

All day long, as I worked in the fields, I dreamed about that cold melon. I dreamed of digging into that melon with my dirty little fingers while the juice ran down my arms and soaked into my shirtsleeves. I dreamed of putting my dusty little face right down in a big slice of melon and blowing bubbles. I wanted to roll in the rinds like a hound dog and spit seeds at the moon. I wanted to act like a two-year old in a highchair and put melon in my hair and melon in my ears.

I was shocked when I came in to do chores at five-thirty and saw the Colonel leaving the cookhouse with a full half of our cold melon under his arm. He had his head down, walking quickly and with a hasty resolve, beating a retreat back toward the big house. I was incensed because I had seen him take a full melon to his place just that morning when he gave us ours.

I felt violated, cheated and robbed. I had earned that watermelon, it had been given to me and I had big plans for it. The situation was made especially onerous after watching the Boss Man and his dog eat cantaloupe and ice cream in the shade of the porch several times over the past few weeks. That melon was my one and only treat in a very long time, and my precious pearl had been cast before the swine.

When the Colonel walked out of there with half of my watermelon, it was like he had put a pebble in one of my boots. I walked on it for a long time and it made a sore spot that never healed.

A Wolf On The Doorstep

We went through a couple of cooks that summer. It was hard for Virginia to hire a woman to work in such a remote location. I don't think she ever considered hiring a man as a full-time cook. In our world, women cooked and men worked in the fields.

I'd been there for just a short while when they hired an older woman to cook. She lasted about a week. Her downfall was assured from the moment she got there because she brought with her a big dog, an ugly German Shepard that served as her companion and protector. The Colonel told the new lady cook that she would have to keep her dog outside. Only Brody ranked high enough for house-duty.

She chained the beast to the front porch and he protected her so well that the rest of us had a tough time trying to get to the bathroom or even into the cookhouse to eat. Her companion and protector was vicious. Joe and Humbert both complained to the Colonel, but nothing was done until after the morning when Brody had a chance to be a hero.

The Colonel was in the habit of having a war-council with the troops each morning, and on that particular morning he came toodling around the corner of the porch humming a happy tune, his head down and his thoughts somewhere in the South Pacific. Before he realized what he'd done, he walked right up on ol' Fang who was sleeping on the porch.

The dog came off the rug like a coiled spring, snapping and snarling. He pinned the good Colonel against the cinderblock wall of the cookhouse, not biting him by some miracle, but barking and growling and slobbering and daring the man to make a move. The Colonel was standing on his tippy-toes, facing the dog, torn between a need to climb the cinderblock wall with his shoulder blades and a need to keep both hands clamped tightly over his private parts to keep them away from the slashing teeth. The old lady who could control the dog was off in the back somewhere, and she must have been cleaning her hearing aids because she was a long time in getting to the door.

Joe and I came running from the cookhouse and were shocked at what we saw. Joe yelled something to me about a shovel and I started for the truck; he ran back inside to round up the dog's owner. The Colonel did the drill he had apparently rehearsed in his dreams and he started to sing out "Brodee . . . Brodee . . . save me Brodee!" Unfortunately, Brody the wonder dog was off chasing peacocks somewhere and missed his shining moment in the sun.

The dog-lady cook landed heavily on the porch with Joe steering her by the shoulders, and she managed to call off her rabid beast. The Colonel retreated to the big house and I'll bet he needed a paper bag over his face to resuscitate himself from hyperventilation. I didn't blame him. It was a vicious and frightening attack.

I got there just a little too late to take Brody's place and be a hero. I was bitterly disappointed. Had I been able to slap the Big Bad Wolf on the butt with the shovel I might have been able to reclaim the war bonnet feather I lost to the badger.

The cook and her wolfhound were gone by the next afternoon.

The Colonel was not bitten, but his mantle of manly dignity was forever ripped to shreds. It was a cruel world we lived in, and any act of embarrassing indiscretion was pounced upon by the bullies at school and turned against you without mercy.

For many weeks thereafter, there was a little inside joke amongst the troops. Whenever one of us would get in a tight spot, like when an old cow in the corral would blow snot and threaten, or when we found a rattlesnake in the field, or even when old Joe idly offered to beat me and Humbert up, the standard response was to put both knees together tightly, clap both hands over the crotch in fake distress and squeal in high falsetto, "Brodee ... Brodee ... save me Brodee!" Of course, the Colonel never knew.

The morning the cook left, a cowboy showed us all how to do it. He was a young man, probably in his mid-twenties, and he strolled in that morning like the Lone Ranger. I never knew his name, where he came from, or where he went. I think he had stopped by to ask for a job.

He parked a pickup truck in the yard and came walking up on the porch, not knowing about the dog and finding out about him before any of us could put down our coffee cups to warn him. The dog came at him the way he had come at the Colonel the morning before—but this time things were different.

That young man, as cool as ice, jerked his hat off as the dog came at him and held it out to the side at arm's length. The sudden motion distracted the dog, and when he turned to it, the cowboy kicked him square in the face. The boot made contact with that slobbering snout with a crack like Babe Ruth's bat and the dog went spinning off into a corner, baying like a road-kill.

The cowboy straightened up his hat and walked on by to the Boss Lady's house, unruffled and unconcerned. Those of us who were mortals stood transfixed with our noses against the screen door and watched as the young man passed by. Clint Eastwood couldn't have done it better.

Cooking School

Joe was the designated substitute cook when we didn't have a full-time cook, and he did a pretty good job. It was okay for a man to be a substitute cook. His potatoes were sometimes greasy and his coffee too stout, but he always made sure we had plenty to eat. Joe did get tired of it though, and once in a while he would have someone else try their hand.

I was truly shocked when one afternoon old Joe told me to quit the field early and go to the cookhouse and fix supper for everyone. I protested vigorously, letting him know that I had never done anything like that before, but he was insistent, and so I did as I was told. I went into the kitchen and looked through the cupboards and finally hovered over the potato bin. I decided I would fry some potatoes.

I had at least an hour to get supper on the table, but I

hurried and peeled a stack of potatoes and put them right in the frying pan. I was a creative little buck and I wanted my dinner to be different, and so instead of slicing the spuds like everyone else, I cut them like French-fries and then diced them, making cute little potato squares. I wasn't smart enough to find a lid for the frying pan.

I set the table, counting out a place for me and Joe and Humbert and Willis. I opened a couple of cans of the ever-present mixed vegetables and put them in a pan to simmer. I got out a stack of wonder bread and put it on a plate and set it in the middle of the table and then went to experiment with coffee recipes.

I watched and waited for the boys to come up for their evening meal, and I turned and turned and turned the potatoes. The grease I had put in the pan was long gone and I had to keep turning the potatoes to keep them from burning. I thought about putting them on a plate, but decided not to do that because I was afraid they would get cold. I was so engrossed with the potatoes that I didn't notice that nearly all of the water had evaporated from the vegetables and they were fast becoming wrinkled and mummified.

At long last, the guys came in and sat down and I served up my very first home-cooked meal.

It is important to understand that there was a code of behavior among ranch hands that was never breached, and the code was, that you never, ever complained about the food. No matter how bad the grub, you simply didn't complain. The rule was that the man who complained got to be the next cook, and besides, complaining was considered to be bad manners and a real man just didn't do it.

Those cute little potato squares sounded like marbles as they made contact with the stoneware plates. I was embarrassed but didn't know what to do other than apologize and explain how I had tried to keep them warm. The mummified vegetables came next. They were dry and strangely discolored and they smelled like freezer burn, but I was probably smelling the smoldering aluminum from the bottom of the pan. Willis picked up a slice of wonder bread that had been sitting out on the table in the afternoon heat for over an hour and it had dried to the texture of toast. He had to crease it to tear it in half. The coffee had been boiling for so long that there was only half a pot left and it smelled and tasted scorched. The coffee had also condensed down into a thick, black mass that could have been put directly into a gearbox.

I was so embarrassed, but I do wish I had a roll of movie film, taken from some discrete vantage point of those brave and silent men as they ate that evening meal.

Humbert kept his head down and never looked up. He soaked his cute little potato squares in half a bottle of ketchup and let them set for about ten minutes to soak-up a little moisture and then he ate them. He scooped up the mummified vegetables on a piece of dry bread and choked them down with his jaw set like a real trooper. I noticed that all three of my dinner guests were using cream and sugar in their coffee that night.

Willis sat and looked at the wall and chewed those cute little potato squares like a man. He had a resigned, suffering look about him as if he were carrying out a sentence imposed upon him by a judge. He chewed and chewed and crunched and crunched with a sound like a big horse walking on gravel. I was afraid he was going to break a tooth. He ate it all and cleaned up his plate and then got his hat and left for the night. He didn't say anything to me when he left, and I was painfully aware that he wouldn't even look at me during his evening meal.

Joe was boiling. He would crunch down on a cute little potato square and his head would jerk convulsively toward me and his jaw would jut out and his eyes would flash with fire. It took every ounce of self-control the old dragon possessed to seal his lips and not slay me with obscene verbiage. He ate only about half of his meal and then got up silently and dumped the rest of it in the trash and went to read his paper and seethe in the comfort of a good cigar.

I found myself all alone to do the dishes that night, and I was never asked to cook again. In fact, it was two or three days before any of them would even speak to me again.

Chapter 7

Cowboys

The King Of The Cowboys

In late June, I actually got to be a cowboy for the Nutter Ranch for a couple of days. It was the fulfillment of that boyhood dream of mine, but it wasn't quite what I had expected.

It was a common practice at the ranch to separate any of the cows that were poor, weak, and not doing very well for special treatment. This was usually done during the fall roundup. Any cows or calves that were poor, but too young to sell or who still held promise as breeding stock were taken to the farm and fed baled hay through the winter to get them back with the program. Also, any new cattle that were recently purchased were often held at the ranch for a while to quarantine and acclimate them before taking them on the mountain. The spring I was there, there were about forty cows and calves in the farm herd and it was time to introduce them to the rigors of being range cows. Humbert and I were given the job of escorting them back to the land of green grass and clean water and turning them over to the real cowboys.

I had met Eldon Kettle by then, the man who was the range boss and the king of the cowboys. He stopped in on his way from town and stayed overnight with us before going back up to the cow camp. Eldon was one of those rare characters that makes such an astounding first impression that a person never forgets that first encounter. He made a big impression on me;

I'd never met another man like him.

Eldon made a living as a cowboy and the boss of other cowboys and he played the part for all it was worth. He dressed and acted like he was performing in a John Wayne movie. He had a powerful stage presence and he performed artfully and with style. He smirked and he swaggered and he was quick on the draw with witty one-liners that dripped with sarcasm and racy cowboy humor. He knew that everybody wanted to be just like him, and he looked down with pity on all lesser beings who grubbed-out their daily bread without a rope, a saddle, and a good horse.

He looked like the leading character in a Louis L'Amour novel. He was tall and thin and weather-beaten and probably in his early fifties. His hair was streaked with a little gray and he had a face with strong cowboy-hero features that were right out of central casting. His hands were large and bony like those of a boxer.

He wore a big, black felt hat that was shaped in an antique style of the 1920s and '30s. A hat like a cowboy from the silent movies might have worn, a ten-gallon hat with a wide, flat brim and a tall crown. He wore a black leather vest that was unlined and unadorned but made from expensive leather, and he wore it all the time, even in the summer heat. He wore plaid cotton shirts under his black leather vest and the sleeves were always down and buttoned. He wore Levi Strauss jeans and fancy, custom-made western boots with long, antique-styled dog-eared pull-ups that almost touched the ground on each side of the boot. He had a fine pair of soft leather riding gloves hanging out from a back pocket. He rolled up the cuffs on his pant legs the way my grandfather and other men of the early 1900s generation did, and like my grandfather, he often used his pant cuff as an ashtray when he smoked in the house.

I was impressed that he always looked clean, a virtue that

set him apart from most working cowboys, and every time I saw him he was shaved and washed and wearing good clothes. He didn't wear thin and ragged work clothes like those of us who wallowed in hay for a living. His clothes always looked new and he wore them with pride. His cleanliness gave him an air of authority around workingmen and he carried himself with the pride and bearing of a knight in the service of his queen.

Eldon was also the first man I ever knew who wore a bandanna knotted around his neck like the movie cowboys. It was more of a costume prop than an article of true utility and it gave his appearance a flamboyant and theatrical touch. Cowboys of the eighteen-eighties, who lived in the saddle, wore bandannas as sun protection and to keep dirt from going down the necks of their often-collarless shirts. It could also be pulled up over the nose and mouth to keep the dust out while making those long and arduous trail drives between Texas and Dodge City Kansas. And then of course, Tom Mix and other silent-movie-era cowboys always wore bandannas when they rode the range and made the frontier safe for sod bustin' settlers and the likes of Mae West.

Eldon wore his bandanna in the shade of the porch and at the dinner table, and like Joe's long hair, it looked unnatural and out of place to me. I think the bandanna betrayed him. It was the final straw that put his outfit over-the-top. It was like a flashy, fake-diamond ring waved under your nose at a dinner party. It whispered, even to a kid like me, that the man was playing a role. His outfit and his rough and tumble cowboy persona were both just a little too showy and over-scripted.

Like most men, Eldon had some vices that were readily discernable. One of them was that he smoked with almost the same enthusiasm as Joe the dragon. When at the cow camp, he smoked roll-yer-own Bull Durham cigarettes like the old-time cowboys, but when he came from town he smoked little black

THE SPLIT SKY

cheroots that were imported from Turkey or Afghanistan or some other wild and exotic place. They came in boxes about the size of a cigarette pack and every time I saw Eldon he had a box in his shirt pocket and a cheroot in his mouth. They burned with the intensity of a dynamite fuse and they smelled suspiciously like a cow chip campfire to me. I secretly fantasized, and giggled to myself, that they were made from Turkish camel dung dipped in tar and I smiled every time I saw Eldon light one up. I never smoked one, but Humbert, who was fond of cigarettes, told me they were strong enough to knock your socks off, and even Joe the dragon, our world champion cigar aficionado, said they were too stout for him. I was surprised. I didn't think there was anything that burned and smelled bad that was too stout for Joe the dragon.

When Eldon came into the cookhouse that first afternoon, Joe and Humbert greeted him like a long-lost big brother. They gave him the best chair and the best spot at the table and Humbert even hung his hat up for him. Even the Colonel came over to the cookhouse to talk to him, which was unusual because the Colonel usually sat in his command bunker at the big house and waited for people to come to him. The simple act of the Colonel going out of his way to talk to Eldon demonstrated for me just how high this fellow stood in the pecking order at the ranch, and I was impressed. The cowboy range boss was obviously at the very top of the food chain.

Eldon loved the attention, and he sat back and drank coffee and smoked his cheroots and entertained everyone with his stories. He was a man's man and the big dog in the kennel that night. The others fawned around him and catered to him and listened in rapt attention to what he had to say—and he had plenty to say. I sat back in awed silence, not having enough whiskers to join in on the fraternal camaraderie, but fascinated nonetheless.

And then I was thrown onto the center of the stage.

One of the guys mentioned to Eldon that I was mad because Virginia wouldn't let me go up to the cow camp that summer. The remark greatly embarrassed me, and I felt so childish and so very presumptuous to have even dreamed such a dream now that I was in the presence of this real-life Cowboy Range Boss. I blushed and tried to make myself very small.

All was quiet for a few moments while Eldon sized me up with a dramatically raised eyebrow. I cowered and glowed red in the spotlight. And then, with a snort of theatrical contempt, he got up and went to his duffle bag and brought out a small hemp rope. He smiled cunningly as he fashioned the rope into a hangman's noose and then he held his creation up for all to admire. He turned with a flourish, tossed the noose to me and told me to go outside and climb a big cottonwood tree and tie the end of the rope to a limb and put the noose around my neck and jump from the tree to see if I could fly. He said that if I could fly he would take me on the mountain tomorrow. If not, I would have to hang around the farm for a while. He said it would be a good idea if I practiced a few times before they set a place for me at the supper table.

The guys all laughed at his joke and Eldon sat back with a self-satisfied smile, enjoying his own cleverness. Even I laughed half-heartedly, still blushing like a schoolgirl. Eldon then proclaimed that there weren't any real cowboys anymore, and anyone who wanted to be a cowboy nowadays should be drowned as a pup—or hanged.

In spite of being the butt of his joke, I was captivated by the way the man looked and by his magnetic personality. He was the glittering movie star version of my manly ideal and I wanted to be just like him. I would have followed him to hell for just a pat on the head.

Unfortunately, my juvenile judgment was bad. Virginia had

done the right thing by keeping me away from the man. I was too young and too impressionable to be spending the summer marinating in the influence of a character like Eldon. He was a tough old stud horse, and steeled in the manly virtues, and I'm sure I could have learned a great deal from him, but at sixteen I was not ready for the big leagues yet. I still had a lot to learn.

I was soon to hear some horror stories about how Eldon got some young men hurt who worked for him. Given the right circumstances, I could easily have been one of his casualties. I was so inexperienced and so desperate to be accepted and so rapt by his charm that I'm sure I would have done anything he said . . . and therein laid the trap.

The men told me of instances where cowboys working for Eldon had been badly injured by doing what he told them to do. They told me that Eldon thought it was funny that the boys would actually do some of the ridiculous things he suggested and he seemed not to have any bad conscience about it at all. In his mind, he transferred full responsibility to the cowboys for being so stupid, even though he was the boss and had told them what to do.

In the first instance, I was told that the cowboys had corralled a particularly wild and angry old range cow and were trying to load her into the back of a stock truck. She was on the fight and had tried to jump the corral fence several times. I was told that Eldon told the newest, youngest, and most inexperienced cowboy to, " get in there and see if that old bitch is givin' any milk." The cowboy, probably in his late teens and dumb as a sheep, dutifully climbed over the fence and tried to get hold of a teat. The terrorized old cow caught him against the fence and broke some of his ribs and they had to haul him off the mountain to the hospital.

Another story was about the time the cowboys were trying to extricate some obstinate old cows from the willows along the river. All along the Green River, the willow and tamarisk grew like a jungle and some of the old cows had learned to run in there and hide when the cowboys approached. Eldon had a habit of burning the brush along the river to drive the cows out, and every summer the BLM Rangers were at the ranch investigating suspicious fires. They never caught him, but everyone knew what was going on. The Colonel defended him because it was much faster and easier to gather cows when the river bottom was on fire, or after the brush had been burned away. And besides, there was never any evidence as to how the fire started. Eldon always said it was lightning—an act of God.

Eldon had another way to get cows out of the willows and that was to shoot them with buckshot. He always carried a .22 caliber revolver and he always had a handful of birdshot cartridges handy. Birdshot is a shell filled with small shotgun pellets instead of a lead slug. He would ride his horse into the willows as far as he could and then stand in the stirrups and shoot the old cows with the birdshot to make them run from cover. The fine pellets fired from the small caliber gun didn't seem to do any permanent harm to the tough hide of an old cow and it seemed to be an ingenious way to move livestock, but then of course, I'm not sure that Virginia and the Colonel ever knew that their precious cows were being blasted out of the willows by gunfire.

On one particular day, some of the boys were trying to get some sneaky old cows out of the tamaracks and the cows had squeezed way back and deep into the tangle of undergrowth. Eldon rode up and started cussing at the hands and told one young man to, " get a run at 'em." He told the kid to take his horse up on a grassy hill and get a good run at the willows and just bust in there and chase the old (expletives deleted) out. The young man did as he was told. He came flying down the hill at a full gallop, cold steel spurs in the horse's belly, and he hit the wall of tamarack with an open throttle. The horse somehow managed to keep his feet, but the cowboy went down in a tangle of arms and legs and willow limbs. The young man suffered several cuts and contusions. He was lucky he wasn't killed. And when the tangle of undergrowth finally stopped the horse's forward motion, the stunned and frantic animal came stumbling back out through the willows, wallowing right over the top of the wounded and bleeding cowboy still lying on the ground, injuring him even more.

I don't know if Virginia and the Colonel knew the full measure of what had transpired in each of these injury incidents, but the ranch hands did, and I was told that Eldon refused to accept any blame in either incident. In fact, Eldon thought it was funny and he often told the stories as part of his repertoire of humorous cowboy tales.

Eldon was a coarse and intimidating old goat. There is a story about the time the cowboys were branding calves and having a pretty tough time. The calves were too big and they were beating the cowboys up pretty bad. Two or three of the boys were roping and tailing the critters down while Eldon branded, docked and ear marked. One of the boys got kicked pretty hard, and he asked Eldon what would happen if someone got a leg broken way up there on the mountain, far away from a telephone, ambulance, or hospital.

Eldon sat back and looked at the young cowboy and then nodded toward the saddle horse tied to the fence. He said he thought an awful lot of that horse, and if one of the cowboys broke a leg he wouldn't hesitate to treat him just like he'd treat old Buck. He grinned wickedly and patted the pistol on his hip and said "I'd just have to put ya outta yer misery and drag ya outta the way so we could get the work done."

The young cowboy walked away from the corral, went to the cabin, got his gear and walked the many long miles off the mountain and into the town of Sunnyside with his saddle over his shoulder. Eldon laughed for weeks.

Another young man was not so easily intimidated. I've heard three versions of the following story, all told by people who were close to the action but not actually eyewitnesses. All three stories have the same basic outline but they differ in details, and so I'll give just the bare essentials.

It seems that Eldon had been riding a particular young man pretty hard. He didn't like the boy and he was trying to get the kid to quit. He was teasing, tormenting and baiting the young cowboy mercilessly, doing what Eldon was famous for doing. There came a day when the kid had had enough. I don't know just what provoked the little incident, but everyone agrees that alcohol was involved. Each story differs in where the booze came from.

Everyone agrees that somehow the kid got drunk and he got the drop on Eldon with the thirty-thirty. He took after the Range Boss with blood in his eye. Eldon ran toward the only cover that was readily available to him, the outhouse behind the cabin that sat by the edge of the wash. He ran behind the outhouse and jumped over the bank and into the wash and then ran for his life down the gully. Too much alcohol had slowed the kid's reactions, and he thought for sure that Eldon had run into the outhouse or was hiding behind it. He put at least three bullets through the fragile building, splintering wood and leaving no doubts about his resolve to get the job done. Humbert just happened to be at the cow camp at the time, and he dove into the stock truck to make a getaway. The kid put a bullet through the boards of the stock rack, just missing the cab of the truck as Humbert beat a hasty retreat.

The cops were called and the kid was rounded up and a quick investigation ensued. When the smoke cleared, nothing was done to the kid and he was put on a bus back to his hometown somewhere in the Pacific Northwest. I don't know if that little incidcnt dampened Eldon's enthusiasm for pestering people or not, but I'm sure it was not one of his favorite cowboy stories to tell. Eldon had a thick hide, but I don't think he was bulletproof.

Pony Jingler

The morning finally came when we were to take the cows to the mountain and I was so excited I hardly slept the night before. I breezed through the morning chores and breakfast with trembling excitement. And then the order came. The Colonel came over to the cookhouse and told me to go to the upper field and bring the horses in so we could select our mounts. Yes! I was going to be the Pony Jingler.

In the world of cowboys, the guy who rounds up the horses in the morning, usually the youngest and lowest ranking cowboy, is called the Jingler. I have no idea where the word came from or what it used to mean. It may be the bastardization of a Spanish word, or it may refer to the sound of spurs as a man walks to catch the horses, or even to the sound of a bell sometimes worn by one of the horses to make it easier to locate the herd; I just don't know. I was well aware that the job of Pony Jingler was considered to be a low and demeaning job, but I didn't care. It was cowboy work and I'd been dying for a chance to do it.

I put on my best hat, and then I went to the granary and got some oats in a bucket. I selected a couple of good hay strings and knotted them together into one long string. Joe asked me what I was doing and I told him I was going to catch a horse and ride it back to the corral. Joe rolled his eyes and snorted something to the effect that it was no wonder they wouldn't let me go to the mountain . . . I was too damn dumb. He told me to put the hay string down and go get a bridle from the tack shed. For the first time ever, I ignored him, and he was mumbling obscenities under his breath as I jumped the fence and started for the horse pasture.

It was early morning in the canyon and the air was cool and the shadows were long. I walked through tall grass that was wet with dew and my pants below the knees were soon wet and cold. The horses, eight or ten of them, were in a field about a mile or so from the ranch buildings and I found them standing in the first warm rays of sunlight enjoying an early breakfast of wet clover and sweet grass.

The horses saw me coming and stood with their ears up and their long necks stretched, sniffing the air for the scent of grain. A few started to move away cautiously, not wanting to be enticed from their horsy paradise of tall grass and shady leisure. I imagined that I could see them whispering softly under their breath to their companions to ignore me and not be snookered into putting their heads in the noose. A few others, weak and addicted to grain, moved haltingly toward me, hoping for a treat.

I held the bucket up and shook it to make that swishing sound of oats on metal that horses love to hear, and my tempting had the desired effect. The sound echoed from the shadowy ledges and ten pairs of fuzzy ears snapped to full attention. Three or four of the horses started toward me at a fast walk, eager and slobbering, salivating at the mere sound of the grain. They were helpless in the presence of the high quality fodder and willing to do a full day of hard labor for a single mouthful of that high-octane horse feed. The others were more cautious, but they too started toward me, not wanting to be left out. The hesitant nags were drawn on by the hope of being able to steal a mouthful of oats and then running away without being caught. I'm sure that some were even hoping that I might pour the precious feed on the ground and then go away and leave them alone.

I looked the horses over as they came up. I had no idea about the status of any of them. I assumed they were all good working horses—a youthfully optimistic and naïve assumption I learned later. One young gelding in particular caught my eye. He was a show horse, a deep red sorrel with white stocking feet and a blaze face. He was the kind of mount a teen-aged cowboy dreams about, a flashy, colorful and beautiful horse, the kind of horse a young man would want to ride around an arena while carrying a flag. The sorrel was cautious and he stayed in the middle of the crowd, planning to slip in, steal a mouthful of grain and then escape back into the pasture.

I let each of the first arrivals get a mouthful of grain as they came to me, but I held my hay string in readiness for the sorrel. I pretended to ignore him, never looking him in the eye, looking instead at his knees while talking softly and reassuringly as he got closer and closer. Finally, it was his turn to put his head in the bucket and I knew he was mine. I reached up quietly and looped the hay twine around his neck. He startled and stiffened as he realized he was caught, but I continued to talk to him quietly and gave him a second helping of the grain to seal our contract. I then poured the rest of the feed on the ground and led my prize a few steps away from the other horses as they jostled for the tiny seeds of oats in the dirt.

What I did next was something I had practiced and dreamed of doing for a long time. My dad had shown me how to use a single piece of twine or rope to tie what he called a "war bridle." It was an ingenious way to loop the string into a complete headstall with two reins just like a real leather bridle. Dad had told me that this war bridle had been a field expedient way for the Cossacks or the Mongols or some other of those Euro-Asian cowboys to steal each other's horses or to commandeer a stray on the battlefield. I had practiced tying the war bridle on the horses at home and I had dreamed of the day I could use it in earnest. Today was the day. I looped my hay string war bridle over the sorrel's nose and head and adjusted it up just right and it all came together perfectly.

I gathered a handful of red mane and swung up on the horse's back. The sorrel bowed his neck and high-stepped sideways for a few feet—just what I would have expected from a handsome and high-strung show horse. I hung the empty grain bucket on my arm near my elbow and I sat there like a Comanche warrior, proud and tall and eager. I had to plow-reign the sorrel to get him to turn around and I slowly began to circle the small herd of horses, gathering them up.

A few of the older, more seasoned nags now knew that the game was over and they started to move dutifully toward the ranch buildings and corrals. It was early morning and it was cool and the horses were feeling good. The leaders started to trot and then lope leisurely toward the ranch house. At that point, I knew the proper thing to do was to back off and let them settle down and bring them in slowly. Horses that have been run and are all worked-up are difficult to catch, saddle and work with. Unfortunately, I was stewing in the impatience of youth and in the excitement of the moment, and more than anything right then, I wanted to show Joe and Humbert that I could ride. With my heels I gave the sorrel the green light to run and he jerked his head and tail up and we zipped in behind the other horses, following closely and goading them to move ever faster.

In a matter of seconds we were flying over the wet grass and the whole herd was in a full charge toward the ranch house and the corrals. The cool air was washing over my face and the ground was flying by and I was completely exhilarated. The horse and I were both young and strong and we fit together perfectly. I wanted to yell like a Banshee and fan the red horse on the rump with my hat like a rodeo cowboy, but somehow I managed to restrain myself. Instead, I leaned low over his neck like a jockey and dug my knees into his shoulders and scanned the ground ahead, anticipating his moves, leaning and balancing and grabbing a handful of mane once in a while to help keep my perch.

We crossed the creek at a full lope, down a steep bank and through the willows, splattering the dark and shallow water in the wake of the other horses and then charging up the opposite bank in the wet sand. The sound of the hooves shattering the cold water ricocheted up through the ledges and rippled through the morning shadows. The icy water stung my legs and splashed high enough to spot my face. I pushed my hat down further on my head and the empty grain bucket rattled against my ribs. The sorrel was running in earnest now and trying to keep up with the others who ran free and wild and without a burden on their backs. The long mane was blowing in my face and the sound of hooves beating into the dark soil was meshed with the sound of my heartbeat and the rhythm was quick and overpowering. I was so excited that I just wanted to keep on going: past the corral, past the ranch, down the canyon and into the boundless and open spaces of the desolation wilderness.

I was jarred back to a more earthly realism when I saw all of the commotion near the corrals up ahead of us. Joe and Humbert and even the Colonel himself were scrambling to open and line up the gates to accommodate the stampeding herd of horses. We were bearing down on them like a run-away train. I winced and got that sick, deer-in-the-headlights feeling deep in my belly. I knew I was going to get my butt chewed good for bringing the horses in on the fly like that. There was nothing I could do about it at that point, however; the stampede was beyond my control.

The horses hit the open corral in a cloud of dust and did a

couple of laps to slow down and stop. The sorrel and I came right on in with them. Joe and Humbert closed the gate and we had our herd of horses. The nags were starting to sweat and they had flared nostrils and were all excited and giddy with their blood and their tails up. I knew that Eldon, the range boss, would wring my neck like a skinny chicken for bringing in his saddle horses like that, and I knew I deserved what I was surely going to get. I enjoyed one final lap around the corral as I mentally prepared to be beat-up for screwing-up my first real cowboy job.

I looked over toward the gate and Virginia was standing there in her riding clothes with her hands on her hips. She looked concerned, and her eyes were scolding me for being so brash, but she was also wearing the faint smile of one who has just been entertained by a good joke. I was just a little embarrassed, but at the same time I was proud that she too had witnessed my rodeo performance. I also saw in her eyes that she understood something else that I had just done.

I would never have admitted it, even to myself, but I had used the pony-jingling detail as an opportunity to show that I was more than a lowly hay hand. I had shown them all, in that one reckless act, that I could ride well and that I had the skills to be a real cowboy. It was a plea to be noticed, an act of daring rebellion to make them all take note, a cry of frustration from a free spirit chained to a hay wagon.

I had also just confirmed for Virginia that she did the right thing in keeping me off the mountain for another year. I had shown that I was hopelessly immature, terminally stupid, and recklessly prone to show off . . . just the kind of impulsive joke-bait that Eldon and some of the other cowboys dreamed of.

I rode the sorrel over to where Joe was standing and jumped off. I didn't say anything, but I wanted him to see clearly what I had done with the hay twine. He pretended not to notice. Reluctantly, I pulled the war bridle over the horse's head and turned him loose. The sorrel trotted over to his friends and started trying to kiss up and beg forgiveness for being the one who betrayed them all by being caught by the pony jingler. I put the grain bucket away and stood by waiting for my much-deserved reprimand. Nothing happened. I can only guess that Virginia had said something to the men because no one said a word to me. I looked around cautiously to see how everyone was reacting to my show of juvenile bravado.

The Colonel didn't seem to notice that I was even there. He had a death-grip on a fence rail, his forehead was all wrinkled up and he looked all anxious and fidgety. Humbert was busy untangling straps and buckles on the riding gear, and Joe was leaning heavily on the fence, making love to a fat cigar. Virginia continued to stand by the gate with her hands on her hips, watching the horses as they milled around, and she smiled faintly and shook her head at me with a look in her eyes like a schoolteacher who is both amused and impressed by the antics of a rowdy student. I looked away quickly and blushed just a little. We all just stood there for a while, waiting for the horses to settle down. No one said anything, and my heart soared like an eagle.

After a while, Virginia walked over, pointed and asked me to catch a big bay mare for her. I did as she asked. I soon found out that the mare was named Cholera and she was the boss lady's personal mount. Humbert caught a horse for himself and one for the Colonel. I put a rope back on my showboat sorrel. Joe had begged off for the day and he was going to stay at the ranch and do the chores and irrigating.

I was brushing my parade horse down and preparing to saddle him when I noticed that Virginia and the Colonel were in a whispered huddle over by the trucks. A few minutes later

Virginia came over and told Humbert and me that they had decided not to ride today but would drive ahead of us in the suburban and open the gates and slow any oncoming traffic. I could tell that Virginia was disappointed. She was dressed in English riding britches and boots and she carried her gloves in her hands. It was obvious that she had planned to ride.

She told me that she wanted me to ride her bay mare. She said the horse needed to be used once in a while and she wanted me to exercise her today. I told her that would be fine with me, but it broke my heart when I had to turn the sorrel back into the corral. Cholera turned out to be a fine mount; she was mannerly and well trained. I could never understand why she was named after a disease. I was told later that there were a few horses on the ranch named after diseases. Old man Nutter is said to have preferred to ride mules and maybe that had something to do with it.

Trail Mix: Cows And Raw Eggs

We just happened to have a cook on the place at that time, and as we prepared to leave, the old lady cook came over and handed Humbert and me each a brown paper bag that was our lunch for the day. We stowed these in our saddlebags. We opened the gate to the bull pasture and the cows started spilling out onto the Nine Mile road. All my dreams had come true; I was a cowboy.

Humbert and I rode most of the day keeping those cows going down the canyon. Every side canyon we passed and every wide place we came to a few of those brain-dead bovines would try to make a wrong turn. I was delighted that the cows were so stupid and required so much tending; I enjoyed chasing after them. My spurs jingled and I yelled hee-yaw and I slapped a rope against my leg. I steered old Cholera through the thickest part of the bushes and through mud puddles and down steep and sandy embankments, trying my best to make a real adventure of it. I found an excuse to cross the crick and bust through the willows and chase a calf up a steep side hill in the rocks, and then I sat back in the saddle, tall and proud, admiring my shadow in the gravel as I punched them Nutter cows.

About noon, the Colonel and Virginia came back past us in the suburban. They were going back to the ranch for lunch and maybe a quick nap. Humbert and I shaded up in the shadow of a ledge and got out our lunches.

I wanted to ride back to the ranch and beat somebody up when I looked in that brown paper bag. I was a growing boy and I needed lots of groceries. I guess she didn't have much to work with, but that contemptable old lady cook had given each of us an apple and one sandwich. That wouldn't have been too bad if she had made a real sandwich. But what she had given us was a warm, wet and slimy, sunny-side-up and barely cooked fried egg between two slices of bread. It was an over-easy and sorry excuse for a sandwich with no butter, no bacon, no mayo and no salt and pepper—just bread and raw egg. And to complicate matters, our raw egg lunch had been festering and growing bacterial cultures in our sun-baked saddlebags all morning.

I knew from the cowboy movies that a fella could get poisoned from bad water, but I'd never suspected that one day I might have to boil my lunch. It was kind of scary too, because I knew that it wouldn't be the first time a cook had poisoned people at the ranch. I'd heard the story of an old lady cook who went to pick flowers in the back yard of the ranch house and discovered a fine batch of rhubarb growing along the fence. She picked an apron-full of the sprouts and made the guys a fine rhubarb pie for supper. The men all took a piece of pie after their evening meal, but it was so bitter that none of them could eat it all—and good thing. The next morning everyone was sick with headaches, fever, stomach cramps, and a roaring case of Montezuma's revenge. They were fighting each other for a turn on the toilet.

When the old gal was asked where she got the rhubarb, she took them out by the back fence and pointed to a nice clump of burdock—better know to cowboys and farmers as cocklebur—a noxious week in anybody's book and apparently toxic in pie.

Humbert was a real old-time cowboy. He stayed true to the Code Of The West and didn't complain about the grub. He did make fun of it a little, holding his sandwich up with two fingers and sniffing at it like a dog. Then he pretended he was going to bury it in the dirt. He made me laugh, but I was mad and I cussed and blustered and practiced using a whole lot of the new words I was learning from my mentors that summer.

Humbert ate his sandwich with the same resolve that a Special Forces Ranger might eat a snake or a big bug, and then he cleansed his palate with warm canteen water and soothing cigarette smoke. I picked around the edges of my alleged sandwich and managed to get a little uncontaminated bread crust, and then I threw the bacteria bomb into the bushes where I hoped it would kill a badger or a coyote or some other deserving vermin. I ate my apple, core, seeds and all, and then licked the juice from my dirty little fingers.

Humbert was either the bravest or the dumbest cowboy God ever put guts in—for sure he was the luckiest—that or the bile in his belly could trump swamp algae. I watched him closely over the next couple of days and he never even got sick.

I was starving when we got back to the ranch that night and I was glad when that old lady cook left in just a few days. She said she felt trapped in the canyon because she couldn't see out and she was afraid the canyon walls would fall on her. I was rooting for the canyon walls, but she made her getaway before the earth could swallow her up and I was disappointed.

That first day, Humbert and I took the cows into Cottonwood Canyon and closed a gate behind them and then rode the ten or twelve miles back to the ranch. The next morning we hauled our horses in Humbert's truck to Cottonwood and resumed our cattle drive where we had left off. That second day, Virginia told me she wanted me to ride a big bay gelding named Mickey, the same horse that Humbert had selected for the Colonel the day before. She seemed to be steering me away from the showboat sorrel like a good mother who doesn't want her teen-aged son to get into trouble by driving the Corvette. She kept routing me toward the Buicks and the Oldsmobiles. It never occurred to me until years later that the young sorrel may not have been well broken and that good woman was trying to keep me from getting my butt and my ego bruised. That may have been why she had that impish, knowing smile on her face when I rode the sorrel bareback into the corral with a hay string for a bridle—she just might have known something I didn't know about that horse.

Mickey was a good horse and he had just a little more pep than the boss lady's bay mare. I truly enjoyed working with Mickey, and Mickey knew how to herd cows. I never did get to ride the flashy sorrel again. A few weeks later the cowboys came and took the whole herd up on the mountain. My dream horse was gone forever. From then on, whenever I dreamed of being a cowboy, I saw myself on that handsome red horse with the long white socks. I had daydreams for years about all of the young girls' hearts I could have broken if only I could have carried the flag in the grand entry of the Black Diamond Stampede while riding that showboat sorrel.

The Colonel and Virginia didn't go with us the second day, and Humbert grinned and told me that the Boss Man didn't get along well with horses. I don't know any of the particulars, but Humbert said it was a good thing the Colonel was in military intelligence and not in the cavalry. Humbert was a true gentleman and he left the rest of the story to my fertile imagination. It didn't take long for me to figure out why the Colonel was leaving stress fractures in the fence rail with his fingertips while those excited nags jostled and bumped and acted crazy in the corral. I never did see the Colonel or Virginia on a horse, but I'm perfectly convinced that the lady could ride.

In the interests of self-preservation, Humbert and I told the cook lady that we didn't need a lunch that second day and that we would be just a little late for supper. We then raided the cupboards like a couple of pack rats while she was in the bathroom. We absconded with cheese and crackers and raisins and a tin of sardines and a whole loaf of bread, and we went deep into the apple bin. We smuggled our loot out to Humbert's truck, giggling like a couple of school kids, and then headed for Cottonwood.

That second day we pushed the cows up Cottonwood Canyon, up the dugway and onto the plateau at the top of the canyon. It was beautiful up there. The sun was shining and the air was clean and we could see for miles and miles. To the West, the jagged crest of the Tavaputs Plateau was still blanketed in snow, and on the tops of the ridges, groves of Quaking Aspen shimmered with new leaves. The scent of sage blossoms hung heavy in the air and fur trees painted the deep canyons dark. To the South and East the wide benches were covered with pinion and sage and the country plunged down the slopes toward the Green River and Desolation Canyon.

We put the cows through a fence and closed the gate and Humbert said that Eldon and the cowboys would take over form there. We then rode our horses back down the canyon to

Humbert's truck and went back to the ranch.

Those two days were my brief, shining moment in the sun, and my career as a working cowboy was behind me by that second afternoon. Luckily, I didn't know it yet; it would have broken my heart.

THE END OF THE TRAIL

Many weeks later, I was alone and sweating it out in a dusty hay field when I saw Eldon riding up the canyon to the ranch. Horses were the only transportation the cowboys had most of the time and Eldon liked it that way. He preferred to ride his horse off the mountain the way they did it back in the eighteen hundreds. It was part of the cowboy dream he lived in and a good way to remind the younger men that he was still a tough old Timber Wolf—the dominant male and leader of the pack.

I remember it was a beautiful late-summer afternoon, the sky was filled with cottony clouds and the light kept changing from bright to muted tones against the sandstone ledges. Eldon looked like a vision from the past century, an out-rider from another age. He was riding a good horse, a big black horse with a white blazed face, and he rode tall and proud and he knew I was watching him. He was sitting his old-time, Newton Brothers high-backed saddle with its Mexican tapaderos (stirrup covers) nearly touching the ground and with silver conchos sparkling in the sun. His black, old-time hat was pulled low over his eyes and his colorful bandanna sheened in the natural light, bright against the background of his black leather vest. His rope was coiled tightly and tied to the saddle and his saddlebags were fat and full of gear. The long saddle strings and the ends of his reins hung low and danced with the motion of the horse.

Like always, he was putting on a show. He didn't break the spell by waving or by acknowledging that he had even seen me;

he was forever playing the part—cattle boss, rounder, and king of the cowboys. I sat down on a stickery hay bale and watched him ride by.

I wished I had a camera that day to record the image as he passed by me and disappeared forever. Oh, he stayed at the ranch for a few more months, but I never saw him again. I think of him once in a while, like when I see some kid wearing spurs in the airport and pretending to be bad like Clint Eastwood, and I contrast that pitiful image with what I remember of what a real cowboy looked and acted like.

Eldon personified the dream. He was the embodiment of the Old West and all it stood for. He was crass and irreverent and even mean at times, but he was also tough and self-reliant and true to himself. Real cowboys are hopelessly romantic and shamelessly idealistic and I hope the breed survives forever. The cowboy ideal is an honorable and a noble model for manhood and I wish that Gene, Roy and Hoppy could be dusted-off and put back on their pedestals.

I still want to be a cowboy.

CHAPTER 8

INCIDENTALS

THE LAY OF THE LAND

The ranch kept about six hundred breeding cows on the mountain and the operation ebbed and flowed with the changes of the seasons. In the winter, the cows were kept in the lower elevations along the Green River where there was less snow and good winter feed in the canyon bottoms. As spring came, the cowboys would start to move the cows higher up the slopes to new pastures. They followed the advance of the new grass up the slopes as the snow melted and the mud dried. The cows were taken ever higher up the mountain until by mid-summer they were at the highest elevations and in the pines and the quaking aspens. In the fall, the boys would round up the steers to be marketed and then they would point the old cows downhill and start the slow descent from the high country. As the winter clouds gathered, the cows would be in the low country again and would remain there all winter.

Upper Nine Mile Canyon.

It was a great system, and the ranch controlled enough ground that the cows could walk from the river to the top of the mountain and back again and never leave Nutter ground. The ranch controlled about 180,000 acres (281 square miles) and was the largest privately owned cattle operation in the state of Utah. I asked Eldon once if he had seen it all and he gave me his condescending Clint Eastwood smirk and told me that he had only worked for the outfit for eight or ten years but he thought he had seen most of it. I never knew if he was telling me the truth or if he was just making fun of me again; Eldon was like that.

At measured intervals along the route, usually near a good spring, the ranch had set up cow camps—line shacks they were sometimes called. Nutter's had a couple of cabins that were made from rocks and one that was an old railroad caboose, but most old-time line shacks were log cabins from the past century that were patched up with tarpaper and tin with asphalt shingles. Cabins like those could be found all over the mountains in Utah, at every ranch and cattle operation. Often they were in the world's most beautiful places, high in the pines and aspens, sometimes with breathtaking views of the mountain country. They were not resort cabins. They usually contained one or two rooms and were built to provide shelter and not comfort. Most were not places where people lived year round. Even the most picturesque were abandoned in the winter when the deep snows cut off access into town and civilization.

In recent years, camp trailers have replaced a lot of the old cabins. It's always sad for me to see those old cowboy camps contaminated with seedy-looking tin trailers with cracked windows and chipped paint. A camp trailer squatting in front of a neglected old log cabin always rubs my nose in the soiled facts of the changing values of my own generation. The old cabins were built with skill and care and with a permanence that revealed the owner's dream to keep and maintain them forever. The camp trailers always seem so cheap, so expedient, and so transient.

Most of the old log cabins sit empty now—open to the elements and slowly falling apart like the dreams of the old-time ranching families. Few people can make a living at ranching anymore. Ranch land is fast becoming real estate. The sons of ranchers are now aspiring to be doctors and lawyers and real estate brokers. There are few men left who have the stomach to put in the endless hours of work and worry for the meager economic rewards of ranching when the very dirt beneath their feet is worth a fortune. I guess we can't blame them . . . but it's a sad situation anyway. The heritage, the pride, the self-reliance, the family ties to the land, faith in the future and the very dreams of the pioneers themselves are being sold with the acres.

Ranching used to be a poor man's way to make a living. Land was cheap and a family with a few cows or sheep and a good vegetable garden could scratch out a humble living with hard work and good luck. Today, ranching is a rich man's sport. Land is so expensive that only millionaires can get into the business from a cold start . . . and rich men don't want the land for a working ranch anyway. They want to sub-divide and make more money. They want to turn the old ranches into five- and ten-acre Ranchettes; secluded luxury home sites for the rich and famous. Today a big ranch is a tax shelter, a corporate write-off, a status symbol, a movie star's retreat and a millionaire's plaything. With enough money, a rich man doesn't have to get the dirt of his empire under his fingernails; he can hire serfs to do all the work, guard the gates and cater to his celebrity quests.

I was lucky enough to have worked for Virginia while the

great, family-owned ranching empire of Preston Nutter was still a working ranch. The cows paid the bills and the fortunes of the operation rose and fell like the tides of the sea with fluctuations in the weather, market conditions and interest rates. It took a good deal of management skill and a real investment in time and effort to keep the operation profitable in the wake of ever-higher taxes, government regulations and a flood of imported Argentine beef.

Virginia loved the ranch and she knew what her empire was worth. One afternoon I was washing dishes when she and John, the California surfer-turned-writer, came into the cookhouse, sat at the table and talked for a while (the Colonel was in the seventh inning of a doggy ballgame out on the lawn). I couldn't help but overhear what was said. She was telling the sandal-clad foreigner from California that she had been insulted when a Texas oil company offered a million dollars to buy the ranch. She told the man that she would never sell her ranch, especially to a damned oil company. She said the ranch was worth more than money to her, it was her whole life. She also said that a million dollars wouldn't make a good down payment on the ranch if she ever did decide to sell it.

I was impressed. A million dollars sounded like a lot of money to a kid who worked for four dollars a day. I figured it up that night with a stubby pencil and found that I'd have to haul hay for six hundred and eighty five years to make that much money—assuming I never got a pay raise, of course.

I was touched to hear Virginia say that the ranch meant that much to her. I could understand her feelings. I knew that if I had a million dollars I would want to buy a ranch like hers and I couldn't understand how anyone could give up something as valuable as a ranch for money. After hearing her talk about how much the place meant to her, I tried even harder to keep the yard clean and make the place look good for her.

OLD HUNKUS

To me, the Colonel seemed to spend an awful lot of time playing with his dog while the rest of the world went on without him. Brody the wonder dog had a special place in everyone's heart, but he was not the only pet on the ranch; Tommy, old Joe's sheep was one, and the mountain lion the cowboys kept chained to a barrel at the cow camp was another. The lion wasn't as warm and fuzzy as old Brody, and he wouldn't chase a ball or pee on the porch, but he was the official mascot for the cowboy side of the ranching operation. The cat was a real live, tooth and fanged, wild-eyed and dangerous part of the cow camp experience.

BYU has a cougar for a mascot, but theirs is a BYU-nik (eunuch?) dressed in a fuzzy cat suit. Eldon the range boss and his motley crew had the real thing. This special pet was just what I would have expected a man like Eldon to have, and the cat's name was Hunkus or Hunker, depending on whom you talked to.

Somehow, having a wildcat for a pet didn't seem out-of-place for the cowboys. The days were long and boring on the mountain and there was never any TV or other genteel amusements. The boys sought their fun in the ways available to them. Sometimes they would shoot, rope, whittle or read, and when they tired of those challenges, they sought excitement in practical jokes and mischief. What better way to while away the hours and add some excitement to your life than by feeding and tormenting a wild and dangerous beast that really would rip your liver out if given half a chance?

In those days, before wolves were our friends, any predator was trapped, poisoned, or shot on sight, and a single lion track in the snow was indictment enough to call out the government trapper. The government trapper was named Willis Butolph and he lived in Wellington and he had the job my friends and I all wanted. Like Eldon the range boss, Willis the trapper was a rough and tumble and take-no-prisoners sort of guy. He was famous for his exploits with wild animals—sort of the Steve Erwin (crocodile hunter) of his day. Willis would climb up in a tree with a hysterical and slobbering wild cat and put a rope around his neck. The lion hunter was the town hero. When we kids saw his truck with all the dog pens and lion cages parked in front of the local café, we all ran to see what type of creature he might have in a wire box on the back of the truck. As a kid, I went lion hunting with Willis once, and we spent one day hunting lions and two days hunting dogs—but that's another story.

Willis the trapper killed a female cougar in the canyon a couple of years before I was there and he captured her two young cubs. Normally, the cubs would have been killed too, but Eldon the range boss thought it would be cool to keep a lion as a pet and he was such a sweet-talker that Willis the trapper let him keep one of them (the range boss could have charmed the spots from a Leopard).

The cat was just a tiny thing when first captured and the cowboys kept him in the cabin and fed him by hand. He was a fussy little fur ball and the boys doted over him. They fed him with their fingers and played with him and teased him and packed him around like a housecat. When they moved from cow camp to cow camp they carried him in a pannier on a packhorse. One of the cowboys told me that they trained some good packhorses with the little cat. If a man was cowboy enough to sweet-talk a packhorse into carrying a live and wiggling mountain lion, you could bet that horse would carry anything else. Of course, there were a few instances of legendary rodeo action involved in the early stages, and the fact that the boys got the job done at all speaks volumes about their cowboy skills and abilities. Little Hunkus was a rodeo star at an early age and he bucked out some of the best the outfit had to offer.

As the cat got bigger, he became more and more aggressive and started to be dangerous. His claws and teeth were growing and he began to assert himself in ways that made the cowboys duck and run. His table manners were still rooted in the wilds and he was intolerant of innocent bystanders while enjoying his meals. In the interests of self-preservation, the cowboys chained the cat to an oil drum and made him live outside by himself. They kept a soft blanket of grass on the bottom of the barrel for Hunkus to sleep on, and the boys kept him chained to the barrel for almost three years. The cat became a permanent, sulking and snake-eyed resident of the cow camps.

In spite of his tender age at capture and his constant contact with the Human species, old Hunkus never got to be man's best friend in the traditions of Gentle Ben or Smokey Bear. Hunkus had never watched Walt Disney or the Animal Planet and he didn't know that wild cougars could be warm and cuddly. He hunkered down in his oil drum and plotted and dreamed of the day he would tear the face off of one of the cowboys who fed and tormented him, and he tried to make his dreams come true every chance he got. The cowboys had a couple of close calls with old Hunkus and he seemed to carry a particular grudge against George Cook. He was moved from cow camp to cow camp in the back of a truck: chain, barrel and all, and the boys got very good at the art of handling the beast.

Feeding a lion on the end of a chain might have been a challenge for some, but it was no big deal at the cow camps. Old Hunkus enjoyed a steady diet of fresh venison and he waxed fat. Every few days the cowboys would shoot a deer and feed it to the lion. The wild beast would eat his fill and then cover the remainder with dirt and twigs to save for tomorrow, in true mountain lion style. There was always a mound of dirt in front of the barrel where Hunkus kept his larder close. He supplemented his diet and whiled away the long hours, deep inside his barrel, by lying in wait for magpies, jaybirds, rodents and unsuspecting housecats to be drawn to the scrap pile. The cowboys kept a few housecats to control mice in the cabins and Hunkus was on a twenty-five foot chain. The lion didn't feel any compelling bonds of kinship toward his little housecat cousins and he would pick them off every chance he got.

It was not at all unusual for the cowboys to poach deer. Deer were plentiful and they were shot for camp meat on a regular basis. One of the old hands told me that when old man Preston Nutter was running the ranch, part of every grocery delivery to the cow camp was a box of 30.30 bullets so the men could supply their own meat.

Virginia and the Colonel kept the tradition going, but in a more subtle sort of way; they couldn't legally tell the boys to shoot deer, but they always made sure the hands had plenty of 30.30 bullets to protect the stock from marauding predators. They seemed not to notice the many chunks of deer hide, deer feet and bones that lay scattered in the grass around the cabins and the cat barrel. They were realists however, and sometimes they would take an especially fine hindquarter or a slice of back strap home to the ranch house after a visit to the cow camps—a gift of "mountain veal" to the Colonel and his lady. The State Fish and Game Department wardens knew what was going on of course, but they were surprisingly tolerant about the poaching. At that time it seemed that the deer herds were endless, and there was a prevailing attitude that since the deer were eating Nutter feed, the outfit was perfectly justified in taking a few for the frying pan—or to feed their hungry lion—or both.

As old Hunkus got bigger and bigger, he became more dangerous and more difficult to move between cow camps.

Each visitor was warned to stay away from the cat barrel. This presented a special challenge to Brody the wonder dog. Brody was a handsome dog, but he was a slow learner. Fortunately for Brody, he was an aristocratic and upper class type of dog and he lived fat on cantaloupe and ice cream. The rotting bone pile was no temptation to him. His weakness was the smell of saddle leather. Every chance he got, he cocked a leg on someone's saddle as it sat innocently on a rail by the side of the cabin.

Sticky dog pee in their stirrups annoyed the cowboys and they grew to hate the boss man's pampered kid. They started to bait old Brody by putting the cat barrel near the saddle pole when they knew the Colonel was coming for a visit. The cowboys smiled, took bets, and secretly cheered for old Hunkus. They even helped the big cat get in shape. They tossed innocent and unsuspecting housecats near the saddle pole to help the lion get the range and practice his sprints. They hoped and dreamed and schemed, but alas, it never happened. Old Brody lived a charmed life. The Colonel never knew that his special friend was being set up as lion bait, but he learned to keep his dog secured in the suburban when he visited just the same—call it Mother's intuition.

Eldon kept the cat chained to the barrel for the better part of three years. The cat got bigger and bigger and finally he became such a nuisance that something had to be done. The fate of old Hunkus culminated in an incident that will live forever in the folklore of the canyon. The particulars of that incident, however, will be discussed in another chapter—so stay tuned.

A Chance To Own The Ranch

I always dreamed of owning a big ranch, and according to old Joe, I could have had one. In fact, according to him, I could have owned the Nutter Ranch and I could have gotten it for free, or . . . almost free. I passed up my big chance when Virginia's two teen-aged nieces, daughters of her sister Katherine, came to visit the ranch for a few days that summer.

The girls were about my own age and I was excited to have them around the ranch, even though I was never able to spend any time with them or to even speak to them that I remember. I was at an age when giggling young girls held a special charm for me, and I had been purged of all female contact for many long weeks and I was antsy. When I saw those young ladies disembark from the suburban and go to the big house with their suitcases and overnight bags I was thrilled, and for the next few days I made sure I wore my best work clothes and kept my dark hair combed . . . just in case.

I saw the girls several times over the next few days as Virginia showed them around and took them on the mountain in the suburban. They looked so cute in their frilly, girlie clothes, all decked out with ribbons and bows, wearing shorts and summer blouses. The girls stayed at the big house and I didn't see them often, but once in a while a faint squeal of girlie laughter would come floating past on the afternoon breeze and my pulse would quicken. The young ladies were a refreshing change from the bib overall and cigar smoking creatures I was used to, and I was completely tweeterpated by the very thought of having them near.

I wished for a chance to meet them, and I dreamed of having some glorious opportunity to sweep them off their feet and be a handsome Prince. I waited patiently for fate to intervene and give me a chance to come to the rescue—to save them from a fire, a flood, or a killer badger. I could just imagine myself being a hero like that handsome Northwest Mountie, Dudley Doright, and then riding off into the sunset with the two of them, cool and studly like Alan Ladd or Clark Gable. I could see a saved and grateful girl hanging on each arm, cooing softly and batting those long eyelashes like Mae West and Veronica Lake.

I secretly dreamed and fantasized about it, but I must add a disclaimer here in the interests of what my young Grandsons might think about all of this. It is important to remember that I was a good Mormon Boy Scout and as pure as the wind driven snow. I looked upon those young ladies with neither longing nor lust, but with a pure heart and a brotherly sense of righteous chivalry—scout's honor (wink).

Joe, of course, had a different perspective. He was an old Tomcat and he saw my wistful mood and my new interest in combing my hair. Life at the ranch was dull and boring, even for an old goat like Joe, and he was never one to pass up an opportunity to harass, intimidate or humiliate someone for entertainment. He sat me down at breakfast one morning and told me that this was my big chance. He reminded me that there was a good chance that those girls would one day own the ranch, and it was my duty to my future posterity to sneak one of them off down by the crick and knock her up—get her pregnant!

I was so shocked he would talk to me like that, I must have turned fifty shades of red. Old Joe laughed and laughed and then told Humbert all about "our" secret plan to inherit the ranch. Humbert jumped in on the fun and the two of them tortured me for weeks. They were merciless. Joe had found a crack in my armor and they probed and jabbed and used the wicked lance of ridicule to knock me from my horse of pleasant daydreams. They teased me endlessly. They had discovered that I was very sensitive about my relationships with young women, and they were completely delighted in how I would blush and cringe and duck and run whenever they peered through that magnifying glass into my inner soul.

They were relentless. Every hour or two one of them would come up with some trash about having seen one of the girls and that she didn't look pregnant yet. Then one of them would ask me, "what's the matter kid . . . ya need lessons or what?" or "Come on kid, make us proud . . . we're countin' on ya." or, "Good hell kid, don't ya got no lead in yer pencil . . . or what?"

The language and the sexual innuendos made me cringe, and to be teased by the older men about such a sensitive subject tore my insides out. I was used to being the little dog in the kennel, but now I was a baby seal with an open wound and the blood in the water drew sharks that took full advantage. As the sharks fed on me, I would blush and cower and finally leave the building and sometimes my unfinished supper just to get away from the torment, and they would laugh and laugh and laugh.

This treatment became especially harsh after the day Virginia asked me to saddle a couple of horses so the girls could go riding. Joe told me that Virginia was trying to help me out. He said: "She likes you and she wants you to inherit her ranch. It's your duty to her and to the outfit to sire an heir to the throne. They'll only be mad at you for a little while—and then you'll own it all, and me and Humbert can retire right here and be your advisors."

I was sure glad when those young ladies finally went back to town, but Joe and Humbert teased me for the rest of the summer about how I had blown my big chance to own the Nutter Ranch.

CHAPTER 9

A TRIP TO TOWN

PIONEER DAY

All summer long I kept track of one special date on the calendar. Pioneer day in Utah is the twenty-fourth of July and I had asked Virginia for that weekend off. It would be my one and only weekend away from the ranch that summer and I counted down the days with the eagerness of a little kid waiting for a birthday.

Pioneer day was a big deal in Utah when I was a kid. The twenty-fourth of July was the day Brigham Young led the first band of Mormon pioneers into the Salt Lake Valley back in 1847. It was the date of the first settlement in the State of Utah and the day the fledgling Mormon Church found a permanent home. Each year the Church and the state of Utah commemorated the date and it was the biggest celebration of the year. The Twenty-Fourth trumped any other holiday. It was the Fourth of July, Founder's day, Statehood day, Pioneer day, Church History day, May day and Thanksgiving all rolled into one. It was a day when patriotism, faith and heritage were celebrated with religious zeal.

Almost all of the little towns in Utah could trace their beginnings to the Mormon pioneer heritage, and in the early decades of the twentieth century they celebrated the twenty-fourth like a religious obligation. All over the state there were parades, flags, programs, speeches, fireworks, rodeos and dances. It was a magic time when the whole state turned out to have a good time. The only other holiday to be celebrated with such passion was the opening of the deer hunt—but we'll deal with that phenomenon a little later.

As children, my brothers and I waited for the twenty-fourth like we waited for Santa Claus. We pined away the weeks and months, dreaming of that big day and all the fun we were going to have. All year long we redeemed pop bottles for two cents each, cut lawns, sold rabbits, did chores for neighbors and anything else we could to make a nickel or a dime so we could have spending money for the twenty-fourth. We each had a jar or a tin tucked safely away at home where we hoarded our treasure of dimes and pennies as we waited for our one big splurge of the year. On the twenty-fourth we didn't hold anything back. It was our civic and religious duty to spend every last dime because the church ran the concessions and the money raised went into the coffers for next year's celebration. A kid had an obligation to make himself sick with cotton candy and go home at the end of the day with more sugary loot and dime-store trinkets than he collected on Halloween.

As the sun topped those sacred Utah Mountains on that one special day of the year, the whole state came alive with the magic of the day. Flags were unfurled and old soldiers saluted. Sons and daughters of handcart pioneers solemnly took their places at the head of small-town parades, and church leaders and politicians hastily reviewed their speeches over toast and scrambled eggs. The towns and valleys had been in preparation for several weeks and the hymns sung in church for most of the preceding month were anthems of the pioneer migrations: *Come, Come Ye Saints—For the Strength of The Hills—High on a Mountain Top* and *Put Your Shoulder to the Wheel.*

The little town of Wellington celebrated with strength and vitality that was far beyond her normal ability. Like little boys who saved nickels, the whole town stored energy and stockpiled resources for that one big event of the year, and when the magic day came, the town too felt a civic and religious obligation to let it all hang out.

The rituals followed the same basic pattern every year. The festivities began early in the morning with a parade down Main Street. The local volunteer fire crew, sitting in and on the town fire truck, always led the parade with the siren and bells going full out. The most envied kids in town were the ones with fathers or uncles or brothers on the fire crew who would let them steal a ride on the fire truck at the head of the parade.

Behind the fire truck, spaced at respectable distances and shining in the sun, were numerous floats sponsored by the various Church auxiliaries. The floats were fabricated with crepe paper and painted cardboard that was nailed and glued and strung with chicken wire to hay wagons and truck beds. Some were pulled by farm tractors and others by automobiles. Most had religious, pioneer or American patriotic themes. On many there were gaggles of children dressed like sunflowers, or like pioneers and Indians. On others were old folks in rocking chairs and shawls, real live and honest-to-goodness sons and daughters of the pioneers, people-relics from the town's early days and a special link to our heritage.

Interspersed between the crepe paper floats were troops of boy scouts and war veterans, the local high school marching band, aspiring politicians, rodeo queens, sports teams, and anyone else in the community who wanted to dress up and join the parade. Proud mothers wore pioneer skirts and sunbonnets and pushed carriages filled with fat babies while older children walked and pulled little red wagons spilling over with dolls, puppies and little brothers. Little kids decorated bicycle tires with crepe paper and weaved in and out of the slow procession showing off their riding skills and lack of training wheels while proud grandparents sat on the hoods of cars all along main street and clapped and shouted encouragement.

There were always two or three riding clubs mounted on horses and led by color guards with flags draped on long poles. Each club was dressed in a distinctive uniform of matching shirts and hats while sitting horses of any color, size or description. The one exception was the county sheriff's posse. The posse was an elite outfit that helped in search and rescue and they all rode colorful palomino horses with fancy matching saddles and tack. Posse members wore park ranger type uniforms with badges and tan western hats. Sometimes the clubs did equestrian drills as they came down the street, the horses weaving and changing formation to the command of a shrill whistle clenched in the teeth of a drillmaster.

Behind the horses were always a few young men dressed up as clowns who made a great show of scooping up the horse droppings. They wheeled large metal trashcans around on hand trucks or go-carts with hand painted signs that said *Wellington Sanitation Department*. The Horse Biscuit Brigade was always at the very end of the parade and they entertained the crowd while performing a valuable community service. They would scoop up an odious pile and then bow to the crowd or act stupid like some NFL star who has just made a touchdown, and then promenade to the next target with brooms and scoop shovels over their shoulders or held at port-arms like marching soldiers. It was all great fun.

After the parade, the whole community went to the Mormon Meeting House where there was a special program of patriotic music mixed with church hymns and discourses from honored community elders who recited the history of the town and the heritage of the Mormon People. The stage was draped with American flags and the dark blue flag of our native Utah.

After the program everyone spent the remainder of the day in the city park. There was food, games, water fights, concessions, baseball games, touch football, horseshoes, foot races, cotton candy, tubs of soda pop, firecrackers and a merry-go-round. Everyone in town was there and out-of-town relatives and neighbors who had moved away years before came back to get reacquainted and to socialize. It was a great family reunion and summer picnic for the whole town. As the day progressed toward evening there was a rodeo featuring the local talent and then a dance for the whole community. The twenty-fourth was the big event of the year; there was magic in the air and it was good to be a kid.

A Trip To Town

Out on the ranch, I watched the calendar as the days ticked slowly by. I was keeping a countdown to the twenty-fourth and I marked off each day. I dreamed of my weekend off when I could go home and join in the festivities and see my friends, my family and my cute little girl friend. I had been in semi-isolation in the canyon for several weeks and I was beginning to feel like I was serving a sentence in solitary confinement. The days seemed to drag on forever.

And finally the big day arrived. One morning I reminded Virginia that I had asked for the twenty-fourth weekend off and the day was fast approaching. She said she remembered, and since Humbert was going into town Friday after lunch, she would have him drop me off. The news was like ice cream on my dusty tongue. I had expected to call my parents to come and get me Friday evening after the chores were done, but now I didn't have to. By the good graces of the boss lady, not only was I going to get Saturday and Sunday at home, I was going to get half of Friday too. This was an unexpected head start and a much-appreciated bonus. I thanked her liberally.

And then the question of money came up.

Virginia asked me if I wanted to draw all or part of my

wages. The question embarrassed me and it shouldn't have. I had earned the money; no one ever worked harder for the Nutter Ranch than I did. I think I was embarrassed because I wanted to take a lot of money to town and I worried that the adults would look down on me and be disappointed by my greed and my audaciousness. I felt very presumptuous. It was like I was breaking the rules. I was a kid and I'd never had more than forty dollars at one time before and a kid wasn't supposed to have a lot of money. I felt like a pretender, a boy who would dare to mimic a real man and be brazen enough to ask the Boss Lady for a lot of money to spend in town.

I ducked my head and scraped my boot in the dirt and then timidly croaked that I would like to have a hundred dollars to take to town. Virginia seemed relieved and she smiled. "I'll have you a check in the morning before you and Humbert leave," she said cheerfully. I understood later that if I had drawn everything coming to me she might have taken it as a signal that I wasn't coming back. That sort of thing happened fairly regularly at the ranch but I didn't know it at the time. The thought of not coming back had never crossed my mind.

I thanked her and then wandered off to get a drink of water and mop my beaded brow. One hundred American dollars, holy cow, I'd never dreamed of having so much money, and Virginia had acted as if it was okay. She didn't seem unhappy or disappointed in me after all. I lay awake most of that night, too excited to sleep and dreaming of all that money and the big shopping spree I would have the next afternoon.

The next day we came in to eat at noon and I showered and put on my best clothes and my best straw hat. Humbert washed up and put on a clean shirt, and Virginia, true to her word, came over to the cookhouse and handed me a check and told me to have a good time. The check was made out for one hundred dollars, just like I had asked, and I felt like I'd just won the lottery.

I handled that check as if it were the holy grail. I doubled it over so it would fit in my shirt pocket but I tried not to fold it or make a crease in it. It was too precious to disfigure. When I got off by myself, I looked at it for a long time, intrigued by Virginia's signature and admiring all of the perfect little zero's she had penned onto the face of it.

All the way up the canyon I leaned forward trying to make the truck go faster. For once I didn't look at the ledges or the deer or the Indian writings; I was focused on getting to town. I was homesick and eager and the check was burning a hole in my shirt pocket.

Humbert dropped me off at my home in Wellington and my little brothers came tumbling out of the house to meet me. I relished that homecoming. I had returned as the conquering hero, the big brother with a real job, the brave soldier home from the war. For that one weekend I could be the big dog in a very small kennel. I frolicked with my brothers for a short while, and then I got down to serious business. I borrowed the family car and went to the big city of Price to reap the rewards of my weeks in the hay fields. I cashed the check at the Carbon-Emery bank, my hand shaking as I endorsed it, and then I went straight to the Price Commission Company.

I stood in that store with the reverence of a pilgrim who has walked to Mecca on his knees. The clean, brightly waxed linoleum floor spread out before me like a magic carpet. The black and white checkered floor was a pathway to the altars of the fruits of capitalism and it beckoned me to follow. I drank in the smells, the wispy incense of the treasures that lined the heavy shelves: oiled leather, mothballs, furniture polish and soap. I stood proud but humble: a new member of the

Consumer's Guild, an Initiate, a Plebe, a Pledge, a raw recruit. I had endured the hazing and the rituals of initiation. I had worked hard. I had paid my dues. It was my first time to enter the Temple of Capitalism with a passport tucked safely in my pocket, a ticket to the inner sanctum—that big wad of green American money.

For the first time in my life I could buy anything I wanted. I could participate in the rituals of commerce as an equal with my parents and other high-ranking individuals in the community. I could expect to be afforded the same levels of courtesy and respect extended to those who had achieved the highest rank within my society—the rank of Consumer of Goods and Services. This was the culmination of my summer's journey. This was what it was all about.

I had rehearsed in my mind exactly what I was going to do on that special day and what I was going to buy. I was resolved to be cautious and deliberate. None of that easy come and easy go crap that Joe and Humbert laughed about. I plotted my strategy carefully, setting priorities and counting up the totals on my fingers. I was painfully aware that I had traded many weeks in the fields for the currency in my pocket and I was very protective of it.

I bought a pair of Levi's for four dollars—a full day's pay—and I bought a couple of fancy shirts for about that same amount each. I picked out a respectable, but not too fancy nickel-silver belt buckle that set me back almost three dollars and a buck-stitched leather belt to go with it for about two and a half. I then went to the boot department and found a fine pair of western boots. I still remember how the new leather smelled and how soft it was in my hands as I tried the boots on. They were fancy dress boots, and I was going to wear them to school all winter and I bought the best pair in the store. The boots fit perfectly and they were beautiful. They cost a whopping thirty dollars and my fingers trembled as I counted up the total. It was the middle of the summer, but I remember thinking about the pretty tracks those boots would make in the snow at the school bus stop and that pleasant thought gave me courage.

I saved the best for last, and when I had selected everything else I wanted, I moved to the hat department.

Nothing is more important to a cowboy than his hat. A man's hat defines him. The shape, style, and how he cares for the hat he wears reveals a great deal about a man's personality and his principles. A man who takes pride in himself will wear a nice hat, and he will keep it clean and treat it with respect. A man who wears a nice hat to town and has the good manners to take it off when he enters a building can be trusted and should be honored. A man who abuses an expensive hat, or who wears a dirty, misshapen and ugly old hat to town has no pride in himself and will kick his dog, beat his wife, drive drunk and spit on the sidewalk.

A man who cares about the way he looks and how he presents himself before others will spend the time necessary to get his headgear just right. For years I had watched my young-buck cowboy heroes come to the school bus stop wearing expensive felt hats and I had dreamed of the day when I too could own a good one. I stood before several shelves of boxed western hats and savored the moment. I was like a prospective bride among the wedding dresses, all starry-eyed and filled with wonder.

The hat had to be black, of course, and the brim had to be at least four inches wide and stiff as a board. I tried on several in front of a small mirror, admiring each with a heartfelt longing, but saving myself for just the right one. It was a big decision, like buying a house or finding a wife.

At last I found her, the hat of my dreams. I opened the box, that door to her lonely cell, and it was love at first sight. She was beautiful, soft midnight black and her crown was lined with rich, red silk.

She had been waiting for me to come to the rescue and save her from that dusty shelf. She came into my arms (my hands actually) and the soft touch of her scented, ebony coat made me sigh with resignation. She pouted longingly and batted her dark eyelashes like a temptress and I knew she was the hat for me. I had always known that somewhere out there, in that big, wide and scary world, there was one special hat for everyone— and I knew I had just found mine. She had been waiting patiently, beautiful and lonely, there in that dark dungeon of a hatbox, waiting for her handsome prince to ride in and take her away. She had longed to be set free, to be cared for and loved, to be taken home to meet Mother, to be worn out in the sunlight where she could charm the good citizens with her radiant good looks and noble character.

With trembling fingers I placed the hat on my head and looked at myself in the mirror. She snuggled down over my curly locks like an old friend and she was everything I'd ever hoped she would be. I peered into that mirror, mirror on the wall, and the mirror whispered to me that I was drop-dead handsome in that hat. I admired my image with a wistful smirk of self-satisfaction. None of my cowboy heroes had a hat better than that one. I tipped the hat just a little to one side, the way a cocky, drunken sailor might wear a hat, and it looked great. I set it on the back of my head and let my wavy forelocks pile up on my forehead like James Dean the movie star and it looked even better. It didn't matter what I did with that hat, I looked great wearing it no matter how I wore it. I looked in the mirror for a long time, turning my head slowly from side to side as the light and shadow played over that beautiful, soft felt hat and across my handsomely smug and suntanned young face, and I purred like a kitten.

The hat, like the boots, was an obscene thirty dollars—more than a full week's wages—but I wouldn't settle for less. That hat was the fulfillment of a dream of mine and it was damn the torpedoes and full speed ahead. I would have traded a month in the hay fields for that hat . . . a couple of months maybe. I wouldn't take it off, even in the store, and I told the sales lady she could throw the box away. The sales lady smiled as she bagged-up my treasures and counted out my change.

The Price Commission Company got most of my money that day, but I left there as happy as a lizard on a warm rock. I walked out of that store with my arms full of packages and with my new black hat tilted just a little cocky to one side. I had spent about eighty of my one hundred hard-earned dollars, but twenty was still enough to take my girlfriend to the rodeo, the dance, and a day of revelry in the Wellington City Park.

My girlfriend was a cute little thing and we'd been going steady for quite a while. We had stayed in touch by writing letters over the summer and she knew I was coming to town for the weekend. We had made plans to go to the park, the rodeo and the dance together.

I took my treasures from the Price Commission Company home and got all decked out in my new duds and then I borrowed the dodge again and went to see her. I just knew she was going to be swept off her feet by my manly good looks and expensive new clothes. She seemed happy to see me all right, but she wasn't all awe-struck and giddy like I expected her to be and I was disappointed. She smiled and said the hat was pretty, but she didn't swoon like Lady Guenevere and I was mystified. I couldn't bring myself to believe that the mirror in the hat store had lied to me.

That pretty young lady surprised me by presenting me with a pair of matching western shirts—his and hers. They were beautiful things and quite expensive, a silky gray and black color with pearl snaps. I was impressed and more than a little embarrassed. I knew she had spent a good deal of her own money to buy the shirts and I had just spent almost a hundred dollars on myself and hadn't thought to buy her anything. And worse than that, if I bought her a present now, I wouldn't have the money to take her to the dance or the rodeo. I was caught, but there wasn't much I could do at that point. I blushed and consoled myself with the thought that I would get her something extra special for Christmas, a jacket or a transistor radio maybe.

Matching shirts was a big thing with the girls at that time. If you could get a guy into a shirt that was identical to the one you were wearing and take him to town in it, it was like painting a billboard on his back that he was taken and as good as married. It was like having "Going Steady" tattooed on your forehead. A real cowboy like John Wayne might have balked at such foolishness, but several of our friends were wearing matching shirts that summer and so it didn't seem like such a big deal—at least I reconciled it that way. We wouldn't be the only couple in town looking like twins. I dutifully put the shirt on and we went to drag Main Street in Price and catch up on what all the other kids had been doing over the summer.

My girlfriend and I spent the twenty-fourth in the Wellington Park with our friends and families and we had a great time. We watched the parade, sat through the patriotic church history program, and goofed off in the park all day. We had a lot of fun. I was in great shape, and I won a foot race while wearing my new cowboy boots. Late that afternoon we went to see the rodeo.

The Rodeo

A rodeo was one of the few opportunities that country people had to get together in large groups and check each other out. It was a great social event for the whole area that was

The Split Sky

disguised as a contest between man and beast. It was at the rodeo where all of the rites of growing up, coming of age, selecting a mate and proving the new generation were performed. It was great fun to be a participant, and almost as much fun to watch.

A rodeo was a great place to meet girls. It gave the young men a chance to show off and strut their stuff in front of the young ladies. In this light, a rodeo could be compared to the drumming ground of the prairie chickens in Wyoming. It was a pre-selected site—a flat place in the dirt—where the rituals of courting took place.

Like the male prairie chickens, the young guys would come to the rodeo all decked out in their regal finery and make fools of themselves to impress the girls. Also like the prairie chickens, the girls remained shy and reserved and sometimes pretended not to notice—at least they acted that way in that by-gone time before the women's libbers poisoned the well. Courting was more refined and civil and steeped in tradition in those days, and the rituals of courtship were a lot of fun, especially at a rodeo.

The young women would show up in their traditional costumes: tight pants and low-cut, sleeveless blouses and fancy jewelry. They were perfumed and painted and curled. Many sported dangling earrings that sparkled like spinners out to tempt a big fish. They wore their hair up with fancy pins or tied back in ponytails, and some of the more daring wore colorful Rodeo Queen western hats in bright girly colors: scarlet, green or lavender. The very young teenaged girls ran around in packs, giggling and whispering and always on their way to or from the overcrowded restrooms, peeking around corners at the young stallion of their dreams. The older girls were much more sophisticated. They traveled in pairs. They were more practiced and skilled than their younger sisters. Like their cousins the female prairie chickens, the older girls were aloof, uninterested and standoffish. They waited for the boys to come to them. Oh, they wiggled the bait once in a while, but most of the time they sat quietly biding their time, cool and reserved.

The young men came dressed like peacocks, desperate to be noticed in the colorful plumage of the mating season: big belt buckles and fancy shirts with bright colors. Those who were really anxious would wear scarlet, electric blue or neon white, sometimes with great, gaudy flowers or shimmering stripes. Pointed cowboy boots were part of the uniform, and a good hat was as important to a young buck as the antlers on a deer—the newer the better and the fancier the better still.

I learned early that wearing a good-looking hat was a great way to meet girls. Some of the more enterprising young ladies had learned to use a guy's hat as a way to gain an impromptu introduction. They would smile sweetly and bat those big eyelashes and purr something like, "Oh, that's a pretty hat . . . can I see it for a minute?" And then of course, a real cowboy had to blush and smile shyly like James Dean as he handed it over for her inspection and approval. You then had an opportunity to talk for a few minutes and exchange vital information. That fancy black hat was girl-bait like I had never dreamed, and worth every cent of the thirty dollars I paid for it.

The rodeo was a proving ground. There were certain rights-of-passage for boys like me in the early sixties, masculine contests of skill and ability that marked a boy's transition into manhood. Getting a job and paying your own way was one of them, riding rough stock in the hometown rodeo was another. Riding a bronc or a bull in front of the hometown crowd was like having a Bar Mitzvah. Once you passed the test you were a man. You showed everyone that you were big enough and strong enough and courageous enough to do the manly deed, and once you had done it, you hoped everyone would see you as grown up. You didn't have to do it all of the time, but you had to do it at least once and out in public where all of your friends and family and the whole community could see you do it. It didn't matter if you got bucked off and got your mouth full of dirt, the important thing was to show everyone that you had the guts to get on in the first place—that you could conquer your fear and be a man.

The whole thing was reminiscent of New Guinea tribesmen jumping out of trees with vines tied to their ankles. It was a ritual whose origins were lost in a distant past, and it was something the young men felt they had to do because their fathers and uncles and older brothers had done it. It was something the community elders and the young women expected the young men to do because everyone had done it in the past. It was a great spectator sport—very dangerous and therefore very exciting. At the same time it was saturated with stupidity. The whole thing was essentially pointless . . . unless you were trying to prove something, which we were.

I didn't ride that summer even though I wanted to. I was still too young and my parents would have killed me if the bull didn't. My turn came a couple of years later. The summer I was eighteen I rode in every show in every town in Carbon and Emery counties. I wasn't very good and I ate a lot of dirt, but I did win the bull riding in Sunnyside, and I've always counted that as one of the feathers in my war bonnet.

The rodeo was held at night under the glare of high-intensity lighting. The arena was on a hill a couple of miles East of town and on the night of the Twenty-Fourth it was bright and could be seen all across the valley. From a distance, it was a great, glowing circle of light on an ocean of darkness, a far-off ship, a great passenger liner leaving port with all her lights on.

In the darkness around the great ship, small dots of car lights snaked out to her in thin, moving ribbons like tiny boats in her wake.

Up close and inside the glow of the lights there was a sensual feast of exotic sights, sounds and smells, with a deep undercurrent of intense excitement. Young boys hung on the fence like troops of monkeys and watched their older brothers and cousins ride. They cheered and clapped and groaned in unison. The boys dreamed of the day when they too could be seventeen and hear their names announced over the PA system as the next rider out. Young cowboys hurried past with anxious, wrinkled brows and with colorful, fringed chaps, bull ropes and bareback riggings over their shoulders. Rodeo queens in bright, fancy costumes sat on pretty horses and waited to be called to chase calves back into the catch pens. Extended family groups sat on the hard boards of the bleachers. Grandparents sat on cushions or folded blankets while babies slept in wicker baskets. Giggling little kids dropped snow cone and bubble gum bombs from the top of the bleachers on unsuspecting passers-by, and naughty boys set off firecrackers under the seats. Lovers sat with blankets over their shoulders and pretended that the people around them didn't know what was going on under the blanket. Drinkers and drunks sat discretely in parked cars against the arena fence. Mothers with small children sat on the hoods of cars, on blankets with picnic baskets, and held their toddlers safely on their laps while small groups of men stood in dark corners and talked and drank beer. In the parking lot and in the shadows behind the bucking chutes, the soft glow of cigarettes could be seen winking in the darkness like taillights on some far off highway.

A running commentary of what was happening was blasted from the PA system: who was riding, who was up next, what the last score was and the name of the next bull. Rowdy polkas or twangy cowboy music took up the slack between events. Rodeo clowns in baggy pants and painted faces ambled around the arena, laughing with the kids who clung to the fence and yelling old and worn-out jokes up to the rodeo announcer who dutifully rebroadcast them over the PA system. The cool night air carried clouds of dust and the tart stink of beer, cigar smoke and horse manure off into the sagebrush. The smell of popcorn and fried onions drifted past from the direction of the concession stands.

Pretty girls on horses orbited the grounds endlessly, trolling for boys and trying to see what their champion and his buddies were doing behind the bucking chutes. Mothers wrung their hands in distress as their babies got bucked off and splashed in the dirt, and fathers stood around in little groups, talking quietly and sizing up each other's sons.

The whole thing was an act of communal bonding. It was like a great dance around the campfire at some Native American village where the whole community comes together to celebrate being alive. It was a testing ground where the young men showed their skills and the village elders nodded their approval. It was a forum for the young women to look over the field of prospective husbands and secretly make their selections. It was a religious observance where the old people took comfort in the continuance of the village traditions. It was school for the children who witnessed the modeling behavior they were expected to conform to. It was also a big, rowdy party where all of these elements were intertwined and disguised so well that few people understood the significance of what was really happening.

The last bull was finally bucked out and the Wellington rodeo was over for another year. There was a mass exodus of dusty cars, aimed at the highway and back into town. The last phase of the Twenty-Fourth celebration was just getting started and that was the community dance.

The dance was held in the Junior High School auditorium, and while it was open to anybody, it was usually just the teen-aged kids and the young married people who participated. A lot of the older folks were stuck on Benny Goodman and just couldn't get in the groove with Elvis and Carl Perkins. Sometimes there was a live band, but more often the dance was a record hop, and it was not unusual for people to bring favorite records from home.

BREAKING UP IS HARD TO DO

My girlfriend and I, in our matching gray shirts, danced and drank watered-down cokes in paper cups and visited with our friends. I was surprisingly unhappy. I had waited all summer for the opportunity to be there, but now that it was happening the whole thing seemed anticlimactic. I was restless and even a little bored and I noticed that she seemed to be that way too. Being separated for the summer had given us both some distance and a chance to reassess our situation. I had taken the opportunity, out in the ledges, to review my life and my priorities and I'd realized that I was beginning to chafe at the strings that bound me.

I was changing, becoming someone else, and I wanted the world around me to change too. I wanted to be free, not just from my girlfriend, but from my life as a kid. I wanted to be grown up and able stand on my own two feet. Free to soar like an eagle, to run joyful and wild like a young mustang out on the prairie: no fences, no restrictions, and no limits to what I could do and where I could go. I wanted to be independent. I wanted to be my own man and make my own choices. I wanted to leave my father's home and the small, sheltered world I lived in. I wanted to strike out and have adventures: climb a mountain, see the world, join the Marines, fight a war, go to college, ride a bull. I was willing to accept the consequences, whatever they might be.

I had quietly decided that I wanted to break off the relationship with that pretty young woman but I didn't know how to do it. We were caught in a trap. Going steady was an easy pool to slide into, but the banks were steep and treacherous when you tried to get back out. It was difficult to reach solid ground again without someone being hurt.

I secretly longed for the freedom to sail away but I was hesitant to cut the anchor chain. There was a negative connotation involved. The person to make such a move would be seen by our friends and families as a traitor and the bad guy. Breaking up with a steady girl was like getting a divorce; the implications were unpleasant. The act would be fodder for the gossips and scandalmongers in our little town. I was a compassionate little pup and I would have chewed my arm off before hurting her feelings, and so I endured for the time being, secretly hoping that she would make the first move. I really thought it might happen too, and soon. I suspected that she was leaning more and more toward a certain good-looking varsity basketball player and I thought that perhaps one day the two of them would ride off into the sunset and leave me in the dust, but so far it hadn't happened.

I didn't have another girlfriend at the time. There was no one waiting in the wings for me to flee to and embrace. I just hoped to have my options back and the chance to do things differently. I wanted to reach out and have those adventures, free from the clutter and baggage of emotional and social obligations. For me to break off the relationship, I needed a reason, an excuse, a push, something to give me the courage to sever the ties . . . and the push came soon and very unexpectedly.

We were sitting on the sidelines on folding tin chairs, holding hands and watching other people dance, when I was completely dumb-struck by the sudden appearance of the most beautiful girl I had ever seen. She was a raven-haired beauty in white pants who could have stood her ground with Annette Funicello from the Mickey Mouse Club. I was mesmerized. I watched in slack-jawed fascination as she materialized like a vision from out of the crowd and walked out on the dance floor with some guy I didn't know. She was radiant, and she danced with the self-confident poise of a movie star and with the grace and feminine charm of a teenaged Aphrodite. I was enraptured. I tried not to stare but I couldn't take my eyes from her.

I watched her dance for what seemed like a long time, while everything else around me faded into insignificance. I was no longer aware of the noise of the crowd or of the other people sitting nearby and talking. All else was completely forgotten. My whole being was focused on that one pretty girl and the way she danced. I had never seen anything like it. She was so very graceful and her face so pretty. Her white pants and long, dark hair shimmered in the dim light. I was her prisoner, bound, gagged and helpless.

And then a most remarkable thing happened, something I would never have dared to dream. With stunned disbelief, I became aware that she was looking back—at me!

There was a pause between dances and she was standing on the dance floor with a large group of people when our eyes met. She was looking at me over the shoulder of the guy she was with, and she smiled sweetly and gave me one of those playful, come-on looks that would have made Mae West and Marilyn Monroe proud. She then blushed like the teenager she was, and ducked her head and looked away quickly like she had been caught being a bad girl. I sat there stupidly with my mouth open, holding my breath. She glanced back demurely, smiled again, and then dropped her eyes submissively like an Arabian princess and my heart sputtered to a stop.

I was suddenly out-of-breath as though I had run a mile. Oh my . . . oh my . . . oh my . . . what should I do! The most beautiful girl in the whole world was making eyes at me and I was sitting there holding someone else's hand . . . what to do . . . what to do? I was in a panic. My mind raced and my palms got sweaty and I was suddenly filled with a terrible resolve. I whispered to my girlfriend, "Let's go."

I drove her home and braced myself against the steering wheel and let her have it as gently as I could. It was the old, "I like you a lot and maybe it will work out some day but for now I don't want to go out with you anymore," speech. I don't think my pronouncement was a complete surprise to her, but I felt like a creep just the same. She didn't argue or fuss. She got out of the car quietly and went into the house. I dropped the dodge in reverse and went back to the dance.

She was gone.

That beautiful girl with the dark hair was gone. I looked all over for her but she wasn't there. She had disappeared in the same way she had materialized, back into the crowd—melted away and gone forever.

We never spoke. I never knew her name. I didn't know where she came from, who she was with, or where in the world she went. She was in and out of my life in a matter of minutes and she changed the course of my life forever with just a smile—and she never knew.

I never saw her again—only in my dreams.

I spent Sunday with the family. Mother cooked a wonderful meal and we watched some television and I packed my things to go back to the ranch. I filled another box with books and clothes and I packed a portable radio—I would deal with Joe the dragon when the time came. I raided mother's cupboards for snack foods and treats and I brooded most of the day because I was embarrassed and ashamed that I had hurt the feelings of my long-time sweetheart, but the deed had been done and I didn't want to patch it up, at least not yet.

Dad drove me back out to the ranch that afternoon with my little brothers tagging along and I didn't fret about it. My attitude had changed. I wasn't embarrassed about my little brothers following me around anymore and it was okay if Dad wore his old work hat out to the ranch. Those things didn't matter to me now. I was different.

A transformation had come over me. My trip to town had helped me to see myself in a new light. I realized that my brothers and my friends now looked up to me as one of the big guys, and for the first time in my life, I had felt the pride of looking my heroes in the eyes as an equal. I was doing the same things that Leon Rich, Smokey Clark and George Cook were doing, and more important than that, I realized that I could see myself as one of my young-buck cowboy heroes now. I felt pride in myself on a level I had never experienced before.

I knew that working on the ranch was going to be different from now on. It was an adventure now, a welcomed proving ground for my manhood. I no longer had doubts. I was still a little coyote in the wolf pack, but I wasn't intimidated or afraid anymore. I was suddenly a young man, and I wore the badge of my new rank and status, that beautiful black hat, like it was the Medal of Honor.

I got out of the car wearing my new black hat and I put my box of personal items under my arm and invited my dad and little brothers to come into the bunkhouse and see my little corner of the ranch. I led them into the bunkhouse through the front door and Apache Joe and his newspaper moved back and out of my way. I tipped my new hat respectfully and said quite sincerely, "Excuse me, Joe."

I took my family on a short tour of the ranch buildings and the corrals as the evening gathered and I proudly pointed out some fine haystacks I had made with my own good hands. I was proud and I felt like I was home again. I hadn't realized until that afternoon just how much a part of my life that ranch had become in just a couple of months.

Chapter 10

Wilderness

Treasures Of The Canyon

After my adventures on the Twenty-Fourth of July, I settled back into the routine at the ranch. There was still an ocean of hay to put up, and chores to do, but things were different after the Twenty-Fourth. Coming back after my weekend off was like starting all over again on a better foot. I was much more confident—things were familiar to me and I felt like I belonged on the ranch. I understood the operation and how things worked and I was better able to act on my own without asking permission or waiting to be told what to do. With an enhanced self-confidence, I was more prone to speak up and join in on conversations instead of sitting quietly in the corner; and the ability to speak my mind and joke and have fun with the guys made my life much simpler. My new sense of assertiveness was not lost on my co-workers. The men around me all seemed to accept me more as an equal and they treated me less like a kid. I reveled in my newfound status.

I stopped using the back door to the bunkhouse all of the time and I started listening to my radio for a short time each night before the generator was shut down. Joe didn't say anything about the radio, which surprised me after the lecture I'd been given on my first day at the ranch. He seemed to have softened his rabid, "none of that rock-n-roll garbage" policy. I stayed tuned to radio station KOMA from Oklahoma City, the premiere rock-n-roll station in the whole world. I did keep the radio turned down as low as possible so as not to disturb old Joe. I was still pretty leery of the old dragon and there was no sense in provoking a fight. After all, we did have to live together.

KOMA became my best friend at the ranch. The radio station helped reduce my sense of isolation and kept me updated on what was happening in the outside world. It also brought to me that vibrant, youthful and rhythmic music that made me want to dance, and I resolved that one of the things I wanted to do as soon as possible was to learn to play an electric guitar like Beau Diddley and Dwaine Eddy.

Even though we spent eleven or twelve hours a day, six days a week with the chores and the hay, it seemed to me that there was always plenty of time off. The summer days were long and the light lasted until almost ten o'clock. And then of course, there was always a day off on Sundays to look forward to. No one cared what I did with my time off and I was left to fill the hours by myself. To me, this was like having Christmas every afternoon. There was no place on earth I would rather have spent my time than in the ledges of Nine Mile Canyon. It was a magic and mystical place.

The canyon was a treasure box of history. Everywhere there were reminders of the past. Weathered wagon wheels and rusty old horse-drawn farm machinery sat in front of abandoned log cabins. All up and down the canyon sandstone walls were covered with rock art made by the hands of ancient artists, and rusty, iron telegraph poles from the past century marched up the canyon for miles.

There was a popular story about the telegraph poles. The story was that the army at Fort Duchesne had installed the iron poles because the Indians kept using the wooden poles for firewood. It made a good story, but anyone with common sense could see that telegraph poles would have made much better building material for settlers than firewood for Indians. Firewood was plentiful and could be gathered with a lot less work than cutting up telegraph poles. It was long, straight fence poles and roof beams that were in short supply.

All along the canyon road pioneer inscriptions and the names of freight wagon teamsters begged to be noticed. Some of the old-time names peeked out from the willows and brush that lined the road like nosy neighbors peeking through the curtains. Often the inscriptions went unnoticed, partly hidden by the brush and the shadows, but they were always there. They were the graffiti and roadside litter of the last century, faceless names scratched into the soft sandstone walls with a nail, or smeared on the rock with axle grease, or written free hand with charcoal from a smoky campfire: Warren Sulser 1849—S Goosbeck 1867—Orson Strong 1886—J L Willson 1893—Mary P. Corbett 1911. Each weathered name was a cry for recognition by some lonely traveler who had secretly hoped that the scribbled testament of having touched that spot would somehow preserve the fact of an otherwise unremarkable existence. Each inscription was a document, a witness and a memorial—haunting testimonials of lives lived and people gone and buried.

Abandoned log cabins and the remains of several farmsteads dotted the canyon bottom, ruins from the pioneer past and relics of that optimistic time when land was free and every man believed he could own a good farm with only enough faith and hard work. The ruined cabins stood as monuments to the hopes and dreams of immigrant ancestors who had poured their blood, sweat and tears into the soil of the canyon, only to be beaten into submission by a cruel Mother Nature and then driven back to the towns and cities with calloused hands and empty pockets.

The Split Sky

I explored some of those abandoned homesteads, and in the weeds and brush around them, where the litter and trash had been discarded, I found hand-forged square nails and purple bottles and shell casings from antique firearms. Sometimes there were bonus treasures like mother-of-pearl buttons or a rusted bridle bit or even an old copper penny. While searching through rusted tin cans and broken crockery of a long abandoned cow camp, I found a brass bar token: *Fitzgerald's place—good for one drink or one cigar*, a treasured memento from a cowboy I never knew.

More exciting and more important to me than the pioneer relics was the great abundance of Native American remains. Everywhere in the canyon were traces of the handiwork of the ancient inhabitants: the Desert Archaic people, the Fremont and the Utes. By tracing clues that were hundreds of years old, I followed ancient footprints through countless miles of rocky rims and shadowy overhangs with the zeal and curiosity of Henry Schleimann uncovering the mysteries of Troy and Mycenae. In the early 1960s a good many of the sites were still unexplored and the canyon was unknown outside of the local communities.

People in my hometown knew that the canyon had ruins and "Indian writings," and there had been some remarkable finds made in the early days. That was one of the reasons I was so excited to work there and to have a chance to try my hand at exploring in such a prime area. To actually live in Nine Mile Canyon was to be surrounded with the bounty of a treasure hunter's dreams, and I was careful not to waste a precious moment in searching them out.

For that one glorious summer, Nine Mile Canyon was all mine. I saw very few people in the canyon that summer and there were no tourists at all. As far as I know, for those few precious months, I was the only person in the whole area doing Indiana Jones style archaeological reconnaissance—and I was loving it.

The fifties and sixties was a great time to collect artifacts. There were some very large private collections made in the Eastern Utah area during those years. There was still an abundance of things to be found and no one cared if people picked them up and took them home. The Federal Antiquities act of 1906 had been on the books for a long time but it was almost never enforced. I knew of Forest Service and BLM rangers who collected arrowheads, and a deputy sheriff who worked with my father spent every weekend digging for artifacts in the dry caves in the area. Even Boy Scout troops in my hometown often went into Nine Mile and the San Rafael desert to camp out and look for arrowheads.

There were prominent and professional people who joined in on the collecting. The District Judge, Fred Keller, had an extensive collection of Anasazi pottery, and when Carbon College (The College of Eastern Utah) started its world-class prehistoric museum in the early 1960s, the Board of Trustees sponsored an expedition to dig and collect artifacts for the new museum. They did this without professional help, advice or permits, just a group of prominent citizens out to help stock empty shelves in the new museum as a community service project. The 1950s and 60s was a different time; there were different attitudes about collecting—and about a lot of other things.

Many people had searched the canyon before me and countless others have left their mark in the years since. The most famous of my predecessors was Dave Nordell, a man who owned a ranch in the canyon in the 1950s and who spent as much time digging for relics as he did in tending his livestock. I knew Dave personally. He bought a house in Wellington from my father and he employed a couple of my young-buck cowboy heroes to work for him on his ranch and help dig artifacts on the weekends. I heard stories of his many discoveries firsthand from those young cowboys turned archaeological looters. Dave would often send those young men down the canyon walls on ropes to explore difficult-to-reach caves and granaries.

Like many of the men who gravitated to Nine Mile, Dave was a bachelor and unencumbered with domestic responsibilities. He could spend all of the time he wanted with his hobby, and he did. When he left the canyon in the early 1960s he had such a large artifact collection that he started a small museum and tourist trap just outside of Wellington on Highway 6. His venture was not profitable and it was soon closed, but for a brief time his full collection was on display and I had a chance to see it all. The man had made some truly remarkable finds.

Dave Nordell, the toughest cowboy in Nine Mile Canyon— about 1957.
Photo Courtesy of Bill Larsen

I went arrowhead hunting with Dave a couple of times, south of Wellington and out on Cedar Mountain. Those were days before I had a driver's license, and a couple of friends and I, shameless beggars, would finagle a ride with anyone who would take us arrowhead hunting. Dave was good to me and tolerant of my puppy dog eagerness and uncontrolled lust for anything made from chipped flint. The man was one of my boyhood heroes and I learned all I could from him about where and how to find artifacts.

Nine Mile has always been more famous for its rock art than for the artifacts and ruins it contains. The canyon is the world's longest art gallery and everywhere on the ledges are found magnificent panels of ancient rock art. Some of the images are painted with hematite or ocher, but most were deeply incised into the living rock (pictographs are painted on the rock, petroglyphs are incised into the rock). The images are everywhere and the natives of the canyon must have passed down the traditions for many generations. The sheer volume of the work is astounding.

It was like a big Easter egg hunt to explore the ledges and look for petroglyph panels. They were everywhere and a person never knew what was going to show up next. There were great panels of lines and dots and squiggles that looked like maps or mindless doodling, and there were figures of hunters with bows and arrows who chased deer and buffalo across sandstone prairies. There were shaman and great chiefs in elaborate headdresses, posturing provocatively, haughty, bold and arrogant. There were warriors with clubs and shields and people wearing masks. Snakes, spirals, rainbows and abstract designs were frequent, and playful, impish little mountain sheep peeked out from the shadows at regular intervals. Some of the carved aborigines wore necklaces, kilts and ear bobs, and some of the men wore a single feather that tipped jauntily over their handsome faces. Some of the people were dancing, some stalking game on their knees with bow and arrow ready, and some were posing formally to have their portraits made. Majestic deer and elk, adorned with great, improbable antlers, strutted across sandstone panels with their heads held high.

Each panel is as unique as individual handwriting; no two are ever the same. Some are bold and beckoning, disrupting the natural flow of the scenery and begging to be noticed like gaudy billboards. Other panels are hidden, unobtrusive, timid and discrete, cowering in the shadows. There are countless thousands of them. I'm convinced that no one person has ever seen them all, nor ever will.

A view from high in the ledges.

You are alone and the canyon is quiet. You find your way around the corner of some high and broken wall of a sandstone ledge and there before you lies the foundations of an ancient and ruined dwelling. You are at first surprised, even startled, because you have been in the ledges for hours and have seen little to suggest that anyone has ever been there before you. You stand frozen in your tracks for a moment and take it all in.

From the way it looks, you know that you may be the first person to see this site since that last longhaired farmer walked away from it eight hundred years before.

The place has a feeling of sanctity, accentuated by the fact that you're alone with no one to share the find with but your inner self. There's a haunting peacefulness about it and you can actually feel the lingering presence of those long-ago people. It's the same feeling you get when you walk through a cemetery by yourself, or stand alone in a quiet chapel, or enter an occupied but silent and empty house. It's a humbling experience, and you feel almost guilty that you are about to intrude and make footprints in that hallowed spot. At the same time you are excited to see what the ancients may have left behind for you to discover.

The ruin is in a sheltered place, tucked below an overhanging rim of sandstone, shielded from the rain and snow. There is a circular wall of rocks extending out from the ledge, just a foot or two high and without mortar. A few mummified roof beams of pinion and juniper lay scattered about and everything has a thin layer of gray dust. There are coyote tracks and bobcat scat mixed in the dirt, and here and there a clump of cedar bark, rye grass, or a small lump of charcoal peeks out from the rubble.

You make a quick survey of the ruin, searching for that elusive cooking pot or basket that the ancient homeowner might have abandoned along with the house, but none are there—they seldom are. You step back and take a second look, and for the first time you see the two little mountain sheep who stand as sentinels, scratched into the sandstone wall at the back of the shelter. You search the ground closely around the structure and discover a few shards of blackened pottery and a dozen small flakes of chert: blue-green, chocolate-brown, and stark, translucent white—stone shavings—clues to where an individual of your own species has labored to make tools from the rocks beneath his feet.

You stand for a while and look out over the canyon and soak up the mystery and the wonder of the place. You muse quietly the question of why in the world anyone would put a house in such an improbable spot, and you wonder what the canyon would have looked like from that same vantage point all those many years ago. You then continue the quest, following the ledge around another corner and on down the canyon.

Ruined "forts" guarded the rocky promontories. They were usually large circles of thick, brown rocks, some still standing tall enough to preserve doorways and peepholes. They stood as sentinels on the high places, the stone walls sagging with the weight of the years and the roof timbers long melted back to dust.

The biggest treasure hunt was to seek out the small beehive-like granaries that could be found tucked away in the secret, secluded places high in the ledges. These tiny structures were often made from willows and mud and it was always a challenge to find them because they were purposely hidden and camouflaged. Some of the little storage bins still held beans and corn. Often the granaries were placed in spots that seemed to be completely inaccessible and it took mountaineering skills and sometimes ropes and ladders to reach them.

Virginia caught on very early that I had a passion for Indian relics, and she would sometimes go out of her way to show me things and tell me of discoveries that her family had made during their many years in the canyon. She knew of a lot of places that she didn't share with most people, but she shared some of them with me. It was not unusual for her to call me aside during one of her visits to my work area and point across the canyon and say something like, "Do you see that ridge over there? Back in the '30s some people from the University found some interesting things over there. You might want to go have a look one of these evenings." She put me on some good tracks and I found some nice things because of her help.

Joe and Humbert were amused by my passion, but they too gave me directions and helpful suggestions. Humbert knew where some of the better sites were and he shared his knowledge with me. He always smiled and seemed a little entertained by the fact that I would actually go up into the rocks and ledges by myself after a long day's work and stay there for hours at a time. He and Joe both thought I was crazy and they told me so on several occasions.

Virginia helped me in another important way that proved invaluable to me. After I had been at the ranch for a few weeks, she began to notice that I was walking farther and farther away from the ranch by myself in the evenings and sometimes getting back after dark. She spoke to me about it one morning and told me I could take one of the tractors to go exploring if I wanted to. In fact, she told me I could take her tractor every afternoon and on Sundays if I wanted to. She asked only that I be careful and make sure the tractor had fuel for the next day's work.

I could have dropped to the ground and kissed her feet. The tractor gave me the mobility to do the canyon in style, and some Sundays I would drive several miles to sites I wanted to explore. I still came in after dark most evenings, but now I had headlights and wheels and I didn't have to worry about cougars or killer badgers or stepping on a snake in the dark.

I found some good artifacts in the canyon and I did it with almost no digging. I was too young and too impatient to dig for very long and I almost never carried a shovel into the ledges. I depended on my athletic prowess and the ability to cover a lot of ground quickly while looking for surface manifestations of hidden treasures. Most of the artifacts I found were sticking out of the dirt or were tucked away in secret places where the Indians had hidden them. I was blessed with perfect eyesight and I would search out likely storage locations and cache sites and climb up to test my intuition. Most of the time I was wrong, but my percentages improved as I learned by hard experience where and what the Fremont had been doing in the canyon.

ALONE IN THE LEDGES

My explorations were always exciting, terribly interesting, physically stimulating and spiritually uplifting. I loved the time I spent in the ledges like nothing else I've ever done. An afternoon in the ledges was freedom. I was master of the universe. I was where I wanted to be and I could go anywhere and do anything I wanted. I owned the place. The possibilities were endless.

Everywhere I went the canyon was new and exciting and it was made just for me. The canyon spoke to me. The birds and the lizards knew my name. Shadowy rock shelters and high mesa tops beckoned me to come and explore, and faint, ancient Indian trails called out for me to follow them into the rim rocks.

It rained a lot that summer and the rocks and bushes were always washed clean. The smell of dark, damp soil and wet sage and juniper was like perfume on the cheek of Mother Nature herself. It was late afternoon by the time I finished my work at the ranch and the shadows of the ledges were always cool and inviting after a hot day in the fields. I remember the sky filled with great, billowing clouds that shimmered and sometimes glowed red and orange as they reflected the late-afternoon sun. I remember the air was clean and cool like mountain water. I also remember a hushed stillness up in the ledges when a person went there alone, a deep quiet that permeated everything. Small sounds seemed to echo for miles. Even birds respected the sanctity of the stillness and they called to each other in hushed and whispered tones. I tried to be quiet, even reverent when I ventured there by myself. A rolling rock, a cough, or a snapped tree branch disrupted the tranquility with a heresy that made me wince.

There is a spiritual element about being alone in the ledges that a person must experience to understand. There is a feeling of blending-in that comes over you when you are alone in such a wild place that makes you feel close to God and nature. It's like being absorbed by the place. You become a part of it. You melt into the background. The clutter and background noise of your everyday life is left behind and you are stripped to the very core; your thoughts and feelings turn inward and you can think and reflect without distraction. You know that you are isolated from other thinking and feeling beings, and yet the trees, bushes and rocks seem to be alive, aware and responsive. The sounds of your breathing, even your innermost thoughts, come back to you as if they belong to someone else and the effect is comforting. You are alone but you don't feel alone. There's a feeling that someone else is with you, a comforting presence that is reassuring. It's like your mind and spirit are communicating with your surroundings on a level that is deeper than your natural senses and beyond your ability to comprehend.

When you go for a long time without utterance, you begin to feel that the trees and the rocks can discern your innermost thoughts. The Ravens and Pinion Jays communicate to you without speaking. It's like experiencing a new dimension, a sense of awareness beyond your normal faculties. It's a humbling experience, and it puts things in a new perspective. It whispers to you that you are not the most important thing in all the world; you are but a very small part of a boundless creation—a speck of dust in the countless eons of time and space. The stillness makes you aware of your fragile mortality and it reminds you that most human pursuits are vanity and destined to be lost in the sands of the centuries. That awareness makes you search your soul for the real meaning of life.

The experience can be very positive and uplifting. The stillness and the closeness to the natural world leaves you with the conviction that there is order and structure in this world and that nature itself bows to an unseen hand. There is power and intelligence manifested in all things. Everything has a purpose, a place, a function to perform. When you accept that fact, you become aware that you are part of something truly great and noble. Your life is a gift and it has meaning and purpose. You get a feel for the promise of your existence and for the opportunities that are yours. You come away with a deeper conviction to do something meaningful with your life. You acquire a new understanding of the depth of time and of the timelessness of creation and the wonder of it all. Alone in the ledges you have an opportunity to think and reflect and ponder what it all means. It makes you feel vulnerable and humble, and yet so very much alive.

The experience helped me to understand how Native Americans can be so spiritual in their worship of the natural world. People who live out-of-doors and away from the comforts and protections of our modern world, see, feel and experience things that our culture has forgotten. God speaks in the stillness of the desert and we can't hear him over the din of our busy lives.

Being alone in the ledges helped me to understand God. His work and his glory is everywhere. In the canyon I was able to commune with Him in a way I found difficult to do in the distractions of a formal church setting. I felt that I could actually speak to God in the canyon as if he were standing with me. I felt his presence and I drew comfort from his company. I discovered, in a very personal way, that an anguished soul could be healed with sunlight, solitude and prayer.

Aborigines

God was in the canyon, and so were the ghosts of countless generations of Native American hunters and farmers. I traced the clues and followed the tracks and sometimes I would find things that would make me feel very close to those ancient peoples. Artifacts are made by human hands, and every one, be it an arrow point, a cooking pot, or a fragment of braided string is unique and personal to me. Finding a hand-made tool or ornament is like meeting the person who made it. The essence of that long-ago personality can often be discerned in the works of the hands. Some arrow points are perfectly symmetrical with long, parallel flaking patterns and deep, precise notches. It's easy to see that the flint knapper took pride in his work and had a sense of balance and artistry. Other points are field expedient, made with little care and no sense of pride. They are little more than crude notches dug into a sliver of chert that is crooked and too thick, anything to get the job done and get on with the business at hand. It makes me smile to know that people were the same in that distant time as they are today.

It was a special experience to find a small, hidden granary with perfect little fingerprints still clearly outlined in the mud plaster after almost a thousand years. The imprints reached out and bid me to follow them back through a time-tunnel to a distant past. I put my fingertips in those dimpled impressions and felt as if I could touch that other person across the centuries.

The world has changed so very much since those tiny fingers pressed into that malleable clay, and yet the canyon itself has remained much the same. The seasons and the years have come and gone with a cyclical rhythm, but the rocks have endured as endless and silent witnesses. The rocks still stand in their familiar places, just as the Fremont knew them, and they compassionately guarded the little granary, refusing to let the

The Split Sky

uncaring wind and rain wash the fingerprints away.

The granary with the fingerprints sat undisturbed for centuries in a sheltered alcove hidden in the ledges, watching the centuries march past and many generations of farmers come and go in the fields below. The people who built the structure filled it with precious seed corn and beans and never came back to reclaim the treasure. Over the years the dust settled in and buried the seed and drew moisture from it until the corn kernels and the beans were as dense and as hard as small, multicolored pebbles. I tried and tried and tried, over a period of several years, to grow some of the seed, but it refused to germinate. Like the hands that placed it in the granary, the seed was dead, and try as I might, I could not bring it back.

I found a perfect little cooking pot tucked away safely in a sheltered place in the rocks. I suspect that a Fremont woman had hidden it there, expecting to return and use it again. It might have held a quart of water, no more than that, and it still had sooty stains on the bottom from a long-ago campfire. It was unpainted, the simple gray color so typical of Fremont ceramics, and it was obviously intended as an article of utility and not meant to be a work of art. It had a perfect little handle and a flared rim. It was pressure cracked from it's many years in the damp dirt, and when I found it, the whole upper half was sticking up out of the ground like it had been waiting and watching for me to walk by. I was fascinated to see that the vessel bore the signature of the ancient potter. The woman had signed her work in the only way she knew how, by incorporating a small part of herself into her creation. An incised row of fingernail impressions circled the neck of the vessel, creating a design and a lasting memorial of those muddy and delicate little hands that shaped the soft clay.

I found several perfect arrowheads in the canyon that summer, little Christmas trees of chipped stone in colors as varied as the rainbow and as sharp as icicles. I also found a large stone blade, a chocolate-brown stone knife, high in the canyon by a natural trail that deer still use to access the feed and water of the canyon floor. The knife was lying in the gravel of a steep side hill where it had rested for centuries. I sat back and studied the terrain and the knife told me its story.

It had belonged to an ancient hunter who lost it as he butchered a mountain sheep in the snow and gathering darkness. He ambushed the animal on the very trail I had followed into the ledges that afternoon. I could see where he had hidden himself in the shadow of a ledge where the game trail passes close. I could imagine him waiting there patiently, in the shade and the cold, for the animal to come to him, watching and waiting, enduring the long, agonizing hours of being still.

I could imagine the brief explosion of excitement and pent-up energy the man experienced as the little band of sheep finally walked by and he chose a target and heard the smack of the flint point as it bit through hide and bone and soft tissue. I could imagine his excitement when the long hours of cold and patience were rewarded and he stood over the warm and bleeding carcass with a song in his heart.

I sat in the dirt and ran my finger along the sharp and ragged flint blade and the knife painted for me a picture of that longhaired hunter with his hands and arms all bloody as he gutted and skinned his prey and tied the meat up in the skin so he could carry it away. I could see him hurrying to be gone, tired and cold after a long day of waiting for the sheep to come. It was getting dark and he gathered up his bow and quiver of arrows, and in his excitement and haste he forgot about the blood-covered stone blade he had left lying in the snow. I could imagine the blade waiting faithfully for him to return, for a day, then two, and then knowing that he was never coming back.

The blade had been washed clean by the rain and snow of centuries when I found it. It was shining in the sun, flashing a signal to attract my attention, and it was happy to be found again. It had waited patiently for hundreds of years to tell someone the story it knew about that longhaired hunter. I was honored that the winds of fate had allowed me to find it after all those years. One day I would be able to show the blade to my children and my grandchildren and tell them the story it had told me.

I climbed up on a high, rocky prominence and found stonewalls and pottery shards and dark ash stains in the dirt that told me the Fremont had lived there. It was a highly improbable, even impossible place. I looked down on the fields so very far below and marveled at the fear and desperation that would have driven those poor people to select such a site for a village. The promontory village site was at the end of a very steep and arduous climb and a long haul for wood and water. The only positive feature of the place was that it was defensible. It was located on a high pinnacle that was a natural lightning magnet and it lay exposed to the harsh winter winds. The whole site reeked of fear and trepidation, a stain on the beauty of the place even after centuries of scouring rain and healing sunshine. The Fremont must have faced a terrible fear to flee high into the rocks like that. I can only imagine the numbing, mortal terror that must have gripped those people to drive them to such desperation. To stand in such a place and imagine how they must have huddled together to stay warm, and rationed out the water, and counted the precious sticks for the fire, and kept a constant grip on the babies to keep them from toppling over the precipice, makes me sad even today.

It has been popular in the world of academics for the past many years to paint the Anasazi and the Fremont as perfect little environmentalist farmers who ran around naked and embraced all of the liberal Hippie ideals of the 1960s—like the professors who study them. I've spent many long days tracking those peoples through their abandoned lairs, and I've seen too much evidence with my own eyes to believe that they were members of the Age of Aquarius. I don't believe they were "peace and love" and save-the-whales types, and I have doubts they would have fit in well at Woodstock in spite of what the park rangers at Mesa Verde might have told you. I submit that those who promote such sentiments have a terrible time making the facts fit their theories. There is ample evidence that the early farmers fought often, and over a period of many years.

I will concede that the Anasazi and the Fremont lived in a time when People were in tune with nature and the natural world. Men were free to follow the dictates of their own hearts, unencumbered by the restraints of law and civilizing traditions. Charles Darwin's principles of natural selection and survival of the fittest had free reign. Men lived much like animals and the strong preyed on the weak. Wilderness was a scary place.

The Anasazi and the Fremont farmers were vulnerable. They were tethered to a piece of land by the way they made their livelihood and that made them an easy prey. The evidence that those peoples were harassed, stolen from, and brutalized, is everywhere.

The Fremont farmers in Nine Mile Canyon lived high in the rocks and labored mightily to maintain a household in such inhospitable places. They built houses and raised children on the edge of dizzying heights and scattered the meager fare of their pantries in the dirt among the rocks. They hid seeds for the next growing season far from where they lived. They walked long and steep trails to tend their fields. They built places of refuge along narrow shelves in the ledges and fortified them with rock walls and tiny doorways. They carried wood and water on their backs up long and tortuous pathways. They made forts and lookout sites and wickedly barbed arrow points designed for fighting. They carved images of their antagonists and their own brave warriors into the sandstone walls—hateful and hopeful posturing men of war with shields, clubs and arrows.

They didn't do those things because they wanted to. A specter of fear still permeates those sites. If they had been peace-loving hippie farmers they would have lived in the bottom of the canyon near the wood and water and where the children could play in the grass near the fields. If they had a choice, they would have abandoned their high and windy, bleak and confining homes in the ledges.

They may have been innocent victims. It might be that a nomadic or less sedentary people overran them, a warrior people from somewhere else—but the evidence so far suggests that they were fighting amongst themselves.

It may have started out as garden-raiding or wife-stealing expeditions, or even as scalp and trophy hunting enterprises that got out of hand over the years. It might have been a war of farmers, each little village attacking and harassing others in some age-old Hatfield and McCoy type of blood feud. It may have been a war of desperation triggered by environmental stresses—a man had to steal or his family starved. It may not have been a war at all, but a centuries-long orgy of lawlessness and violence brought on by religious bickering, clan rivalries, or simply the lack of a central authority to keep the peace. However it happened, and just what it was that happened, is still unknown to us. We do know that the phenomenon seems to have been universal throughout the Southwest. Both the Fremont and the Anasazi cultures apparently collapsed sometime in the mid thirteenth century. In 1540, Coronado found a poor remnant of the once numerous peoples of the four-corners area living on high mesa tops in central Arizona.

It seems that the last aboriginal group to occupy the canyon had things a little better. The Utes occupied the canyon after the Fremont and they lived there until recent times. They didn't farm or live in pit houses and they didn't make rock walls and granaries. They were hunters and gatherers, more flexible and more mobile than their Fremont predecessors. They may in fact be ancestors of the Fremont, a noble remnant who gave up farming and permanent homes as being too risky, and who fled to the mountains to pursue an ancient lifestyle and live off the land.

They made a distinctive type of arrowhead, a very small, triangular point with a notch in either side and a notch in the base (real archaeologists call them desert side-notch points). The desert side-notched points were generally smaller and better made than Fremont points. They were thinner and sharper and often much better flaked. I found some very good ones in the canyon.

There is a story, told from early trapper's journals, that General William Ashley, one of the first white men to organize a trapping company to venture into the mountain west, floated down the Green River in May of 1825 with a few of his men in bull boats. They were exploring and trapping for beaver. In the

Uintah Basin they met two trappers who worked for Provost and LeClerc and who were wintering near the river. The trappers told Ashley that four members of their party had descended the river "to a great distance" and found the country barren and the Indians hostile. Ashley continued anyway, and by his own estimate he traveled down the river for about thirty miles below where the White River enters from the East. If his reckoning was true, he quit the river somewhere near the mouth of Nine Mile Canyon. He left the river because of the scarcity of game and the foreboding nature of the country. He was into the mouth of what John Wesley Powell would later call Desolation Canyon. Ashley described the country as, "a barren heap of rocky mountains."

Near where they quit the river, Ashley and his three men found an Indian trail and followed it for a few miles up the river and finally made contact with a band of Utes. He wanted to buy seven horses for his men and his goods, but was only able to purchase two and at considerable cost. He said he found the Utes to be rich, well armed, and the best-dressed Indians, "west of Council Bluffs."

One hundred and thirty-eight years after that event, as I was exploring the canyon and finding some fine Ute arrowheads, I found carved on a ledge what might be the Indian account of that historic meeting with General Ashley and his men. I was climbing around on a steep, rocky side hill when I found some magnificent rock carvings of Indians with long, flowing headdresses and long spears who were mounted on horses. To the right of the Indians there is a long crack in the rock that may represent the Green River or Nine Mile Creek (It was not unusual for Native Americans to use natural rock features as part of a petroglyph). Across this natural barrier, there are figures that depict three white men on foot with brimmed hats and firearms. The Indians have their horses turned facing away from the white men, exposing their backs, and one of them has his right arm up and raised to the square, a native sign language signal of peace and goodwill. The white men are facing the Indians and have their long guns held in their left hands while they point what appear to be pistols at the Indians with their right hands.

This petroglyph panel has intrigued me for years. Could it be that this is indeed the story of the Utes meeting Ashley and his hungry band of trappers just back from an unsuccessfully attempt to explore the depths of Desolation Canyon? It could be. Many of the basic elements of the story are present: the white men are on foot while the Indians are mounted. The crack in the rock may represent the river. The Indians are dressed in their finest garb and they are showing the sign of peace. If not General Ashley and his band, the panel is surely from the same era and tells of the Utes meeting a band of white men under similar circumstances. The one negative element in the panel is the fact that the white men appear to have hostile posturing, holding rifles at the ready while pointing what may be handguns at the Indians.

I'm happy to report that this treasure of Native American

art is still there in the warm sunshine of the canyon. The proud Ute Warriors with long headdresses still ride prancing horses across that sandstone wall and the site is still unmarred by vandals or well-meaning tourists. At least that's how it was as the Twentieth century made way for the Twenty-First.

I feel I should add a few words here about antiquities and antiquity law. The nineteen sixties and early seventies was a different time, and we lived in a different world. Attitudes about collecting and a lot of other things were much different, as I have mentioned before. Unfortunately, there was a lot of damage done to many ancient sites. Many artifacts and clues to the past were destroyed by vandals and by well-meaning tourists and collectors; even our own government—Lake Powell and non-archaeologically surveyed cedar chaining operations, to name only a couple.

Today, antiquities laws are being enforced with a vengeance, and in some circles, artifact collecting is a more heinous crime than stealing cars or selling dope. There is a greater social awareness now, an understanding that the treasures of the past are priceless, irreplaceable, and finite. People should visit places like Nine Mile canyon and enjoy them, but they should leave only footprints and take only photographs.

SPOOKS

Wilderness places have always been areas of mystery, and so it was in the unexplored little corners of Nine Mile Canyon and in the depths and shadows of the foreboding Desolation Country to the South and East. It was a remote and isolated country, known to few and most often seen from the air while passing over at a few hundred miles an hour. A good many of the nooks and crannies of the area had been bypassed by the early explorers, even though the rivers, streams and canyons were well defined on the map. There were still areas in the 1960s where a white man had yet to place his foot.

There were legends and tall-tales about the country, whispers of lost mines and Spanish gold, hidden treasures, ancient cities and outlaw hideouts. A few contained a grain of truth, but most were old wives tales. Even the Indians told fanciful stories: about Sasquatch (big foot) of the mountains, a tribe of red-headed giants who lived on the Nevada desert, and mysterious little beings like Irish Leprechauns who lived among the rocks and played tricks on people.

Most people laugh at such foolishness, but every once in a while evidence will be found that gives some slight credence to one of these old tales: Spanish coins found along the Price River, a rotting saddlebag filled with 200 silver dollars and hidden in a pack rat nest in the Uintah Basin, an ancient six foot tall and red-headed mummy from Lovelock Cave in Nevada, and the apparently adult but only fourteen inches tall Pedro Mountain mummy found in a cave near Casper Wyoming. There are many other stories and many other mysteries.

There are many representations in the rock art of the canyon of what may best be described as supernatural beings. Some are fantastic personages with impressive, even improbable headdresses and with long, reaching fingers. Some seem to be part animal and part man. Some are represented as humanoid but without arms or legs, which may mean that they depict spirits or ghosts who didn't need appendages and who traveled in other ways, like floating through the air. There are other more mortal appearing beings, great shaman probably, medicine men or witch doctors who could cure ills and cast spells and travel into the depths of time and space in the underworld and then return while in a trance or a drug-induced

THE SPLIT SKY

Spooks who guard the ancient trails—Barrier Canyon Utah.

coma. The shamans on the sandstone walls are bold and arrogant figures with elaborate headdresses and provocative postures. Many are depicted with horns like bulls. Later Indians said that horns on the head of a man or a spirit told of his great strength and power.

I've found many representations of these ghostly shaman and supernatural beings frozen in eternity on the sandstone walls, and I've felt the power of the figures through the images themselves. I've often wondered what stories the Fremont could tell me about those phantoms, if only I could hear.

In 1534, the shipwrecked conquistador Cabeza De Vaca was journeying across the wilderness that was to become New Mexico and Arizona. He was searching for Mexico and the Europeans he knew to be there. He was one of a handful of survivors of the Narvaez expedition to Florida in 1528, and he had been held as a slave to a group of Indians in Texas. In the narrative of his journey to Mexico, he tells about a ghostly apparition that stalked the Indians and caused great fear and consternation among them.

De Vaca was told that about fifteen years before he met a particular group of Indians, in about 1519—the year that Cortez and his little band first challenged the empire of the Aztecs—an evil little man appeared among the villages. The little man had a beard like the white men and he had magic powers and no one ever saw his features clearly. The Indians said that when the little man approached, the people would tremble and the hair would stand up on the backs of their necks. They said that the evil little man would enter any house he chose and he would grab a person and open his stomach with a large flint blade and cut off a length of intestine and throw it into the fire. He would then sever an arm from his victim, taking it off at the elbow, and when his victim had screamed and bled and started to die, the evil little man would heal the wounds and reattach the arm by molding the flesh with his hands. The Indians said that the little man could heal the damaged flesh instantly with his fingers.

The natives said that the little man would show up unexpectedly during their dances and ceremonies, and sometimes he would be disguised as a woman. He would appear and disappear and no one ever saw him approach or saw him leave. They gave him offerings of food but he never ate with them, and when they asked him where he came from he pointed to a crevice in the earth and told them his home was down below.

De Vaca and his comrades were much amused by the story and laughed scornfully at the fanciful tale. And then the Indians brought to them a long line of victims who bore the scars on their bellies and arms of the evil little man's flint blade.

In the early 1970s, there was a rash of cattle mutilations all across the Western United States. The phenomenon touched Eastern Utah and the Nine Mile and Range Creek drainages were not exempted. Hundreds of cattle were found mutilated, most of them in remote and isolated areas. Cattle were found with their eyes and tongues and sexual organs removed and with all blood drawn from their veins. In most cases, no blood was found on the ground. There was never any evidence as to how or why these crimes were perpetrated. Law enforcement officials could never find any tracks, and it was surmised that the attacks could only have taken place from the air. During the same period of time, people in the area reported strange lights in the sky and strange sounds and vibrations in the air. The mystery has never been solved.

Was it little green men from outer space? Was it our own military conducting weapons tests on unsuspecting cows? Was it secretive government scientists in black helicopters collecting tissue samples to track open-air bomb tests of the 1950s, or covert biologic tests from the 1970s? Or was it a group of devil-worshiping perverts who performed bloody rituals on sleepy bovines? Each of these theories has been promoted by people who are smarter than I.

There is always some risk involved in exploring the wilderness alone, and that risk was much greater just a few short years ago. I was alone in the ledges long before the era of cell phones, walkie-talkies, global positioning satellites and airborne thermal imaging devices. In those days a person really was isolated and on his own when he ventured into the outback. My co-workers at the ranch never asked where I was going, when I would be back, or if I had the skills and resources to spend the night if need be. I was completely on my own. I had no weapon, no signaling or communications device, no medical supplies, no extra food or water, not even a registered flight plan—and climbing around in the ledges is risky business. A person might fall, get bit by a snake, jumped by a wildcat, squashed by a falling rock, drowned in a flash flood, gutted by a killer badger, hit by a meteorite, or abducted by a flying saucer.

A young man named Everett Ruess wandered away from the town of Escalante in the mid nineteen-thirties and simply disappeared from the face of the earth. They found his burros, his wilderness camp and his boot tracks in the sand, but the man was never seen again.

I was way up in the ledges late one afternoon, and I had climbed much higher than I normally went. I was in one of those wild and unexplored little corners of the canyon, a place without tracks or trails, and I had found no evidence to suggest that a man had ever been there before. The sun was dipping low toward the mountains to the west, and long, ragged shadows were spilling down into the deep side canyons. Everything was deathly still.

I was negotiating some large boulders when I felt something behind me. I turned around very quickly but nothing was there. I was stunned. I had felt a presence just as plainly as if I had passed another person on the sidewalk, and yet nothing was there. I stood quietly and looked around for a few moments and listened carefully and nothing seemed amiss. There was only the silence of the canyon and the towering rocks and ledges and the darkening amber sky of sunset. I began to feel uneasy and decided it was time to go. I turned my face downhill and started the long descent to the canyon floor, climbing down a steep and rocky side hill.

I had gone only a short distance when I felt the presence again. I whirled around, defensively this time, fists clenched, wild-eyed, and afraid. Again, I saw nothing. I stood for a while, breathing heavily and looking around desperately, trying hard to swallow the fear I felt creeping up my throat. Everything looked normal but I felt terrible. A cold chill soaked into my body and I felt a rising panic coming from deep in my guts. This was insane. I could see nothing to be afraid of but my mind was screaming at me to watch out like it knew something that my eyes didn't know. The hair was standing up on the back of my neck and I had goose bumps on my arms. I had never experienced anything like it. Everything looked tranquil, but my mind was screaming for me to run . . . run . . . run!

I stooped down and picked up a couple of rocks about the size of baseballs and held them tightly in my sweating hands. I started to walk backwards down the steep hill, not wanting to turn around, unwilling to expose my back and feeling very vulnerable. No sound came from my lips but my mind screamed at the absurdity that I could not determine the nature of my antagonist. I could feel in my very soul that something absolutely evil and dangerous was out there, and very close, but I could not determine what it was and the canyon was growing dark.

I stumbled and slid in the gravel. I went to my knees several times on the steep hillside as I scrambled to get out of that canyon. I kept turning around and around, trying to cover my back. The evil presence had me surrounded. My hands were clenched white on the two rocks that I carried and my knuckles were bruised and bleeding from using my clenched fists to help me over large rocks and dead trees. I had cactus tines in my pant legs and bruises on my shins and elbows.

I was breathing in great gulps of air by the time I reached the road in the bottom of the canyon and I did an out-of-breath sprint to the tractor a few hundred yards away. There was hope now that the tractor was near and I was so glad that I had outrun the dark as it washed down over the canyon. The sky was lit with a cold, otherworldly glow from the fading sunset. I vaulted to the tractor seat and hit the starter with a panicked hand.

The engine roared to life, shattering the stillness and filling the air with smoke. I jerked the machine into gear, popped the clutch and sped away madly, trying to push the steering wheel hard enough to make the lumbering machine go faster. I quickly turned the headlights on and ducked low over the steering wheel, still expecting some night creature to jump up on my back. I zoomed up the canyon in high gear, the sounds of the tractor echoing from the dark canyon walls, and I kept looking back over my shoulder into the night. I wouldn't have been at all surprised to see the glowing eyeballs of some ghostly apparition following me in the gathering darkness.

The speed, noise and light of the tractor gave me some comfort, but my skin was still crawling when I got back to the ranch. I parked the tractor and hurried to the light and shelter of the cookhouse and other people. I could no longer feel the evil presence but I was badly shaken and I had a hard time sleeping for a couple of nights. It was also a few afternoons before I could make myself go back up into the ledges like I loved to do.

I never told anyone at the ranch about what I experienced that afternoon. I was not on the same wavelength as my bunkhouse compatriots and I was afraid they would laugh and make fun of me. I never did know what it was that panicked me so badly that night and I never experienced anything like it in the canyon again.

Was it the ghost of some ancient Fremont Shaman chasing me away from a sacred spot? Was it a cattle mutilator? A Sasquatch? A space alien? Did my mind perceive the presence of a mountain lion or a bear in some unknowing way that my cave man ancestors might have recognized? Or did I sink into a self-induced hysteria simply because of the lateness of the hour and the spreading darkness of the canyon? I don't know.

I do know that the experience forever changed the way I did things. From then on, whenever I went up into the ledges by myself I carried a gun—and I still do.

Now, I'm acquainted with the movie *The Exorcist*, and I've seen *Star Trek* and *King Kong*, and so I know that a .357 magnum is useless against ghosts, illegal space aliens and determined monsters. I still carry it anyway and I carry it for two reasons. The first is the same reason the war hero Audie Murphy gave when a reporter asked him why he carried a gun. He said it was for therapy—he felt better when he had it with him. The second reason is the reason the cowboy Gus gave to the kid in the book *Lonesome Dove*. Gus said it was always better to have a gun and not need it, than to need it and not have it. I couldn't have said it better.

Take it from someone who knows. When you're all alone in the depths of the outback and you start to feel a little creepy, a .357 on your hip beats a rock in your hand—any day.

CHAPTER 11

GUNS

GUNS

Guns are evil, scary and sinful things to a lot of people today, but it wasn't always that way, especially in places like rural Utah. Guns were common things; they were tools, and objects for entertainment like golf clubs or fishing poles.

My cowboy heroes have always carried guns. Not for gunning each other down in the middle of the street, like in the western movies, but for real and practical reasons like hunting, protecting livestock and saving yourself. Roy Rogers, John Wayne, Eldon Kettle, Leon Rich and Arnold Adair all carried guns when they rode the range and chased after them cows.

A gun is a wonderful signaling device in the wilderness; it makes a loud noise and a cowboy down with a broken leg could alert his pals as to his whereabouts. Even without a broken leg, a cowboy could shoot a couple of times in the air and wait for the answering bark of his buddy's six-gun to let him know which ridge, which canyon, or which oak-bush pocket his pal was riding down so they could meet up and coordinate their efforts. I've even had old cowboys tell me they carried a gun to shoot a mad cow or even their own horse if need be. Good horses outweigh good cowboys by as much as eleven hundred pounds, and a lonesome cowboy tangled up in a rope, or the stirrup of a fleeing horse is dead if he can't stop the animal. Such things were not uncommon when men worked on horseback. Also, a cowboy was expected to "protect" the livestock, and any cat, wolf, coyote or rattlesnake was a target of opportunity. A deer close to camp was a gift from the Gods.

I was never a stranger to guns. There were always guns in the house when I was growing up. Guns were normal and natural things. Dad was a deputy sheriff and he carried a big gun on his hip when he went to work. And when he was at home, his big gun sat quietly in its holster on top of the refrigerator near the back door of the house. It was always there and it was always loaded. The gun was as much a part of the furniture in the house as the refrigerator itself. Dad also kept a shotgun and a deer rifle in his bedroom closet and there was a second shotgun in the police car that he drove to work.

We were careful around guns in the same ways we were careful around horses that kicked and farm machinery with whirling cogs, wheels and belts. Guns never held any terror or dread for anyone. Like the horses and farm machinery, we knew there were certain hazards inherent in having them around, but there were ways to manage and control them without being hurt. Education, and a clear understanding of the hazards is a key element.

We had a rule at home that every gun was loaded. Most of them weren't loaded, but the rule was that every gun was treated as if it were loaded. It was a good rule and dad raised five little boys without any of us ever having a firearm accident. My brothers and I knew that we didn't touch dad's guns. If we wanted to see them we only had to ask and he would show them to us. We never touched them when he wasn't there.

Dad taught his boys to shoot when we were very small. We would go for picnics out in the cedars, and dad would let us shoot his short-barreled .38 revolver at cans and rocks. He kept the little gun for undercover work for times when he had to wear a suit and appear in court or go on an airplane to bring a prisoner back to the county. It had a small frame and it didn't kick too badly and it was a gun that a boy could handle. The big gun on the refrigerator was a .357 magnum with a long barrel.

My grandpa wasn't a cop, but he had more guns than my dad. He had half a dozen rifles and at least three pistols. Grandpa carried a nine-shot .22 revolver with him in his pickup truck almost everywhere he went. He kept it under the seat of his truck rolled up in a gun belt. He also kept a .38 revolver in a drawer by his bed.

I got a gun of some kind for Christmas every year that Santa Claus put my presents under the tree. I started out with popguns and then cap guns and finally I got a .BB gun the year I was eight. The .BB gun was a Daisy Red Rider and I learned to shoot it at barn sparrows and blackbirds. The Red Rider wasn't powerful enough for big kids and I graduated to a Daisy pump-action .BB gun when I was ten. The pump gun was much more powerful, and we kids learned to enhance the power by pouring a small amount of white gas (kerosene) down the barrel. We discovered that with a little white gas in the barrel, the gun would shoot like a pellet gun. I don't know why. I've guessed it was because the gun was compressing gas fumes instead of air. A .BB shot from a kerosene-coated barrel would shoot clear through a pop can at twenty feet, and pop cans in the 1950s were much more robust than those in use today. An Alka Seltzer bottle filled with white gas, pilfered from one of our dad's Coleman lanterns, became as common as Davy Crockett's powder horn for my friends and me.

I got my first real gun for Christmas right after I turned thirteen—and that was late. Some of my friends had gotten real guns for Christmas when they were eleven. My first gun was a .22 rifle, a bolt action Winchester model 72A that was tube fed and would hold twelve rounds. It was a quality gun and I was very proud of it. Santa Claus sacrificed to buy me that gun. He never owned one as good.

The Split Sky

For the next two or three years my friends and I spent almost every Saturday and many nights after school walking along the river at the bottom of the farm fields south of Wellington. We hunted jackrabbits, prairie dogs and muskrats. We would walk for miles, two or three of us boys, each with a rifle and a handful of ammunition. We learned to shoot and we learned to hunt.

We had a Sunday School teacher who told us we should never shoot anything we didn't eat. We knew right away that she was crazy because people weren't supposed to eat a lot of the things we shot. Lizards, snakes and muskrats would surely make a person sick. We knew that. God had made some creatures to be moving targets and they served no other function that we could discern.

Sometimes we would shoot cottontail rabbits and take them home to eat. Our mothers would cook them and they were pretty good, but everybody knew that you only ate wild rabbits during months that had an "R" in them, like November, December and March. Wild rabbits were out of season in May, June and August. Wild rabbits were out of season in February for a long time too . . . until we got to the seventh grade and learned how to spell the month correctly (I know it sounds stupid—February is the only month that actually has two "R"s in it—but trust me—and give me a break, we were just kids).

Our primary targets were jackrabbits. The hills south of Wellington was a jackrabbit haven and they made great targets. The old Jacks would hear us coming and run way out ahead of us. We could see their tall ears over the sage bushes at over a hundred yards out, sprinting for the deep willows or over the next hill. It took some good shooting ability to connect with one of them with a .22 and we considered it great sport. Our parents told us not to bring jackrabbits home. They were not good to eat and God had made them just to feed the hungry coyotes. We knew that hungry coyotes were scavengers as well as hunters and we always felt we were just helping nature out by clobbering an old jack once in a while and leaving him for the starvin' yodel dogs.

We tried to eat a duck once and it was an unforgettable culinary adventure. The duck posed sort of a problem. In a surge of juvenile stupidity we shot at some ducks sitting on the water at extreme range and were truly surprised when one of them tipped over. I think it was Plato who said that little boys throw rocks at frogs in sport but the frogs die in earnest. It wasn't duck season, we didn't have a duck license, and we didn't dare to take him home. Dad was a cop and he might have been less than understanding about our choice of targets. Our victim was a fine duck, and it would have been a shame to leave him for the coyotes, and so we valiantly tried to follow our Sunday School teacher's advice and eat him.

We made a smoky little fire of weeds and sagebrush and skinned and gutted the Mallard and put him on a forked willow like we were roasting weenies. We held him to the flame for a while, pretending we were mountain men camping out on the continental divide, keepin' a wary eye out for hostile Injuns while we had a fine supper of roasted duck.

We took turns holding the duck over the feeble flame for what seemed like hours and he just never seemed to get cooked. I think we were actually smoking him like a ham because we were too stupid to build a robust and healthy fire. Finally, the weenie stick he was attached to burned through and dropped him in the hot coals. That was okay by us because we didn't have to hold him any longer and he would cook even better right there in the fire. We decided we would just scrape the ashes off before we ate him. We kept him in the fire for a long time, occasionally covering him with quick-burning sage twigs and clumps of swamp grass to help him brown, and he started to smell pretty good through the smoky vapors. It was getting late and we had to be home soon to do chores and have our real supper, and so we dug him from the heap of sage and swamp grass embers, and with our pocketknives we divided him up.

I've never tasted anything so nasty. That duck was singed black on the outside, but he was raw, cold and greasy in the middle, and he stank like smoldering swamp grass and wet bird guts. At first, none of us wanted to admit that he tasted terrible. We each continued to pick at the carcass while waiting for one of the other guys to make the pronouncement. Finally, and almost in unison, we started to giggle, and then gag, and then throw chunks of raw duck at each other. "Here . . . you look like yer starvin' . . . you can have my part too."

That was the end of my duck-hunting days. I did penitence and made restitution for my duck-poaching career by never shooting another duck or ever buying a duck license as an adult. That one raw Mallard cured me forever. On the list of things that people should never eat, ducks are right up there with snails, raw oysters and swamp water crawdads. I've always made it a point of honor to stay away from duck's unlimited banquets.

Many years later, my sweet young wife and I were shopping for Thanksgiving dinner when she picked up a bottle of cold duck and asked if I'd ever tried it. I told her I ate a cold duck once, but had never considered that they might be good to drink. I suggested a nice burgundy instead.

My dad, being a cop and familiar with guns and gun accidents, made sure that my brothers and I, and even some of our friends, took a hunter safety course. Hunter safety wasn't required in those days and it was something new. Dad hauled all of us to Price for the classes that were taught by a Fish and

Game guy named Lee Robertson who was later famous in Utah for the statewide hunter safety programs he implemented. We learned hunter safety from Mr. Robertson and we practiced it—and we only had one bad accident.

It happened on my friend David Rich's fourteenth birthday. (I was still thirteen.) David's older brother Leon took us rabbit hunting in Clark's Valley. Leon was big and had a driver's license and a fifty-five Chevy. We spent the morning in Clark's Valley and I shot up a whole box of bullets and had a great time.

Leon had been working and had bought himself a new gun. It was a .22 caliber semi-auto pistol, and like a good brother, Leon let his little brother Dave use the new gun for his birthday hunt. We all knew revolvers, but the semi-auto was a new girl in town and Dave was just getting acquainted.

We were in the car and headed home when Dave took the pistol out and decided to take the clip out of it. He was sitting in the middle of the front seat; Leon was driving and I was riding shotgun by the right door. We were cruising down the dirt road, coming out of Dugout Canyon when the gun went off. There was a flash and a bang and then everything was still. For a moment, the only sound was the car engine and the crunch of tires on the gravel. And then Dave started to sing out. "Leon! . . . Leon! . . . I'm shot Leon! Right in the leg! . . . Right in the leg! . . . My God! . . . My God! . . . I'm shot Leon!" And as he said those things, he started to thrash about wildly.

Leon pulled the car over and we got out to see. Dave was squealing with pain but there was no blood and so we knew he couldn't be hurt too badly. Leon made him pull his pants down and we found the telltale mark, a little round hole in his thigh. Strangely, it wasn't bleeding at all. There was a clear fluid oozing from the wound and I was amazed. It was the first real-live gunshot wound I ever saw in a person and it was not at all like in the movies. There was a perfect little round hole with a powder burn around it and a clear liquid leaking out like tear drops. I had never heard of such a thing.

Dave was going crazy. His leg was cramping and he screamed with pain. His toes were all doubled up and his foot was sucked up like a claw. Leon took care of the pistol and then loaded Dave back into the car and we headed for town. Dave couldn't put his boot back on and he couldn't sit down in the car seat. He dug his fingers into the back of the seat and chewed his shirt collar in pain. I sat in the back seat and watched, helpless and alarmed. Dave was not following the script. On the silver screen, I had seen John Wayne take a rifle bullet in the shoulder at least a dozen times and he always just put his bandanna in his shirt to stop the bleeding and then beat the bad guy up. Dave was not responding at all like John Wayne.

We stopped at Dave's house to tell his mother and I got out and ran for home. I wasn't afraid that we were in trouble or anything; it's just that I had seen the wound and I knew Dave wasn't going to die and I had a whopper of a story to tell. I didn't want to go to the doctor with them anyway and get trapped in that stinky old hospital all afternoon while they fixed Dave up. I ran for home to spread the news.

We found out later that the bullet had entered the upper part of his thigh and exited just above the back of his knee. It then penetrated the back of his calf and exited again near his shinbone and through the top of his cowboy boot. The bullet passed in and out of him twice and never hit anything important. It made a little round hole in the floorboards of the Chevy and then kicked up dust in the road—but we didn't see that part. Dave was back in school in just a couple of days and for a few weeks he was the town hero. He couldn't keep his pants on at school for showing everyone the nifty little bullet holes in his leg. I was envious.

I spent a lot of time at the Rich home when I was a kid, and they were big on hunting and shooting. I think every bedroom in the house had it's own gun rack on the wall with a rifle or two on prominent display. The family had roots in the Nine Mile country and every year they would go there as a tribe to hunt deer. They usually didn't come back until the middle of the week and I would sit on the front porch of their house and wait for them to come home so I could see the big deer when they hung them in the garage. Some of the deer they brought home were monsters.

In the 1950s and 60s, the annual deer hunt was Utah's second largest holiday and it lasted for eleven days. The hunt came in late October and the schools shut down for two days so families could go hunting. The deer hunt was like a social obligation, and the whole population of the state migrated into the hills dressed in red shirts and hats.

Deer hunting was a time-honored Utah custom and it was the patriotic thing to do. The fall hunt was a pioneer tradition and everyone participated in the ritual. It was like a great harvest celebration that happened in the fall when the farming was done. It was a great family event and an opportunity for people to top-off their pantries with wild game for the cold winter months. Venison was considered premium food, and deer steak and biscuits was a meal you served to company.

Deer were plentiful in those days and the rules were simple. You bought a deer license and you shot a deer. You could hunt anywhere you wanted (if it wasn't private ground that was posted), and you could shoot any deer that took your fancy: buck, doe or fawn. Horns didn't matter to most hunters back then; people were hunting for meat. There were big buck contests in my hometown that were based on the dressed weight of the deer and the antlers were not even measured for the contest. After the deer hunt, the Wellington city dump was littered with deer heads and antlers that people had thrown away, and some of the discarded racks were quite impressive. We never dreamed that people would make such a big fuss over deer horns in the years to come.

It seemed to us that the whole population of the state of California migrated to Utah to help us celebrate our deer hunt. The service stations and beer joints were full of out-of-staters, and for two weeks each fall, I would have bet that every other car on the road was wearing a California tag. We joked and made fun of the Californians, but in some ways we were envious of them. They seemed to have money, and they were much better equipped than most of the locals.

Most of our camping gear was army surplus, the tent, the gas cans, the grub boxes and even the sleeping bags. It was good stuff, but it was not fancy and it was cheap. Most of it was gear left over from World War II that was sold through Allied War Surplus in Salt Lake. Almost all of the people I knew hunted with military surplus rifles, Springfield ought-sixes or Craig Jorgensen thirty-forties or British three-o-three's. Surplus rifles were cheap and could even be bought from mail-order magazine ads. The Californians and some of the better-heeled locals had store-bought factory guns: Winchester Model 70s or Savage 300s. My dad hunted with an old Enfield 30-06 with buckhorn sights that had been cleaned up by Remington after the First World War and sold on the civilian market as the Remington Model 30. A few people, like my grandpa who was an old man with bad eyes, carried a store-bought 300 Savage with a four-power telescope.

Only Californians and old men with bad eyes used telescopic sights when I was a kid. It was a point of honor. To use a telescope on your gun was like cheating. We told each other that we were real sportsmen and were giving the deer a better chance, but in reality, most of us couldn't afford a riflescope anyway. It really didn't matter that much in those days. There were plenty of deer around, and if a guy couldn't hit the first one he shot at, there would always be another.

In the '50s and early '60s, the Wellington Mountaineer Riding Club sponsored a Deer Hunter's Ball on the Friday night before the big hunt. The Deer Hunter's Ball was without a doubt the most rowdy social event ever held in our sleepy little town. The one I remember best was the first one I ever attended. I must have been eight or nine years old. Dad was an official of the club and so I got to go while dad helped officiate and mother worked concessions. It was a romping, stomping good time, and a real treat for a little kid like me. There were other kids there of course, deer hunting was a family affair and the macho, scarlet-coated Nimrods wouldn't think of leaving the "little woman" and the kids out of the pre-hunt celebration.

The Deer Hunter's Ball was like a combination tribal hunting rite and a low budget costume party where everyone came dressed in their deer hunting outfits. Everyone, even the women and kids, showed up wearing red shirts and red hats and the whole crowd was armed and dangerous. There were revelers with bullet belts around their waists and partygoers with bandoliers criss-crossed over their shoulders like Mexican bandits. Some of those guys must have been carrying fifty or sixty rounds of 30.06 or 8mm ammo, and everyone was wearing a big knife of some sort hanging from a belt. They were the most well-armed dancers I ever saw outside of a John Ford western movie.

The whole thing was like a big Native American dance around a campfire before the spring buffalo hunt. Dozens of the happy deer hunters were drunk and disorderly and they stomped around the dance floor in a big circle while the band played rowdy polka music. It was dangerous for a little kid like me to get in the way and so I hugged the wall closely, fascinated by the out-of-control antics of the adults in my life. It was very exciting stuff for a little boy. Everyone was wearing hunting boots on the hardwood floor and the sound of the ruckus should have scared all of the deer out of the valley.

I remember I was awed when one of the more brazen celebrants came into the dance with a handgun on his hip. The pistol was a semi-auto with a checkered, wooden grip, and I think it was a German Luger. No one seemed to pay any attention, and I watched in fascination as the man joined in the dancing and strutted his stuff. Cowboys in the movies often wore handguns to the dance, and so the action was not without precedent as far as I was concerned. And actually, the Pistolero was in compliance with the Utah State Code. A man could wear a gun out in the open where everyone could see that he had it. It was when a fellow tried to be sneaky and put it under his coat that he got into trouble.

In those days, wearing a pistol to a Deer Hunter Dance was considered to be a little cheeky, but not completely off the clock. It showed bad taste to be sure, but it was treated more like a social faux pas than a reason to freak. Almost all of the people at the dance were armed, especially on that night before the big deer hunt, but most were discrete enough to leave the firearms in the pickup truck. Everyone had a big knife; it was part of the deer hunting costume.

It seems incredible now that such a thing could actually happen, but it did, and it wasn't that uncommon. I remember another time when a gun was brought into a dance and no one seemed to notice. It was in October of 1964, and the event was a costume party at Carbon High School. In the 1965 Carbon Year Book, on page 114, there is a picture of Bert Bunnell and

Angelo Halamandaris dressed in police uniforms they had borrowed from the County Sheriff's Department. In the picture they are in the school auditorium, standing in the middle of a crowded dance floor, and Angelo is holding a very real, twelve-gauge, pump-action shot gun—also borrowed from the county sheriff. Times have certainly changed.

Whenever I see some pundit on TV wringing his hands and preaching that guns cause violence, I have to smile. If guns caused violence, everyone in the little town I grew up in would have been dead before Nixon was president. It's what's in a man's heart that causes violence, not what's in his hand.

It is true that we lived in a small, close-knit, rural community and not a big city. In Carbon County Utah, we didn't worry about people freaking out and committing indiscriminate mass murder. It just didn't happen. People feared God and they feared the law and they had reason to fear the wrath of other people at the event. It was an era before kids were taught at school to be "tolerant" of bad behavior, and before they were encouraged by Bevis and Butthead to act out in anti-social ways. There was a code of conduct that was expected and even demanded of people. Everyone knew what was right and what was wrong. Bad behavior and bad language were not tolerated in public. A man who spoke obscenities at a public function was in danger of immediate retribution, and if the first guy to call him on it couldn't beat him up, surely the second or third guy in line could. There was a price to pay for uncivil behavior. There were times when a drunk would get out-of-line at a dance and half-a-dozen young men would spontaneously come to the rescue and escort the bad apple outside and see him on his way. It sounds terrible to say it, but in those days it might have been dangerous for some punk desperado to brandish a gun in earnest at a public function. His was surely not the only weapon in close proximity, and the crowd might have beaten the bad actor to death before the county sheriff could rescue him. That was the mindset and those were the facts. People knew those things, and even the worst of human rubbish behaved themselves in public.

At least in my little corner of the world, good people banded together in those days the way bad people band together now. We were all members of a gang that we called a congregation, a community and a nation. We shared common values and common goals. "Diversity" was not a virtue—a house divided cannot stand. People who immigrated to our country were welcomed, but they were expected to embrace our culture, our values, and our language. We looked after each other in those days, and it was the bad guys who were isolated and on the run. Somehow, we need to recapture that spirit.

All was not love, peace and sunshine among the good guys and the God fearing. Whenever young bucks and booze got together, like at the Deer Hunter's Ball, there was always a fight or two, and the combatants would retire to the dueling ground behind the parked cars. It speaks well of my father's generation that there were almost never any weapons used in those close combat engagements. All manner of weapons were readily available, as discussed previously, but when young men fought each other it was a fistfight; they left the weapons out of it. Men were supposed to stand and fight with their fists the way Roy Rogers and Gene Autry taught us at the Saturday matinees. They fought to a set of unwritten rules, a code of conduct that seemed to be universal. Nothing would ruin a man's good name and reputation faster than the charge that he fought "dirty." It was not a disgrace to be bested in a fistfight. It was a disgrace to win by using your boots or knees or by hitting a man from behind.

Men got mad in those days, but they seldom got murderous. Even in the heat of battle there was a measure of self-control. Justice was sure and swift, and God and your neighbors were watching.

After I had been at the ranch for a few days and saw all of the woodchucks (marmots) that hung around the fields, I began to wish I had my rifle. Woodchucks were a nuisance and everyone in the canyon shot and poisoned them on a regular basis. I pondered it for a while, and then one morning I got brave enough to ask the Colonel if he cared if I had my dad bring my rifle out to me. The man surprised me by upping the ante and telling me I could use his rifle. I was amazed. The man who wouldn't shake hands with me was going to let me borrow his rifle and I hadn't even asked for it.

The Colonel went over to the big house and brought back a pump-action .22 rifle. It was a beautiful thing with a deeply figured walnut stock and a high-gloss finish. It looked like it had never been used and it was obviously very expensive and almost too fancy to hunt with. He gave me a box of bullets and told me he had lots more and when I had shot those up I was to let him know and he would give me more. I thanked him sincerely, but I knew right away that it just wasn't going to work out. The Colonel's rifle was so fancy and so expensive that I knew I couldn't have any fun with it. I would be too concerned about scratching the finish or getting it dirty. A rifle like that belonged in some rich man's gun cabinet and not out in the greasewoods potting woodchucks.

My rifle, on the other hand, was a working girl and right at home in the fields, the briars and the willows. I didn't worry if she got a little dirty or accumulated an honorable scratch now and then while crossing a barbed wire fence. The Winchester had a dull, oiled finish and I never worried about marring her pretty face. I also liked the bolt rifle better, it was more accurate and more reliable and I was accustomed to shooting it. I wrote dad a letter and asked him to bring my .22 out to the ranch to me, and the next weekend he did.

I gave the Colonel back his fancy gun and I half-apologized as I explained to him that I preferred to use my own. He was good-natured about it all and seemed happy to have his gun back. He then told me that he would still furnish the shells if I would shoot the woodchucks. That was just what I wanted to hear. I went through a box of shells a week, and I kept score so I could report to the boss man how many woodchucks I had bagged for the price of his bullets. He was happy and I was happy and I averaged at least two woodchucks a day for the rest of the summer.

THE POACHER

We ate pretty well at the ranch that summer, but the one thing we seemed to lack (other than ice cream and cantaloupe), was fresh meat. Early on, a cow had slipped and fallen in a cattle truck and broken her leg. Virginia sent her to town to be butchered, and we got some of the meat, but with one growing boy and three to four grown men plus the occupants of the big house all chewing on that one cow, she didn't last long.

Virginia and her Colonel often brought back a steak or two of "mountain veal" with deer hair on it when they visited the cow camps, but they usually got only small amounts and seldom had enough to share with the hired help. Once in a while one of the cowboys would drop off a hindquarter for the cookhouse, but it didn't happen very often. We ate a lot of potatoes and mixed vegetables, Spam, corned beef and baloney.

One day, we were between cooks and Joe was cooking again, and he said he had had enough. "(Epletive deleted)" he growled, "I can't swallow another stinkin' potato without some real meat." He pointed a cigar-stained finger at me across the table and he said he wanted me to go get a deer.

I was surprised. Who did he think he was talking to? I was a good little Mormon Boy Scout and poaching deer was illegal and my dad was a cop. I couldn't do something stupid like that, my dad would kill me, and besides, my clear and hardly-used conscience wouldn't allow it anyway. Poaching was breaking the law and I didn't break the law and that's all there was too it—case closed.

Joe glared at me across the table and I blinked. The man was serious. I gulped and started to sweat. This was something I hadn't expected. Shooting deer did hold a certain charm, but I had never considered that I might actually poach one. I might have considered it up on the mountain with the cowboys, maybe, but not here at the ranch headquarters with so many witnesses and all. What if someone told my dad? The thought made me nervous.

I'd never been any good at getting away with things, but the more I thought about it, the more exciting the little plot became. I grew bolder. Poaching was a minor crime and everybody did it, and besides, it would be serving a noble purpose—we wouldn't want the hands to go hungry. The scheme began to take on the markings of a juvenile adventure and I became intrigued. Maybe I could bring myself to poach a deer after all. The whole thing began to take on an air of impish fun . . . like plotting to steal cookies.

"Okay," I said to Joe. "If you really want one, I'll get one tomorrow on my way back from the fields . . . but if I get caught it's your fault."

"Nothin's ever my fault and don't you dare shoot one with that damn .22," he growled. "I don't want it all shot full of holes—we're going to eat it."

"We've got a thirty-thirty around here somewhere and you can use that," he said with an air of finality.

"I can get one with my .22," I insisted.

"(Expletive deleted)," Joe shot back. " I'll find that thirty-thirty and you use it or I'll stomp a mud hole in your guts."

The next afternoon, Joe recruited Humbert and the two of them went looking for the thirty-thirty. They found it behind the seat of the cattle truck, but there were no bullets for it. They spent an hour or two ransacking the bunkhouse, the cookhouse, the saddle shed, their personal gear, and under the seat of Humbert's truck, and finally they found three cartridges.

Joe handed me the rifle and the three shells and told me point blank (pun intended) that if I couldn't hit the deer in the head he didn't want me to bring it back. He said he'd been a professional meat cutter and he refused to skin and cut up a deer that was gut shot and bloody. At first I was more interested in the fact that he said he would skin and cut it up than I was with the fact that I had to shoot it in the head. I wasn't worried about making a headshot—until I took a good look at that rifle and those shells.

The rifle was an antique. It was a Winchester 94 that must have been made in '93. It was old, rusted and dirty. The fore grip was broken and held together with electrical tape. The action and the guide rails were pitted with rust and it didn't look like it had seen oil or a cleaning rag since the final days of World War I. It had been bouncing around behind the seat of the stock truck since Moses was a corporal, and I had no idea if it would even shoot or which way the sights were bent last. To complicate matters, I didn't have enough ammo to try it out.

The cartridges were not any better. There were only three of them and they were all different: different brands, different bullet weights, and different spots of green algae growing on the tarnished brass. One of the lead slugs was so old that it was pitted with what I assumed to be molecular decomposition. That bullet might have rattled around for decades in the saddlebags of old man Nutter himself. If I were a betting man,

I wouldn't have given fifty-fifty odds that two of the three cartridges would even fire. My heart sank into my boots.

I started to protest to Joe that I would feel much more confident with my own .22, but he cut me off short.

"(Expletive deleted)!" He roared. "You take this rifle and you go get a deer and you get it tonight! I'm tired of screwin' around with you . . . you be a man and go get us a deer or pack your (expletive deleted) trash and get outta here and go play with the girls." The old dragon certainly knew how to motivate me.

I took the rusted gun and the three decaying shells and stomped out of the bunkhouse and into a gentle afternoon rain. We had agreed that I would take the stock truck to get a deer because hauling one back on a tractor would be too difficult. I got in the truck and slammed it into gear and started down the canyon with the windshield wipers flapping furiously. I was fuming.

I growled and talked to myself as I drove down the canyon, but slowly a cold reality started to settle in and I began to feel anxious and distressed. I faced the fact that I was afraid of that junky old gun. In hunter safety class I had seen pictures of old antique firearms that had blown up when fired with modern ammunition and I tried to console myself with the fact that the mummified bullets were probably older than the gun. I wished I had been smart enough to have insisted that Joe or Humbert shoot the thing first to show me how it's done. I was also nervous about a personal little secret that I had not shared with Joe and Humbert. I'd never shot a deer before.

I knew about killing things. I grew up on a farm and we butchered beef, sheep, pigs, chickens and rabbits all the time. I had helped to shoot, gut, skin, quarter, and even cut up a beef, but I had never killed a deer or even helped to take care of one. I had been deer hunting with my dad and my uncles, but always as a kid and a spectator. I wasn't sure how this was all going to turn out.

I drove the truck down the canyon, past the road to Myton and on toward the bottom fields. I had seen deer in those fields in the evenings while climbing around in the ledges and I suspected they would be out again tonight. The rain was gentle but persistent and I cussed my luck. Everything would be wet and muddy. I knew how hard it would be to take care of a deer in such conditions and try to keep it clean to make old Joe happy.

I drove down the road slowly, watching the fields, and finally I spotted them, three deer in the hay field, eating with their heads down. I drove on past them, hoping they wouldn't spook, and they didn't. I parked the truck down the road and took the gun and tippy-toed back on foot to where the deer were.

The deer spotted me as I found a good vantage point and they all stood with their ears up, watching. Three does. They were standing in a row, one behind the other and about the length of a football field away.

I held the gun against a fence post to steady it and I pulled the hammer back. There was a dull click as the sear engaged and the trigger was set. I stood still for a moment, breathing hard and feeling anxious. The soft rain beat down and soaked my back and ran off the front of my straw hat in a weak trickle. I stood there and watched the deer and the deer watched me, neither of us moving. The soft rain on the straw hat made a drumming sound that only increased the tension.

It was time to do it. I put my cheek against the wet stock of the rifle and looked down the sights. I was about to pull the trigger when it suddenly occurred to me that I had never even looked down the barrel of that rifle. I didn't know if there was a mouse nest, a spider web, or a steel rod in that barrel. I knew the rifle hadn't been cleaned since dirt was invented and the bore might have been rusted completely shut for all I knew. My mind flashed back to those hunter safety pictures of blown-up guns and I could think of lots of things I would rather have happen that afternoon than having a thirty-thirty come apart in my face. "(Expletive deleted)," I cussed to myself. I should have taken more time getting ready.

It was too late now. To check the rifle now meant that I had to jack all three shells out into the rain and mud and try to find enough light to see down the bore. I didn't have a flashlight and it was getting dark fast and I didn't think the deer would stand there all night while I checked it out.

To hell with it. I looked back down the sights. The deer were frozen like decorative statues on a lawn of green grass.

I decided to use strategy. I would shoot at the middle deer. I reasoned that if the sights were way off, maybe I would be lucky and hit one of the deer on either side. The strategy seemed obvious enough to me, but at the same time I was bothered by it. In my troubled little mind, I kept hearing the echo of Joe telling me that if I didn't hit one in the head he didn't want me to bring it back. I winced.

Surely old Joe didn't mean it. He had to be just screwing around with me the way Eldon did. No one was good enough to make a head shot every time, and besides, I was laboring under extreme conditions here and even Joe should understand that. I decided that I was going to get a deer the best way I could and I would argue the finer points of marksmanship with Joe later. If he wanted a fancy headshot he could come out here in the rain and do it himself.

I lined up the sights again. I put the front post on the middle deer, right in the center of her ribs, and I tilted the rifle up until the V notch of the rear sight framed the front post. And then I did something truly remarkable. I held my breath, closed my eyes, ducked my head and pulled the trigger.

The roar of the Winchester shattered the stillness of the canyon and I saw the muzzle flash through my closed eyes. The rifle kicked back and hit me in the cheek and the shoulder and knocked my hat off. There was a cloud of smoke around the muzzle like I'd been shooting black powder, and maybe I was. A couple of those cartridges were older than Buffalo Bill's Wild West Show. The thunderous report of the rifle echoed for miles down the canyon under the low and heavy clouds.

I blinked my eyes to be sure I could still see, and I wiggled my fingers to be sure they were all still attached, and I looked down at the gun to be sure it was still in one piece. Everything seemed to be okay. And then I remembered that I had shot at a deer and I looked up quickly to see how that had turned out. Two deer were bouncing off toward the willows. There was no sign of a third.

I picked up my hat and climbed over the fence and started to walk out into the rain-wet field. The hay was almost as tall as my boot tops and my pant legs were soaked in just a few steps. I couldn't see a deer lying down anywhere, and I counted the two running away a second time. I was sure there had been three of them, and I focused on that area in the field where they had been standing when I shot. I wasn't sure that I had hit one of them. I had seen deer shot before and they usually kicked and struggled for at least a moment or two after they went down. Out in front of me everything was still. The field was placid and calm, a green sea of wet hay.

And then I found her. I almost stepped on the deer before I saw her. She was lying peacefully in the hay like she was sleeping, and a thin trickle of blood ran down from a tiny hole at the base of her ear.

I couldn't believe it. I had deliberately held the sights in the middle of her ribs, but my bullet had taken her at the base of the skull. She never knew what hit her. By complete accident I had shot her in the head just like Joe said. I couldn't imagine how I could have been so lucky—it was Heavenly intervention.

The Gods of the hunt were laughing and having a lot of fun that afternoon, and they were all on my side. I laughed with them. The whole canyon seemed to be laughing. I held my arms out to the falling rain and felt the cool water on my face and then bowed to the four winds as if performing in front of a great audience. "Thank you . . . thank you one and all," I giggled. That famous trick-shooter Annie Oakley never had a thing on me. I wanted to sing like a wet little songbird.

I field-dressed the deer and dragged her over the wet hay to the barbed wire. It was growing dark now and still raining lightly and I was soaked. I pulled her under the bottom strand of wire through the mud. I wasn't big enough or strong enough to lift her over. I brought the truck to where she lay and I struggled in the mud and the rain to load her by myself. I had to balance her on my hip and swing her up and into the back of the stock bed using my leg for leverage. The effort exhausted me and the hernia made my belly and my leg ache, but I was mad-dog determined that I would not go back to the bunkhouse and ask Joe or Humbert to come and help me. Be a man or go play with the girls . . . that's what Joe had told me, and I was still mad.

I drove the truck back to the ranch yard with the headlights on. I backed up to the saddle shed, and that let Joe know that I had a deer. He came out to help me get her in the shed. Humbert and Willis had gone home for the night.

Joe was trying not to get too wet and so we didn't say much as we carried her inside. There was a dim light bulb in the shed, and Joe turned it on. He also produced a flashlight and started to check her over before he would hang her up. With a rising anger, I realized that he was looking for the bullet hole. The hateful old pirate was going to be as good as his word; if she wasn't headshot he was going to tell me to throw her away. I stood back, all wet, bloody and exhausted, and waited for him to find the hole. I didn't give him any clues. I was beginning to hate the man.

He finally found it, there at the base of her ear, and he looked both surprised and disappointed. Joe hadn't given me a real bad time for a few weeks and he was overdue. He seemed to be looking for an excuse to pick a fight with me.

I helped him hang the deer so he could skin it and cut it up like he said, and nothing has ever made me happier than handing him back that junky gun and those two unfired shells. Joe took the gun and the bullets and he didn't say a word. I turned and walked away, cool and professional and swaggering just a little like John Wayne.

I smiled all the way to the shower, and I smiled for the next two or three days. I never did tell any of them what really happened that afternoon. When Joe cooked deer steaks for supper the next day I smiled like a Chessey Cat and ate like a hungry pup. My old Sunday School teacher would have been proud.

CHAPTER 12

WATER

WATER FROM THE SKY

The month of August came with a good deal of rain and the weather complicated the haying process. Wet hay could not be cut, hay in the windrows rotted, and wet bales could not be stacked. The rain made the roads muddy and sometimes when the water was high in the creek we couldn't access some of the fields. There were a couple of long, boring days when we stayed in the cookhouse and drank coffee and watched it rain.

Rain was good for the canyon. It washed everything clean. It cleared the air of dust and pollen and made the world smell fresh and new. The rain made the grass grow strong and made the hillsides come alive with vibrant new colors. Even the pinion and juniper trees seemed brighter, cleaner and more alive. It filled the stock ponds with muddy water and made the springs flow with renewed vigor. The little stream that wandered through the canyon grew stronger and more assertive and there was an abundance of irrigation water.

Rain is one of the key elements in agriculture that a man can't provide with work, sweat and good planning. In spite of his best efforts, if the rain doesn't come, there is no chance for success in farming. It's rain that makes life happen in the fields. Mankind learned early that when water falls from the sky it's a gift from God. The first man ever to put seeds into the ground prayed for rain and his children have appealed to the good graces of God ever since.

THE SPLIT SKY

The very act of farming is a test of faith: faith that the seed will germinate, faith that the rain will come, faith that Mother Nature will stay her fury and allow the crop to mature, and faith that all the work and worry will be rewarded by a good harvest. Only men engage in endeavors that require such faith. Farming is what made men different from animals. Only men will bet today's labor against tomorrow's promise. Only men have the imagination, the vision, the discipline and the faith to see it through.

I loved the summer rainstorms in the canyon. I loved to watch the storm approach, to see it and smell it and feel the power of it from a distance. I loved to feel the cool wind on my face as the storm broke over the canyon rim a long way off—to hear the whisper of the breeze as it bent the grass and shook the willows as it hurried past. I loved the wet smell in the air as the rain approached, and the feel of those first tiny little wind-driven specks of cool water that found my dusty face. I loved the wild and reckless way the dark clouds took command of the sky and chased the sun away and raced with the wind across the vast open heavens, the canyon turning dark in the shadow of the clouds. I loved the excitement of that first crack of lightening in the ledges and the concussion of thunder as it rolled down the canyon.

I was amazed as the approaching storm grew and grew and began to threaten violence. The canyon above me filled with a thick, dark foam of cloud that spilled from the heavens and disappeared into the ground as it moved down the canyon toward me. It was an advancing wall of water, thundering down the canyon like a flood, the sound of the storm increasing in pitch and tempo like an approaching freight train. An angry wind charged ahead of the waterfall, flaying the trees, flattening the grass and fighting me for my hat. The ocean of hay rippled and swayed in the wind, breakers and troughs of green vegetation like the swells and crests of ocean waves.

A primeval fear clutched at my belly as I watched the dark wall approaching. I was fearful, and yet wildly excited, apprehensive, but thrilled to have the monotony of the day interrupted by such a violent display of nature's fury. I made a mad dash to the shelter of the pickup truck as the storm came crashing down the canyon to engulf me.

From the shelter of the pickup I marveled when the first bullets of heavy rain smacked into the dirt along the road and threw little geysers of dust in the air like firecrackers exploding. The rain bullets hit the windshield and the hood of the truck with a thump like projectiles from a slingshot, splattering on the glass and metal surfaces and causing me to duck and wince and laugh out loud. The barrage quickly increased in intensity until it blended into one great explosion as the waterfall broke over me. The truck shook under the onslaught and the sound of high velocity water against the metal skin was deafening. It was like a fire hose attack, an encounter with the drive-through car wash.

I laughed and yelled in defiance as the rain pounded on the tin roof and taunted the windshield wipers to keep up. The storm beat its fists on the truck hood in frustration as I sat warm and dry and ran the engine and the heater to keep the cold chill at bay. I was delighted to sit in the warm shelter of my tin and glass bubble and watch the rainwater cascade down from the steep canyon walls, muddy water tumbling and falling and jumping out into space, creating spectacular waterfalls.

I was awed by nature's fury when the quiet little creek was transformed from a shallow ribbon of clear water into a rampaging flood. In just minutes the little ditch became a mighty river of angry gray liquid that crashed down the canyon, throwing it's shoulders against the twists and turns in the channel, muscling over obstacles and spilling over its banks. I watched with some alarm as the torrent carved new pathways that were straight and deep and rigid, bulldozing through dirt banks and impatiently bypassing the lazy meanders of the old streambed. Big slices of the stream bank sloughed off into the torrent, undercut by the fast moving water and sliding into the chaos of the flood, vast tons of dirt bank collapsing, sinking suddenly and without warning into the muddy water, violently sucking in the hapless greasewood and sage, fence posts and wire.

Little ribbons of water flowed everywhere, scurrying through the sage bushes and searching for the creek channel, hurrying to join the flood in the creek. Slight depressions in the ground, previously unnoticed, became small ponds and puddles, holding the water back and denying it the fun and excitement of racing down the canyon with the flood. The dark, liquid surfaces of the puddles boiled with raindrops and frustration.

I rolled the window down when the rain had almost stopped to better listen to the sounds of the flood in the creek. It was a savage and frightening sound, the roar and splash of angry water and the crack of boulders as they rattled along the channel bottom pushed by tons and tons of muddy water. It was the sound of an unstoppable force, a powerful and relentless energy drawn from the natural world. It was humbling just to sit and listen to the strength of it.

As the storm spent its fury, I drank in the smell of the ionized freshness of the damp air and delighted in the pungent odor of wet sage. I watched the sun discover that first crack in the departing clouds and send a feeble ray to probe a high canyon wall. I was the only witness when a remarkable rainbow burst forth to straddle the canyon and bathe the ledges in a soft glow of light and vibrant color. I rejoiced when the deep blue sky came back to reclaim the heavens from the dark and angry clouds.

I marveled at the calm that enveloped the canyon after the storm had passed by, a quiet peacefulness punctuated by the sound of dripping water and the diminished growl of the receding flood. I smiled when I heard the birds start to sing as the sun came back—the blackbirds, swallows and finches, all singing the same song in a chorus of different tongues, glad the storm had passed, happy to be alive, and giving thanks to God.

MUD PEOPLE

The rain made the road muddy, and the floods that tumbled out of the side canyons sometimes washed the road out. Usually, this posed only an inconvenience because the county road crews were quick to respond and make the necessary repairs, and besides, everyone who called the canyon home or who used the road often drove pickup trucks with a shovel in the back. It was, after all, a dirt and gravel road, and while passable to cars most of the time, the locals knew that on any given day the road might be turned into a four-wheel-drive jeep trail in the wake of a good storm.

One beautiful Sunday morning, the day after a good storm, I was going down the canyon on the boss lady's tractor. It was my day off and I was on my way to a good arrowhead hunting spot. A few miles below the ranch, at the mouth of what is known as Blind Canyon, I came upon a pitiful sight.

I came around a bend in the canyon road and there before me was one of those big, ugly, upside-down-bathtub type cars from the early 1950s, wallowing on her belly in the mud. She was sunk to her running boards in the muck where the road crossed the shallow wash. The big car lay there panting and exhausted like a great, beached whale.

She was a '52 or '53 Buick I think, living a second childhood as a high school kid's hot rod. She sported custom paint, tons of chrome, and a pair of fuzzy dice dangling from the rear view mirror. She looked soiled, desecrated and pitiful in the mud hole. The fancy paint job was hopelessly defiled, and the painted, red flames of fire shooting from the fender wells a cruel mockery as she lay dying on her belly in the slime.

It was readily apparent that the driver had beaten the great beast mercilessly in an effort to make her pull her impossible weight free. She had thrashed and fought gallantly for a while. He had spun her wheels and dug her in until her great weight was sitting flat on the gravel of the bottom of the wash, hopelessly high-centered. She sat so low in the muck that her open doors made drag marks in the mud like snow angels. Two wilted and drooping mud-people stood near the exhausted car.

I rattled up to them on the tractor and just sat there for a minute taking it all in. The story of their struggle was everywhere; they didn't have to say a word. I could see where the mud-man had kicked up sagebrush and gathered flat rocks to try to push into the mud under the wheels. His efforts had been hopeless without a shovel. It was obvious that he and the mud-lady had taken turns spinning the wheels while the other tried to push. They were both completely covered with mud; it was in their hair and their eyelashes. Their nice clothes were ruined and their shoes must have weighed fifty pounds. I was fascinated by the mud-people, not so much because of the mud, even though it was very entertaining, but because I recognized them.

A couple of month's before, they had been Carbon High School royalty. They were the upper crust, star athlete and queen of the senior class, graduating seniors and lords of the sacred halls. He was a varsity jock who wore his letterman jacket like the purple robe of royalty. She was his steady girl, painted, perfumed, and hanging on his arm like princess

Dianna. The two of them had promenaded the halls together, looking down with disdain at all the little people, acting as if those of us who were mere Sophomores should scrape and bow and cast rose petals in their path.

They looked very different as mud-people, and they acted different too. He walked up to my powerful and purring tractor with the demeanor of a beggar seeking alms. He recognized me too and he was doing humble penitence for all the sneers, jeers and haughty looks he had cast at me and my young friends who wore cowboy boots to school.

He was one of the "big guys" from Price who wore penny loafers and white socks, and who laughed and made off-colored remarks and sometimes even mooed like cows when we younger boys from Wellington walked past. I could see now that the varsity mud-man was sorry he had ever done that. The humiliation choked him, and he was having a tough time looking me in the face.

I sat on the tractor and smiled and watched him approach. I couldn't believe it. Of all the people to run into out there in the wilderness, this had to be the most unlikely and the most improbable pair I would ever have guessed. I couldn't help but smile at the irony of it all. I didn't mean to be cruel, but there was something so very funny and so inherently deserving about the two of them transformed into mud puppies. I would have traded the farm for a camera.

It was obvious that they needed my help and he didn't have to ask. I was a compassionate little pup, and merciful too. I thought about asking him to moo for me before I pulled him out, but I was bigger than that; he was already humiliated and suffering enough. I gallantly told him I'd be happy to help, but I'm sure I was smiling way too much as I backed the tractor up to his floundering mud-monster of a car.

I hooked the chain to the tractor, then smiled and handed

the other end to him to attach to his soiled chariot. If I pulled the bumper off, or jerked the front axle or tie rods out, I wanted him to be the guy who hooked it up so I didn't have to take the heat. And besides all that, I was clean and dry and not about to wallow in the mud like a little pig if I didn't have to. I smiled even more when he had to get down on his belly in the mud and dig out a place with his hands under the bumper to find a place to hook the chain. While he was doing the alligator low crawl, I made small talk with princess mud-lady.

At the high school, she would never give me the time-of-day. She had stood poised on her fairy princess pedestal, robed in taffeta and lace, a condescending smirk ever present on her pretty face. Her crown was her beautiful hair, and her scepter the strong arm of her lover-boy and varsity hero who now wallowed on his belly in the mud. She would have been embarrassed to be seen speaking to a lowly serf like me at the high school, but today, in the canyon, she was happy to see me. We were old friends. Just for today, I was her handsome prince on a Ford tractor; John Wayne and the U.S. Cavalry come to the rescue; Dudley Doright from the Northwest Mounties. I just couldn't stop smiling.

She told me they had been stuck all night. They had come to the canyon the day before, on Saturday, as tourists, and got caught in the rain and stuck on their way home that afternoon. They were on a date, a leisurely afternoon drive, both of them dressed in nice picnic-date clothes. She was wringing her hands in frustration and distress as she told me the story. They had been out all night and her parents and family and maybe even the Highway Patrol would be out looking for them by now. It had been silly of them not to tell someone where they were going.

She was a humble fairy princess that morning. Her eyes were all red and puffy from crying and lack of sleep, and her fancy hairdo was wilted, wispy, and full of little mud balls and sage bush twigs. She had mud in her ears and her face was streaked with sweat, mud, and the smudges of yesterday's makeup. She looked a lot different from the last time I saw her. She ask me for water and I had to tell her that the closest drinking water was at the ranch house a few miles up the road. I sure wanted her to stop in for a drink, too. I knew that Joe and Humbert would never believe me if they didn't get to see the mud-princess for themselves.

The tractor easily pulled the beached mud-monster from the slime and the big car stood on her own feet again, humiliated and brooding in her coat of filth. It was sad to see the interior of what had been a perfumed and velvet-seated love boat. The inside of the car was almost as muddy as the outside.

The mud-people said thank you with a humble sincerity that almost made me sad, and then he ask me if there were any more mud holes up ahead. I told him there was one that might be a problem, but I would follow them back to be sure they got through.

I followed them to Water Canyon and the next mud hole. I told him I had just come through it on the tractor and it looked worse than it really was. If he hit it hard, I thought he could make it. I bit my lip and stood back in breathless anticipation as he revved up the engine and dug in at the starting gate.

The big car hit the bog hole with the throttle wide open and it sounded like a train wreck. The explosion echoed for miles down the canyon. Water, mud and gravel flew everywhere. The coconut heads of the mud-people bounced off the windows and rattled around inside the car like tethered ping-pong balls. The mud-monster floundered, shuddered and almost stalled, but her mad-dog driver caught a lower gear and dumped the clutch. The monster roared, kicked, caught her footing again and stomped on through the mud, her great chrome bumper pushing a path like a snowplow. It was close, but her great weight and to-hell-with-the-fancy-paint-job lead foot of her rocket pilot carried her on across.

The muddy beast gained the solid ground on the other side of the bog and never even slowed down. She shot right on up the canyon, gobs of mud flying from the tires higher than the car itself and raining down on the bushes along the road. It reminded me of an old-time manure spreader.

I watched them go, the big, muddy, upside-down bathtub scooting along behind the greasewoods like a great, lumbering turtle, the stuttering roar of his exhaust manifold flaying the ledges and echoing back down the canyon from a dislodged muffler and tail pipe.

I sat clean and dry and smiling on my purring tractor and watched them disappear. I could hear the roar of his open tail pipe long after he was gone from sight. It cracked me up to think about how funny it was going to be for the varsity mud-king and his soiled princess to pass through Wellington with his tail pipe roaring so everyone would look. I couldn't imagine a more humiliating and more deserving thing to happen to a haughty pair of Carbon High's finest.

It's amazing how fast the great and exalted ones can be brought to ruin and disgrace by a single sword-stroke of cruel misfortune.

My pretty young wife kept a plaque hanging on the wall near our kitchen table in those years when our little boys were growing up. What it said could be the moral to this little story. It said:

> *Be careful of the words you speak*
> *Keep them soft and sweet*
> *You never know from day to day*
> *Which ones you'll have to eat*

Flood Poker

It was not unusual for us to start the morning in full sunshine and be rained out by noon, and then finish the day with a clear sky and a glorious sunset. The summer storms came and went at will. They were brief and sometimes violent and we never knew when one would creep over the canyon wall and catch us by surprise.

If the storms came down the canyon from the west we could see them coming for a long time, but storms from the south sometimes sneaked up on us. Down in the canyon the horizon was very close and our view to the north and south was limited. If the approaching storm didn't herald its presence with a drum roll of thunder, we might not see it coming until it was almost on us. It was always surprising to be caught that way; to be working in the field and focused on the task at hand and suddenly notice that the light had dimmed, and look up to see the black clouds already overhead and poised to strike.

I got caught in one of those surprise storms and stranded on the wrong side of the creek once. It turned out to be a wild adventure and an incident that makes me cringe when I think back on it. I did something very foolish that day and it could have cost me dearly.

I was hauling hay by myself in one of the lower fields. I was just finishing up a good stack on the hay wagon when the summer sunshine went to low beam and I looked up to see a heavy blanket of clouds spreading rapidly from the south. I hurried to finish the load as the wind picked up and thunder started cannonading far off in the high ridges. I had just a few bales left to put on the wagon and I wanted to finish the field so I didn't have to come back.

The black clouds spread out low over the canyon and blotted out the sun. There was no increase in the wind, or a preliminary sprinkling of rain, or even a close report of thunder to herald what was about to happen. The canyon held it's breath as the dark clouds took their positions.

I knew it was going to rain at any minute, and I was throwing bales like a mad man trying to get them all loaded and be gone. I knew I was going to get wet. I didn't have a pickup to use for shelter and I was a couple of long miles from the ranch buildings. I expected to be caught in the storm, but I had never seen anything to prepare me for what happened next.

A vast sheet of water hit the ground all at once like it was thrown from a bucket. I actually heard the water falling in that millisecond before it hit the ground and I sucked up like a chipmunk in the shadow of a hawk. The cold water hit me like a giant water balloon and I staggered to keep my feet. The water just kept coming. Tons of water caught me out in the open field and it was falling so fast and so furious that it was hard for me to breathe. It was a deluge that old father Noah would have recognized.

I was caught without shelter. I might have crawled under the hay wagon, but in the excitement of the moment I didn't even think of that. I ran to the tractor and pulled the pin to unhook the wagon and then vaulted to the tractor seat and started for the ranch house. The rain beat down on my back like the devil with a wet towel and the soggy brim of my straw hat was pounded down over my shoulders. My boots were full of water. I was desperate because I knew I had to cross the creek before the water got too high.

I bounced the tractor across the field and caught the muddy road at the bottom and slipped and slid to where the road crossed the creek, but I was already too late. The creek was a muddy torrent. I skidded the tractor to a stop in the mud and watched in panic as the water climbed higher and higher up the creek bank. I could already hear rocks sliding and crashing down the channel. As bad as I wanted to get across, I had to admit that it was too risky. I was trapped.

After those first few drowning minutes, the intensity of the storm slacked off to a standard cloudburst and I backed the tractor up to higher ground and sat there wet and cold and exposed to the downpour. There were some cottonwood trees nearby but I thought I was safer on the tractor. Lightning sought out the trees and I had enough problems already, and besides, I was already as wet as a person could get and so shelter was something that wasn't going to do me a whole lot of good at that point. I was starting to shiver with cold but I had no way to make a fire. I didn't know what else to do, and so I just sat on the tractor and endured the onslaught.

The rain let up another notch and settled into a heavy drizzle. The dark clouds were emptying and I could finally breathe without taking in water. The creek channel was completely filled with the flood now, and the muddy water was deeper than the tractor was tall. I knew that if the rain stopped right then, it might be a couple of hours before I could cross the creek again.

I looked out from under the soaked and sagging brim of my straw hat, and I saw the stock truck coming down the canyon on the muddy road. It was Willis coming to get me. Willis was a good man. He had been bailing hay in one of the upper fields when the storm hit, and instead of heading to the cookhouse for hot coffee with Joe and Humbert, he had jumped in the truck and come to find me. It was raining in the canyon where the other men were working, but nothing like the deluge I was experiencing a few miles away in the lower fields.

The flood was between us. Willis stopped the truck on the opposite side of the creek and got out in the rain and held his hands up helplessly. He was signaling that he didn't know what to do. I gave him the same gesture and we looked at each other

The Split Sky

across that wide chasm of churning water.

And then I came up with a plan.

I signaled to Willis to take the truck on down the canyon, and I got off the tractor and started walking down the muddy creek bank. Willis held his hands up questioningly, indicating that he didn't understand, and again I waved him to go down the canyon. He shrugged and got back in the truck and started to do as I said, driving slowly and watching to see what I was going to do.

A few hundred yards below where I had parked the tractor, a large pipe crossed the creek and I was going to see if I could cross on that pipe. I walked to it and stood for a while, sizing up the situation. The pipe was twelve inches in diameter and about forty feet long. It acted as a flume to carry ditch water over the creek. It was placed in an area where the creek banks were relatively close together and the channel was deep. It was suspended ten or twelve feet above the normal level of the stream. It was made of steel and it was cold, wet and slippery.

Willis figured out what I was up to, and he got out of the truck and walked in the mud to the other side of the pipe and looked it over. He then waved me off like some guy on the deck of an aircraft carrier who doesn't want the plane to land. He was hollering something at me, but I couldn't make out his words over the roar of the water and the sound of the falling rain. He shook his head from side to side and waved his arms across his chest and told me to forget it in the best sign language available to him.

I wasn't so sure. I knelt down and touched the pipe. It was cold and wet, but the steel was rigid and it hung four or five feet above the flood. It was a path as straight as an arrow to the heater and the shelter of the stock truck. I decided to go for it.

I sat down in the mud and started to scoot out onto the pipe. Willis was waving wildly at me not to do it and so I quit looking at him. I tried to focus on the pipe and not on the flood. I kept my legs down for balance and both hands cupped over the wet metal. I scooted out an inch at a time, balancing like a high-wire walker, except that my limbs were tucked in close and I was sitting the steel pipe on my wet and muddy little pockets.

I moved slowly and deliberately, and sooner than I wanted, my feet were swinging freely over the raging torrent. I could hear rocks slamming together like billiard balls in the flood below me, and big chunks of cottonwood trees were bobbing past. Big slices of the dirt banks were sloughing off into the boiling water. I was committed now. It was as dangerous to go back as it was to go forward and I had to keep going. I had just placed the biggest bet of my young life. All my cards were on the table—it was win or die.

I inched my way across the pipe slowly and methodically. I concentrated on my balance and the position of my hands. I moved an inch or two and then paused to be sure that I was set for the next move. I shut out the noise of the flood, the rain and the thunder. Inside of myself, I was surprisingly calm, focused and deliberate. On the outside, the part that Willis could see, everything was pandemonium. Willis stood by helplessly, painfully aware of what I was betting. He couldn't help me if the flood still had an ace to play.

I reached the other bank and Willis almost came out on the pipe to get me. He was a big man with long arms and he got right down in the mud and extended one of those big Marine Corps hands and helped me scramble off the wet pipe and onto the opposite bank. The flood roared its disapproval and kicked and slapped at the dirt bank where we floundered on our knees in the mud and finally gained the higher ground.

I was trembling with excitement and exhilarated by my conquest. I had challenged the angry flood to a duel and I had come out the winner. I had bet my very life on my physical and mental abilities, and I had conquered. I was laughing, and ready to run and jump and buck in the rain like a happy baby lamb. I wasn't even cold anymore.

Willis, on the other hand, was cold and wet and muddy and not very impressed that I had done something so foolish. He smiled good-naturedly and shook his head at my wild exuberance, and then he cuffed me on the back of the head almost hard enough to knock me down and told me to get in the truck.

I was still surfing on an adrenaline wave when we got to the cookhouse. I was wet and muddy and didn't care. I was trembling uncontrollably and I was giddy and acting stupid. I laughed and told Joe and Humbert what I had just done, and they sat quietly over their coffee cups and looked at me with the uncomprehending blank stares of domestic livestock. They just couldn't picture it. They didn't appreciate my audaciousness. They hadn't experienced the violence of the storm, nor could they comprehend the intensity of the flood or the daring gamble this stupid little hay hand had just bet his life on.

Willis understood because he had witnessed it. He reached out with one of those big hands and ruffed up my wet hair again, hard enough to make my eyeballs bounce, and then he told Joe and Humbert to take care of me. He then went home to get some dry clothes. I took a warm shower, put on dry clothes, drank a cup of hot coffee and got warm, but it was late that afternoon before I could stop shaking.

Chapter 13

Gaining Control

The Road To Myton

In August we started to haul grain from the Uintah Basin. Virginia owned a farm in Myton and she had a sharecropping arrangement with the tenant farmer. The Colonel, Humbert and I spent a day traveling to the farm to make arrangements to collect the Ranch's portion of the farm produce. It was like a day away from school for me and I enjoyed the fieldtrip to the farm. I enjoyed it even though I was the little guy who had to sit in the back seat of the suburban with Brody the wonder dog. It was the one and only time I ever went anywhere outside of the canyon with the Colonel, and it was quite an experience for me. I learned some things about the Colonel that day, and about my other traveling companions as well.

From my vantage point in the back seat, where I was soon forgotten, I watched with some amusement the interplay between the Colonel and his hired hand. Humbert was shamelessly kissing-up to the boss man and playing him like a bass fiddle. Humbert giggled at the big man's jokes and oo'ed and ah'ed and nodded his head knowingly as the Colonel went on and on in a long dissertation about world affairs and current events. I smiled because I could only guess what Humbert was really thinking. He was completely clueless about anything going on outside the canyon. I kept waiting for Humbert to look back at me so I could wink and rub my nose to let him know that I thought he was a brown-noser, but he never gave me the chance. Humbert sat in rapt attention and hung on the Colonel's every word and he never looked back at me. I think he knew I was going to give him the raspberry. I've always been an admirer of good acting, and Humbert was a master. I also noticed that he wasn't smoking in the boss man's suburban, and I giggled because I knew he must have been dying for a cigarette.

I thought it was funny that Humbert was showing himself to be such a shameless toady, but I was every bit as bad. I was trying to discipline the big man's dog without him knowing about it. Brody and I were back-seat traveling companions and we were not getting along well together. It was like being locked in a phone booth with the boss man's spoiled kid who was wiping boogers on everything and daring me to say something about it.

I was sitting behind Humbert on the right side of the back seat. Brody had the left side and the middle of the same seat. He wanted my side too. He kept crawling along the seat, trying to put his fuzzy head with his wet and snotty nose on my lap. I didn't want to touch the stinky, ice cream eating fleabag, and I would watch the Colonel in the mirror, and when he was distracted, I would push the dog off the seat and onto the floor where he should have been in the first place.

Brody just couldn't understand that I didn't love him. He thought I was playing a game, and he would come right back up on the seat and try to put that drooling snout on my leg again. He even upped the ante by licking my hand with his horse-biscuit-fondling-tongue and I had to summon all my reserves of self-control to keep from jerking the door open and booting him out onto the gravel at fifty miles an hour. I looked down on him with revulsion, and I fantasized about murder. I counted over a dozen creative ways to put that big yellow bag of ice cream and cantaloupe out of his misery.

I tried to warn him off with body language. I put my knee up on the seat to try to keep him back, and when the Colonel wasn't looking, I even raised my hand like I was going to slap him. Brody didn't get it. He had never had anyone raise a hand at him before and he thought I was playing another game. He panted happily and cast those dim and disgustingly Airedale eyes at me playfully, and then he slobbered on the seat cover and waited to see what I was going to do next.

I wanted to snap and growl at him like a wolf and let him know in doggie language that I was about to bite his stupid head off, but I knew if I did something like that I would have to answer to his master the Colonel. And being the coward that I was, and not wanting to force the big man to make a choice between his doggie best friend and his lowly farm hand, I restrained myself.

In frustration, I decided to try to communicate with the dog using telepathy—you know—that superior form of mind-to-mind communication that dolphins and other smarter-than-people animals are supposed to enjoy. I squinted-up my eyes tight and focused on casting a brain wave to old Brody. I told him that he had better back off and leave me alone or there would be hell to pay. Unfortunately, Brody didn't fall into the category of smart animals and my telepathic cablegram bounced off. He still didn't get it.

I looked him deep in the eyes like a hypnotist and told him with mind waves that he was a stinking, flea-bitten, good-for-nothing cur, and if I had my way he would be stomped down a long tin chute into the flashing steel teeth of a fish-food shredder. If Brody understood my brain waves, he still didn't let on. He slobbered on the seat cover and wagged his stupid tail and bowed his neck so I could pet him on the head—not even!

Finally, in desperation, when all else had failed and my brain waves were just ricocheting around and around in the suburban and not soaking into the dog, I took drastic measures. The dog put his stinking head on my leg again for the ninety-second time and I reached down and flipped him hard on the lip with my finger. Brody yipped and jumped back and looked so darn surprised. The Colonel looked up in the rear view mirror and told the dog to lie down and behave himself. Brody retreated to the other side of the seat and sat there looking back at me with big, sad and pouting puppy dog eyes. The Colonel watched me suspiciously in the rear view mirror for a long time.

Brody's heart was broken, and the Colonel didn't know why. He knew I had done something disrespectful to his canine soul mate but he wasn't sure what it was. He watched me in the mirror for a long time and he frowned and wrinkled up his nose. I looked out the window and pretended to be tired and bored, but our eyes kept meeting in that stupid mirror. I put on my very best innocent and boyish face, but the leader of men and defender of dogs was still suspicious. Finally, Humbert distracted the Colonel with a leading question about world events and the man went back to talking and driving and the storm passed. I made a mental note that I owed Humbert a favor, and I smiled because I knew that Humbert and I both should have been nominated for academy awards that morning.

We arrived at the farm, and the farmer's wife told us that the farmer was out in the fields. So we drove out to where a great, ancient combine was beating up the amber waves of grain. All activity came to a halt and the farmer climbed down from his rusty behemoth to report to his lord and master.

We all got out of the suburban and Brody dashed over to be the first to pee on the tires of the big machine. He had just cocked a leg, when from behind the big machine there materialized three other dogs. Brody was delighted. He lived a sheltered life and he thought that even strange dogs loved him too. He bounded over to play with the strangers with a smile on his muzzle and a song in his heart.

The three dogs were border collies, and they were farm dogs and protective of their turf and tires. They had saved baby lambs from coyotes, and they knew skunks and coons and killer badgers. Brody was something new; he was big and gangly, yellow and dumb. He was a rich-man's pet and he smelled of cantaloupe and doggy-salon perfume. He was a creature like none of the working dogs had ever encountered. They sized him up cautiously as he bounced around them with all the finesse of a baby moose, and then one of them confronted him head-on with a snarl while another nipped him on the heels from behind.

Brody was aghast. He squealed like a pig, wet all over himself, and sought safety under the suburban. The Colonel ran to the rescue. He sprinted to the suburban and got down on his knees in the dirt and looked under the oily crankcase at his cowering and shell-shocked comrade. Then he started to yell at the farmer, "Make them stop . . . Make them stop!" And when the farmer managed to call off his dogs, the Colonel scooped the trembling terrier up in his arms and put him back inside the suburban and whispered baby talk to calm him down. It was a tender moment.

He rolled the dog over a couple of times, there on the seat, conducting a combat medic's triage to assess his doggie soldier's wounds. There were none. All that was hurt was doggie pride and doggie dignity—and the Colonel's feelings.

The farmer apologized copiously, groveling like a servant who had spilled the king's wine, and he made a good show of cursing and kicking at his loyal watchdogs as he sent them away. I looked over at Humbert and he was looking back at me.

He smiled ever so slightly and winked, and I had to turn my back and pretend to blow my nose in my handkerchief to keep from laughing out loud.

The farmer and the Colonel finished conducting their business out there in the field. Humbert stood by and chain-smoked half-a-dozen cigarettes, soaking up enough nicotine to get him back to the ranch. I was bored out of my skull and threw dirt clods at a fence post, pretending it was a big, yellow Airedale terrier. Brody sat safely in the suburban, in his wet dog suit. He drooled on the seats, painted the windows with doggie slobber, and waited happily for his hero the Colonel to return.

When we left the farm we didn't go back to the ranch right away, we went to see a demonstration of new farm equipment that was sponsored by one of the big farm implement companies in the Basin. They were showing off a new-fangled device to stack hay. They called it a bale wagon, and it was like a tractor with an attached platform that scooped bales up off the ground and stacked them on the platform mechanically. Once they were stacked on the platform, the driver could empty the platform against an existing stack and he didn't even have to get off the tractor seat for the whole process. The whole thing looked like cheating to me.

Humbert thought it was the neatest thing since sliced cheese, but the Colonel was more skeptical. He pointed out to the salesmen that the finished stack was not tight and water could get down between the blocks of bales. He also noted that the process limited how high a stack could be built, and that the stack would have to be placed on firm and level ground or it would tip over. He then described for them some of the mechanical limitations of the machine.

The Colonel paced back and forth, gesturing with a finger

like a College Professor giving a lecture, and he artfully parried each and every argument the salesmen threw back at him. It was obvious that he had done his homework and prepared himself for this little sales meeting. He was no pushover. The salesmen, in their short-sleeved, pinstriped shirts, bolo ties, pot bellies and obligatory western straw hats, were frustrated and fuming. There were other, less articulate and less prepared farmers there at the sales show and the Colonel was their champion. The other farmers stood by and watched in awe as the Colonel paced back and forth and backed that whole team of salesmen into a corner. He whipped them all. I don't think anyone bought one of those new-fangled bale wagons that day.

I was impressed that the Colonel knew so much about haystacks, and I was impressed by the way he subdued and cowed that pack of eager salesmen. I had never seen that side of the man before. He was not much of a farm hand, but in a toe-to-toe debate the man was a tiger. There was a spark of manly aggression smoldering in the old guy after all; he just needed the right playing field to make it known.

The Colonel embarrassed me, but he made me proud when he placed a hand on my shoulder and told that mob of salesmen that I was his hay stacker and he would keep me until they worked the bugs out of the new machine. At the time, I took it as a compliment, but now, through eyes that have seen a lot of colonels and a lot of years, I see that he was just using me as a prop to make a point. He might have said the same thing about a mule or a tractor. I was too eager to accept a compliment, and I looked for them in places they were not.

Just a week or two later there was a small earthquake in the Basin and the demonstration hay stack, so carefully crafted by the crafty salesmen, came crashing down. When the Colonel heard the news, he walked over to the cookhouse at noon to tell Humbert and me all about it. He was smiling triumphantly and rocking back and forth from his heels to his toes, and he kept saying, "I told them . . . I told them," and we all agreed that he had. I think if I could have stayed there for another season or two I might have learned to like the Colonel. The man had some redeeming features; he just took a little getting used to.

I did receive a compliment about my stacking abilities before I left that summer. Virginia stopped by to chat one afternoon while I was building a haystack, and she took my picture and told me that as far as she was concerned, I had won the all-time best hay stacker award at the ranch. I don't know if she really meant it or if she was just trying to be nice to the hired help. I hoped it was true. I had certainly tried to be the best hay stacker she ever had. For me to hear such a thing from a woman I admired and respected meant a lot to me. I put another feather in my war bonnet—Virginia Nutter's top hay stacker.

Humbert and I started the grain haul from Myton. He used his own truck and I drove the stock truck from the ranch. I was as proud as a stupid peacock. I had a driver's license that wasn't a year old yet and I had never gotten to drive all I wanted to, and now I was going to get paid to drive a truck. I was honored that Virginia and the Colonel would trust me with such manly responsibility.

I followed Humbert to the farm, we loaded up with loose grain from the combine, and I followed him back to the ranch where we unloaded into the granary with scoop shovels. For the next two or three days I traveled the route alone and loaded and unloaded grain in one hundred pound sacks. The farmer helped me load and Humbert or Willis helped me unload.

I completely enjoyed the assignment. The road up Gate Canyon to Myton was the same ancient freight road that my great grandfather had traveled with wagons and teams and I was proud to be carrying on the tradition. It was also nice to be away from the fields for a while and able see some new country and drive the truck. I had been given the full measure of a man's responsibility, and I betrayed the trust placed in me only one time by an act of youthful indiscretion.

I was between Myton and the top of Gate Canyon, loaded and climbing the winding road, heading back to the ranch. The truck was lumbering along, groaning under its heavy burden, when a man and woman in a little foreign car came up behind me and the driver started to honk his horn. It was a dirt road and I knew it was dusty back there. The guy wanted me to pull over and let him pass. He was driving one of those little two-seater sports cars that well-to-do beatniks drove around college campuses in those days. It was a dark, navy blue convertible and it looked out of place on a dirt road in the Uintah Basin.

The road was narrow, winding and washboardy. There was no good place for me to pull over and let him pass, and besides, I didn't want to completely stop the truck anyway. With the full load of grain and the steepness of the hill, I knew that if I stopped the truck and started again I would be stuck in granny gear to the top of the mountain and would probably overheat the engine.

I squeezed to the right as far as I dared to let him around, but he wouldn't pass me. The road was full of turns and I supposed that he couldn't see what was coming and he was afraid to pass. I came to a long, straight stretch of road and I put my outside duals in the grass on the shoulder of the road and with my arm I waved for him to come around me. He stayed back in the dust and kept honking. I finally understood that he wasn't going to pass me no matter what I did. I could only guess that he was afraid the truck would flip gravel on his precious little car and he was insisting that I pull over and stop

The Split Sky

to let him by. He kept honking and honking, and then he started to mouth obscenities and give me the finger. I'm sure his boldness was bred by the fact that he could see me in the mirrors of the truck, and he could see that I was alone and that I was just a kid.

I watched that guy in the truck mirror as he got all red-faced and slobbery and repeatedly jabbed that finger in the air at me, and from somewhere deep within me, a genetic defect common in my Irish ancestry boiled to the surface. I got mad as hell. I didn't fully understand what was happening to me, but I was experiencing my very first case of road rage.

The nasty man in the little car stayed back behind me until we reached the very top of the canyon where the road was wide and I pulled over and almost stopped to let him get by me. He came flying past, laying on the horn, gunning his engine and hollering something that I couldn't understand. He zoomed past in a cloud of dust, peppering the truck with gravel, and for several seconds I could see that finger waving like a flag above the dust cloud.

I was in a big truck, heavily loaded, and gravity was my friend. I caught third gear as my nose pointed down the Nine Mile side of the canyon and I stepped on the throttle. I sat up close to the steering wheel, all of my faculties on full alert and steering for all I was worth. With the load of grain pushing and gravity pulling, I caught the little car and the red-faced angry man before he reached the middle of the canyon. I came down on him like a hammer.

He had forgotten all about me and he was toodling down the canyon like a tourist, admiring the scenery and laid back with an arm over the side of his door. My big truck came around the bend behind him like a charging rhinoceros and I laid on the horn. He looked up and I'm sure all he could see was truck grill in his rear view mirror. He jerked the car over to the right like he was dodging rabbits and I tucked right in behind him and slapped the horn again. I had to hit the brakes and slide in the gravel to keep from running him over.

He figured it out in a heartbeat and he hit the gas and his little car threw gravel and sped down the canyon. His back became as straight as a two-by-four. He had both hands on the wheel and was steering like he was racing in the Indianapolis 500. He tried to outrun me, but his little rice rocket was light in the gravel and it wasn't negotiating the washboardy turns like my heavy truck. Try as he might, he just couldn't do it. I stayed right on him, honking and following his every evasion. I chased him for two or three miles down that torturous, winding and narrow canyon road. His little car fishtailed in the gravel and swung too wide on some of the washboardy turns. God was good to us and we didn't meet any other cars coming up the canyon.

He wasn't giving me the finger anymore. He had both hands on the wheel and he was steering like a wild man. He did wave a clenched fist at me over his shoulder once or twice, but he kept his disgusting finger tucked in close and safe. His face wasn't red anymore either, it was white, and his eyes were as big as paper plates. His lady friend sat rigid, frozen, staring straight ahead like a dime store mannequin.

When we hit the bottom of the canyon he had the advantage again and he left me in a cloud of dust. I wheeled into the ranch yard and half expected him to be sitting there crying to the Colonel about what a bad boy I was, but the coast was clear. The angry man in the little car had zipped right on through the ranch and headed for points unknown. I giggled to myself that he probably couldn't stop to talk until he got his diaper changed.

At supper that night, I told Joe and Humbert about the angry man in the little car and what I had done to him and they chewed me out pretty good. They said I was lucky I hadn't killed somebody and I was damn lucky that guy didn't stop and kick my butt. I'm sure they were right. It was a very irresponsible and juvenile thing to do and I probably wouldn't do the same thing today—but then you never know. Dogs that bite and slobbering, red-faced geeks waving fingers will often change their habits if they get kicked in the guts once in a while.

Slaying The Dragon

There must have been some weird sign in the stars that week. I didn't check my horoscope, but my zodiac chart must have been flashing red warning signals like the lights at a railroad crossing. No one ever accused me of being an Astrologist, but I'll bet the stars were aligned in such a way that Jupiter beat up his wife Venus, Mercury spilled on Mars, Neptune kicked his dog Pluto and Uranus got mooned. It was my week for strange confrontations.

It was just a few days after the little car incident that Joe the dragon and I had a showdown. It was like high noon in Dodge City and it had been brewing for a long time. Joe had bullied me since my first afternoon at the ranch and I had taken a lot of crap from him that summer. There are times when even a cute little puppy will bite.

We were hauling hay, Joe and I, at least I was hauling hay and Joe was driving the tractor. Joe was drunk again. I don't know where or how he got the booze, but he was quite drunk and obnoxious and he'd been trying to pick a fight all morning.

We were going along the edge of a large field. I would pick up the bales and throw them on the wagon and then jump up on the wagon and stack them and jump off again to get some more. Joe slouched over the steering wheel of the tractor and hummed irreverent barroom songs to himself and cussed and growled that I was too damn slow. He wanted to get it done and go back to the house.

I came to a spot in the field where the ditch had flooded over because of a beaver dam and two or three hay bales were sitting in the water. I walked past them and went to get others. Joe stopped the tractor, cursing incoherently, and jeered impatiently that I had missed a couple. I yelled back that they were wet, we couldn't stack them, and we should leave them behind. I told him I would come back and get them later. Joe sat defiantly on the tractor seat with his foot heavy on the brake and insisted that I go get the wet bales. I told him no again, and Joe got very ugly.

He came down off the tractor seat, rolling up his sleeves and cursing like a pirate. He had blood in his eye and he was calling me some vile and filthy names. He was coming fast, and he sneered that he was going to stomp my guts once and for all. Joe had made threats toward me before, but this time things were different. He was drunk and he was actually coming at me, and from the look on his face, I had no doubts about his sincerity.

I ducked behind the hay wagon—he had me on the run. He came around the corner of the wagon very fast, hot on my heels and huffing and puffing like the big bad wolf. His fist was cocked back and ready to go and he had a dark and evil smirk on his drunken face—and then he froze in mid-stride. He slammed on his air brakes and he stood teetering on his tippy-toes, trying to keep his balance.

The pitchfork was aimed at his belt buckle.

The old dragon had been caught completely by surprise and he stood very still with his soft belly exposed to the sharp spikes. His breath and his guts were all sucked up and his eyes wide and suddenly full of panic. He looked down at the cold, steel tines and then blinked and looked up at me, unbelieving.

My dark resolve must have shown through my boyish features because I thought for a moment he was going to wet himself. His face went waxy white as his alcohol-foggy mind absorbed what was happening to him, and he started to sober up real fast.

I was trembling with fear and apprehension but my feet were planted solidly. I had no idea what I was going to do next. I was caught up in the moment like an accident victim, out of control and grasping for hope and stability. I was panicked, terrified and cornered. The pitchfork was a primal instinct, an overriding impulse to self-defense. I held it like a bayonet and I think I really would have stuck him if he had kept coming.

Through tightly clenched teeth I growled at him like a cornered little Bobcat. "Back off Joe . . . I'll gut you like a fish," and I raised the tines just a little toward his liver to punctuate my sincerity. Joe obediently took a step backward and stood frozen again. His right fist was still cocked half-heartedly, but his face had a wilted, disbelieving look about it.

I was as surprised as old Joe. This was not something I had planned to do or would even have thought to do. It had just happened in the heat of the moment. Without even thinking, I had reacted to his attack with a counter attack and I had raised the stakes exponentially. My overriding thoughts were that I was not going to let that drunken old gutter rat beat me up, and I was tired of ducking and running from the man.

My emotions were in a tangle. I was so damn mad at the old dragon for putting me in that position; and yet I was embarrassed that I had broken the Code of the West by grabbing a weapon. I tried to resolve the inner conflict with the consolation that this was not a fair fight in the first place. Joe was older, stronger, bigger, and more experienced. He was mean and drunk and he outweighed me by at least sixty pounds. He had also picked the fight and chosen the ground. I still felt bad but I didn't know what to do about it. I was in a real dilemma. I didn't want to hurt the old dragon, but I didn't know how to release him from the trap I'd caught him in. I couldn't just back away from what I'd done. If I put the pitchfork down now old Joe would kick my butt for sure; and he just might use the pitchfork to teach me a lesson. At least for now the pitchfork was giving me some measure of control and I had to maintain that control to see the thing through.

In the boiler room of my emotions the anger bubbled to the top. I cracked open the pressure valve and let the hot steam escape. I opened the lid to that box of pent-up frustrations I had kept hidden since that first afternoon in the bunkhouse and I let all the bats fly away. I told him what a sorry excuse for a man I thought he was, and I used some of the vile and filthy words he had taught me that summer as adjectives to describe him. He looked shocked, dumbfounded—even hurt. I told him I wasn't about to take a beating from him and I was tired of his crap, and if he ever, ever raised a hand at me again I'd kill him—and I think he believed me. He slowly lowered his doubled fist and went back to the tractor without a word.

I watched him retreat but I didn't gloat in the victory. I knew that even injured snakes can bite and I didn't trust him. I stood with the pitchfork in my hands like a medieval Englishman's pike until Joe was safely back on the tractor seat, and then I stuck the weapon in a hay bale on the wagon where I could get to it quickly.

I was shaking almost uncontrollably, but we went on about our business like nothing had happened. I hauled hay and Joe drove the tractor, only this time he wasn't humming any bawdy, drunken tunes to himself, and he wasn't bitching that I was working too slowly. The three wet bales sat quietly in the sunshine until I went back that afternoon and loaded them in the pickup truck to feed to the stock in the corral.

Virginia and the Colonel never knew about our little discussion around the pitchfork out there in the field. I left the ranch just a week or two after our meeting of the minds and Joe and I never mentioned the incident to each other again. Old Joe was polite and respectful toward me after that, and even years later, whenever I stopped by the ranch to visit, he would treat me like an old friend.

I had gone to the canyon to learn to be a man, and the confrontation with Joe was my final exam. I was ready to go home. In the Gladiator's forum that was the Nutter Ranch, I had met fear, humiliation, anxiety, stress, isolation, hard work and pain. I had fought a dragon, a killer badger, a flood, a phantom, a geek in a little car, physical injury and my own insecurities. Each represented a Gladiator from a different realm: the world of men, the animal kingdom, the physical and natural world, the world of shadow and mystery, confrontation and challenge, the physical self and the deep and private spiritual world within. I had bested them all. I could wear the laurels of victory and drink from the waters of sweet success.

I had climbed the mountain.

Chapter 14

Salutation

The Split Sky

Joe and I lived our last few days together in the shelter of an undeclared truce. After our little discussion around the pitchfork, we still worked together, and we ate together, and we both went our ways like nothing had happened. Joe never raised his voice to me again and we were both polite and very respectful.

I was finally a full-fledged adult member of the farm crew and not the kid anymore. Old Joe and the other hands were finally treating me as an equal. I had flexed and growled and elbowed my way in . . . and I had finally won myself a place around the dog dish. Joe and the Colonel were even learning to call me by my name. All summer long I had answered to "Hey Kid," or "Hey You," but now that I was almost ready to go home, I had earned my own name.

I was anxious to go home. I would be a junior in high school that coming year and I was looking forward to it. Finally, I would be one of the big guys, back from a summer job on a big ranch, wearing my expensive black hat and telling war stories about my adventures. I was excited.

I had mixed feelings about leaving the ranch. I had fought hard to claim a spot among that little group of people and it was hard for me to give it up. I was proud of what I had accomplished and I hated to leave it all behind. It was like abandoning a hard-won homestead after a long season of

The Split Sky

making fence, clearing brush and digging ditch in the rocky soil. I was preparing to walk away, knowing that some other guy would soon come along and take possession of the fields I had plowed.

As I prepared to leave, I knew that my life would never be the same again. In fact, it wasn't just my life that had changed; the whole world was never the same after the summer of '63. In November of that same year, President Kennedy was assassinated in Dallas, and already American troops were being sent to serve as military advisors in a place called Vietnam on the dark side of the world. By the following summer God was ordered out of our schools and silver was taken out of our money. The sexual revolution, the drug culture, the counter culture, hippies, long hair, campus unrest, war protests, race riots and war in the Middle East were all just on the verge of bursting forth upon the world like biblical plagues. The days of innocence, civility, and cowboy ideals were almost over.

The day I left the ranch I knew I was going into a storm. I had an experience, a spiritual experience, if you believe in such things, one afternoon during my last few days in the canyon. To me, it was a heavenly manifestation that foretold of things to come in my life. It was a troubling revelation at the time, and yet it contained an element that has given me courage and hope for all these many years. The vision of it will stay with me always.

I had been sent to tend water in one of the upper fields. It was late afternoon and the Southeastern sky looked ominous. All afternoon there had been a dark shadow over the desolation country and we were expecting rain.

There was a remarkable contrast to the west. The sky was filled with great banks of soft, billowing clouds and the heavens overflowed with a magnificent sunset. The sun was just beginning to sink into the mountains, and long shafts of golden light shot up into the air and illuminated the clouds with a radiance that was truly spectacular. The clouds glowed like they were on fire, deep red and orange, purple, soft pink and shining gold. They were bold and vibrant colors, neon in their intensity, and they showered the heavens with the warm glow of the fire.

The reflected light spilled down over the canyon where I was working and it was like looking at the world through a rainbow. Everything shimmered with a remarkable glow, the ledges, trees, and even the grass. It was a soft and filtered sort of light, amber and slightly hazy like gold dust sprinkled in the air. I basked in the glory of it and marveled at the beauty.

I was the only witness. The canyon was empty and quiet but for the tinkling of the little stream of water at my feet. I stood for several minutes and let it all soak in, and then reluctantly, I went back to my shovel. I had to finish my work before the darkness came.

I was shoveling out a small lateral ditch when I was startled by the sudden crash of thunder behind me—very close and down the canyon toward the ranch buildings. I turned toward the sound with my shoulders up and my head ducked as though I expected shrapnel. Of course the lightning bolt was gone, but the thunder had drawn my attention to something else I was supposed to see.

I was fascinated to see a great, dark cloud spreading from the south and across the lower canyon. It was coming rapidly on a silent wind, hanging low and heavy, and spreading like an ink stain across the sky. As the cloud moved, the earth below it disappeared into darkness and the darkness growled with thunder. The storm was passing parallel to me. I could see it and hear it as it spread its dark cloak over the canyon, but it was not coming for me, and so I held my ground and watched.

It was an incredible thing. I was standing safe and dry and in the soft light of a glorious sunset while watching one of the most violent storms of the summer explode on the canyon below. The black cloud covered everything with a veil of darkness that was so dense, so impossibly thick, that I couldn't see into it. The outer edge of the storm was hung like a curtain that cascaded from high in the heavens to the very ground, and the curtain of darkness was less than a mile away. The storm curtain moved ever northward, the bottom dragging in the dirt and erasing the features of the ground as it touched them: ledges, trees, rocks and hillsides disappearing into the darkness. The storm was alive and devouring the canyon. It was a frightening thing to watch. I could feel the power of it, the ferocity, and the danger.

The blackness boiled and seethed. Deep inside the storm there were terrible flashes of lightning, great angry blades of light that ripped into the sky, pushing back the darkness, shuddering with the effort, clawing for the edge of the storm and then collapsing back into a crash of thunder and darkness. Smaller and weaker splinters of blue-yellow light were quickly smothered by the storm; instant sparks of electricity that flashed like flint on steel. The darkness overwhelmed the light, suffocating it, pushing it back and stamping out the sparks as if jealous to share the heavens. Darkness prevailed everywhere—and from deep in the depths of the darkness came the voice of the storm, a deep and persistent wild-animal growl of thunder, the voice of a dragon, alive and threatening.

I was standing in a field of sunshine. Everything around me was lit with the brilliant hues of the rainbow. The contrast was startling. I looked up at the heavens. The sky was split in two.

It was as if a line had been drawn in the sky. I looked

around me and the whole world was divided. On one side everything was dark, angry and filled with violence. On the other, all was tranquility, light and color, warmth and peace. I had never seen such a contrast, and the thought came to me that I was witnessing a marvelous manifestation of the great dichotomy of life—the clash of opposing forces. It was as though I was standing in a great outdoors theater where the timeless cosmic drama of darkness versus light, good versus evil and virtue versus vice was being played out just for me and with the whole of the natural world as props. I marveled at the splendor and the majesty of it all.

And then it occurred to me that I might have a part to play in the drama too. It was getting late and I had to go. I had to move in one of those directions. The thought was disquieting and I was struck by the profundity of what my mind was suggesting to me. Was God trying to tell me something? Was this a test?

I hesitated. I pondered and I marveled. Could I be so brash? Was I really audacious enough to believe that the God of Abraham was communicating with me personally and using the wonders of creation—this magnificent split sky light show— to impress something on me? Could it possibly be true? Did I dare to be so bold?

I brooded over it. I looked longingly at the last sliver of the setting sun and the glory of the painted sky. The light, warmth, and the quiet beckoned to me. And then, with some trepidation, I looked back down the canyon at the storm. I knew what I had to do. I really didn't have a choice. Like it or not, I had to go into the storm. The ranch house, my job and my life were on the dark side of the split sky.

A few minutes later I drove the pickup into the curtain of rain and the darkness covered me. The brilliant sunset was still there, but I couldn't see it anymore. As the foreboding blackness settled over me and the cold water slapped against the windshield, I knew that I had been given a sign. I knew, just as surely as if God himself had whispered in my ear, that my life would be filled with storm, trouble, fear and uncertainty for a while . . . and it was.

But through the darkest nights of the storm: in a foxhole in Vietnam, and in the tomb-like caverns of a coalmine, and even in the sterilized, liberal halls of academia, whenever I was afraid, or in trouble, or just suffering quietly, I had the vision of that split sky to comfort me. I knew that no matter how bad things got, out there somewhere the storm ended and the sun was shining. I knew that one day I would walk out of that cold curtain of rain and I would see that sunset and it's glorious promise again . . . and I did.

SAYING GOODBYE

I called my parents to come and get me when my tour of duty was done. They were both busy and so they sent my friend David Rich to pick me up. That was okay with me, David was like one of my brothers. We had grown up together and I had spent almost as much time at his house as I had at mine. David had bought himself an old car that summer and he came to pick me up in that. It was an old Chevy, I think, an early 1950s model, as squat and stout as one of General Patton's tanks.

Before David got there, I gathered up my things and put on my best clothes and delighted in wearing my new black hat again. Virginia had asked me to come over to the big house to settle up and I was honored. It was the first time I'd been invited into her home and I wanted to look my very best.

She sat at her desk and showed me her ledger book where she had calculated my wages and my deductions. She already had a check made out for me, and she surprised me by giving me a bonus. She paid me an extra week's pay and thanked me for doing a good job. She told me to come back any time and look for Indian artifacts, and she said she had a job for me anytime I might want one. She told me she would be happy to have me back next summer and she would be sure that I went on the mountain with the cowboys. We both laughed about that, and I thanked her warmly.

I was leaving the house when the Colonel caught me. He awkwardly put a hand on my shoulder and said, "Good job . . . Good job," and then he did something truly remarkable—he extended his hand for a handshake. I looked down at that open palm and a flood of emotions came over me. Had I won that too? With pain I remembered how devastated I was just a few months earlier when that hand was refused me. I looked him in the eyes, and with pride I took his hand and gave it a strong but polite grip.

Over at the cookhouse, Joe and Humbert were having their evening coffee and I stopped to say goodbye. Humbert told me that he had enjoyed working with me and he hoped I would come back next year. Joe was civil but more reserved. I offered him my hand and he took it. I secretly marveled at how different things were between the old dragon and me, on this, my last evening at the ranch. I was standing over him now, reaching out, trying to coax him into being my friend. I was being conciliatory, forgiving, and maybe even apologetic for what I had done to him. He sat passively detached, quietly brooding and smoking a cigar like he always did.

I made small talk for a while, and then, when I thought I heard a car coming down the canyon, I told them goodbye and turned to leave. Joe took me by surprise when he called out for me to be sure to stop and say hello whenever I passed through the canyon. I turned, and I must have given him a surprised look, and maybe even a questioning, raised eyebrow, because he said it again. "I mean it," he said. "If you get a chance . . . you stop and see us." I told him I would . . . and I meant it too.

David rattled into the yard in his old Chevy and I carried my gear out to put in his car. It was getting dark and the stupid peacock cheerleaders honked and applauded at every little sound. David laughed.

As we headed for town in the dark, I felt strangely subdued. I didn't want to talk much and I wasn't very good company to my friend David. I sat quietly and watched the headlights touch every fence post as we left the canyon. Behind us, the ranch settled into another quiet, star-filled, late-summer night. Pale moonlight soaked into the ledges and filled the tracks of my boots that still followed the canyon rims.

The summer of my growing up was over.

EPILOGUE

For almost a year I looked forward to going back to the ranch and reclaiming my spot. I still wanted to go on the mountain and be a cowboy, but like the best-laid plans of mice and men, it never happened. By the next summer the world was different and I was different, and I had wandered off in other directions.

I still dreamed of ridin' and ropin' and punchin' them cows, but I was making a lot more money at another job by then, and the new job was closer to home and closer to the rodeos and dragging main street on Saturday nights with my friends. The early sixties was a great time to be a teenaged kid and I didn't want to miss any of it.

I was actually working two jobs by the time school let out that next year. I was managing a farm for old man Pepperakis out in the Miller Creek area, and I was playing rhythm guitar in a band on the weekends. I had always wanted to play a guitar, and that winter I took some of my hard earned money from the ranch and invested in the dream. I made a down payment on a brand new Fender Stratocaster and taught myself to play. By the spring of '64 I was a member of a rock-n-roll band—The Playboys. My brother Reed was in the band too.

We performed all over the county: the country club, the Elk's, the high school, the college, and after the rodeos. We played anything that was popular: Buck Owens, Elvis and Chuck Berry, The Beatles and Buddy Holly. We did country, rock-n-roll and California surfin' tunes. We mimicked the

Beach Boys and The Ventures. We were amateurs, kids having fun, and we were not very good by professional standards, but we were as good as anything Carbon and Emery Counties had to offer at the time—and people kept us busy. Sometimes we practiced in the pavilion at the city park in Price and our open-air jam sessions drew crowds as big as our dance engagements. There in the city park, we would put on impromptu and free concerts, for all the kids in the county. Kids would dance on the tennis courts and the sidewalks and kick off their shoes and dance in the grass. We'd stay with it until the city police shut us down around midnight. We did the same thing during lunch hour at the high school, out on the courtyard and in front of the school. It was a lot of fun and I didn't want to give it up.

I met Jeannie that winter at the high school. We literally ran into each other on a blind corner of a hallway. I knocked her books all over the floor and had to apologize and pick them up for her. She was a sophomore with a pretty face and beautiful, long brown hair, and she sure smelled good up close. I recognized her the next time we met on that fateful corner as we hurried to classes, and we both smiled and said hello. I found myself watching for her at school, and by the spring of '64 we were holding hands.

Jeannie was a farm girl and we understood each other. I could communicate with her across a crowded room without saying anything, and she held me captive with her beautiful eyes. She was a little thing, just five feet tall and a hundred and five pounds, but she radiated energy, health, strength and character in measure far beyond her physical size. She was a beautiful girl with a charming smile—and when she wore her black skirt to school I surrendered. There was something about the curve of her hips that turned my guts to mush. I was smitten, moonstruck and helpless like a bottle-fed calf. I tried to be cool and studly, but I would have followed her anywhere.

She was unlike any girl I had ever known. She was smart, tough and self-reliant, a real cowgirl who didn't show off, a young woman who made her own clothes and earned her own spending money. She could ride a horse bareback like a Comanche, and she had a love for life that showed in everything she did. She loved horses, babies, sunsets and flowers. Farm animals loved her. She always had a big hug for lambs, calves and baby colts. She talked to horses in their native tongue and they loved her for it. Stray cats followed her through the farmyard like she was the pied piper. She was my princess from a fairy tale, a blending of Snow White and Cinderella; a beautiful chore girl who milked cows and then went to the dance in velvet slippers.

There was another side to her that fascinated me. I had never known a girl so bold and ever willing to take a chance or a dare. She was fearless, and she could ride, shoot, tie knots and drive a big truck better than I could. She could even beat me in armwrestling (wink). She had a wonderful sense of humor and she used wit and sarcasm like the sword of Zorro.

To me, she was like a wild and beautiful horse to be tamed and a prize to be won. She was a challenge to me and I had to earn her respect, her love, and eventually her hand—and that made her all the more precious to me. She was another reason I never went back to the ranch. We were married in December of 1967, just a month before I went to Vietnam.

Over the next couple of summers I stopped in to visit with Joe and Humbert several times when I went back to the canyon and the ranch to hunt arrowheads. They always treated me well and were only too happy to stop whatever they were doing to visit for a while. I was even invited to eat dinner with them a couple of times and I did. I enjoyed those meals in the cookhouse again. Each time there was a new farmhand or a new cook that I didn't know, someone I could show off for. I would kick back and talk to Joe and Humbert about the good old days when I worked there too, and it made me feel like a triumphant old soldier revisiting a battlefield.

Not surprisingly, Joe's health deteriorated quickly over the next few years. The booze and the cigars gradually pulled him down. My dad was called out to the ranch with the county ambulance a couple of times to take him to the hospital when he had bouts with bleeding ulcers.

The last time dad was called out to the ranch Joe wouldn't go with them. He had been drunk and not eating for three or four days, and he was lying in a soiled bed and the ulcer was trying to kill him. He was in terrible pain and bleeding but he refused to go to the hospital. Even Humbert couldn't talk any sense into him. It was not a crime to be sick or drunk, and he had a right to refuse help, and so the ambulance crew left him there in the care of Humbert The Good. Surprisingly, he bounced back that time. Joe died a couple of years later, in 1976, three months short of his sixtieth birthday.

Willis still owns his ranch in the canyon. The old timers still call it the old Housekeeper place, even though Willis has owned it for over forty years and his name isn't Housekeeper. Willis lives in Price, and he's still a good man and one of my heroes. I'll never forget how hard I tried to keep up with him in the fields and how futile my efforts were. Another thing I'll never forget is the day those big hands took me by the arm and helped me up that muddy slope and away from the gaping mouth of the Nine Mile flood. The Marine Corps and the Nutter Ranch were lucky to have a few good men like Willis Hammerschmid.

I got reacquainted with Humbert many years later when I

discovered that he was in a local nursing home. He was an old man, older than his years, and he was recovering from knee surgery. He had developed a staff infection and they had him in the nursing home convalescing. I stopped to see him and he remembered me. We laughed and got along so well and had so much to talk about that I dropped in on him often. He always seemed to enjoy my visits.

His knee was a real mess and he couldn't walk for a long time, and before they got him back on his feet he was diagnosed with throat cancer. Like his friend Joe, his love affair with tobacco proved to be his undoing.

He was a brave man and he didn't complain or bury himself in self-pity, even though he suffered terribly. He took every day as it came and I was proud of him.

Humbert told me that he wanted to go back out to the canyon one more time before he died, and we were dreaming and scheming about me taking him for a final farewell when he got real sick. I felt terrible that I couldn't take him back out to the canyon like he wanted. He couldn't walk and he was all poked full of tubes and needles and there was just no way I could have taken him anywhere. Humbert knew it would never happen, but we talked about it anyway, and we planned and dreamed and pretended that we were almost ready to go.

We went to Nine Mile together in our minds and in our hearts. We took more than one full tour of the canyon while Humbert lay in bed and I sat on a folding tin chair. We went back to the Sand Wash Hotel and rode our horses up Cottonwood Canyon again; we ate raw egg sandwiches, cussed the Colonel and his dog and hauled a lot of hay. Our little game of remember and pretend gave him something to dream about and something to help keep his mind from his suffering. He died without me knowing about it and I was crushed when I read his obituary in the newspaper. It had been less than a week since I had seen him, and I missed his funeral by one day.

I went to the canyon alone, as his proxy, and I visited his ranch in Argyle and his old place at the mouth of Dry Canyon. I drove slowly past the Nutter Ranch and I said goodbye to Humbert in my own way. Humbert was good to me when I needed a friend, and I can only hope that my visits to his bedside paid the interest on my debt. My friend Humbert Pressett died in September of 1988.

Eldon the range boss made history before he left the canyon. Like everything else the man did, he rode off into the sunset amidst fireworks and controversy. I wasn't there to see it, but I heard what happened from people who were in the canyon at the time.

It should be understood that there are two or three slightly different versions of the following story out there. I've tried to track it all down and I've interviewed everybody I know who was close to the action. Each of these people tells me something just a little different, which seriously complicates the telling of the tale. To get the job done, I've had to rely on my best judgment, my personal knowledge and understanding of the players and the circumstances, and my boundless imagination—so trust me. What follows is the fabric of a true story that is forty years old and already clouded in the mists of folklore and legend.

When Christmas of '63 approached, there were three cowboys on the mountain: Eldon the range boss, Arnold Adair and Don Gonzales. All three of them had asked to have Christmas week off. Virginia consented to let them all go at once, even though it meant there would be no one on the mountain to keep an eye on things.

It would be the first time in years that all the cowboys left at the same time, and it became apparent that no one would be around to feed and break ice for old Hunkus the mountain lion over the long Christmas holiday. Carbon County didn't have an animal shelter in those days, and Hunkus was not a trustee who could be released on his own recognizance.

The cowboys asked around, and it seemed that no one wanted to invite old Hunkus home for Christmas dinner with the family. He was not the sort of dinner guest a guy would want to take home to mother. His table manners were crude, he was not housebroken, and he had a special way of dealing with other pets. The cowboys talked it over and decided that Hunkus was getting to be more of a pain in the butt than a novelty anyway, and they decided to put him down.

Without ceremony, animosity, or remorse, the Range Boss shot the hapless feline and made a trophy of his golden fleece.

Nobody really cared that Old Hunkus went under. He was a mountain lion and filled with the original sin of his species and therefore guilty of crimes against humanity. He deserved to be shot. The trouble started because Eldon had been on the mountain too long and his sense of humor was warped. His inclination to get people hurt for entertainment would finally prove to be his downfall.

The boys had no way to weigh the cat, but he was a Boone and Crockett contender and he was only about three years old. He measured nine feet and one inch from the tip of his tail to his wet little nose. He was sleek and fat and his fur was prime. Hunkus had eaten more deer than any other cat on the mountain and it showed. When relieved of his winter coat, the boys noticed that he was in exceptionally good shape and his hams were thick and firm and muscled. Eldon giggled and decided it would be great fun to play a little joke on the boys at the farm.

They cut off one hindquarter, sprinkled it liberally with deer hair from an old hide lying in the snow by the lion barrel, and then stuffed it in a saddlebag. Smiling wickedly, they saddled up their horses and made the pilgrimage to the ranch.

When they got to the ranch they hung the cat ham in the saddle shed. They never mentioned it to anyone; they didn't have to. The farmhands were always pestering the cowboys to bring a hindquarter when they stopped by, and it was not unusual for the cowboys to oblige them. Often the exchange was accomplished without any fuss or fanfare. Poaching deer was technically against the law and it was bad manners to brag or make a fuss about it. Besides, It was the Christmas season, a time of brotherly love, and the farmers would be expecting a gift of "mountain veal" from the land of green grass and sweet water. Surely, one of the farmers would check the meat pole in the saddle shed to see if the Christmas gift had materialized.

Before the Three Musketeers left for town and their winter holiday, they hung their heads sadly and told the farmers about the fate of old Hunkus. Eldon went on about what a fine cat Hunkus was, and how well fed. He showed them the golden pelt and told them what a shame it was that the big cat's carcass had been left for the buzzards, the coyotes, and the mice.

The cowboys were gone for a week, but their tracks weren't cold when someone discovered the hindquarter hanging in the shed. There was a woman cook at the ranch again, and she was delighted to have the fresh meat.

I must interject here again with a little disclaimer. There is no one still with us who actually sat around the kitchen table on that fateful day. All of the details come from people who were not there but who spoke with people who were. One of the people I talked to is adamant that no one partook of the forbidden fruit; however, I have three others who were close to the action and they all believe the cat may have been on the menu. The latter story is the most entertaining, and the one

Eldon would have liked the best, and so, while the exact details may be in question, I shall continue with that version.

Joe cleaned off the deer hair and cut some fine, thick steaks for Christmas dinner. The cook fried them up and prepared a great holiday feast. The table was set and everyone pulled up a chair.

It was Christmas and everyone was having a wonderful time, but while the others laughed and talked and passed the salt and pepper, one of the players became suspicious and sat back and poked at the steak apprehensively. Something just didn't seem right. The meat was gamy, and the texture was somehow wrong. This fellow apparently didn't smoke like the rest of them and his nose was better, his eyes and his taste buds too. He got up quietly from the table and went to the stove to examine a few strips of meat that had escaped the frying pan. He pondered for a few moments, while his companions poured gravy and speared the string beans, and then he made a somewhat hesitant and cautious pronouncement. He pointed out that the meat was pale, like pork or chicken; it had a funny smell and a strange tang to the taste. The fat had a faint, pinkish tint to it, and the meat was stringy—not at all like deer steak.

All conversation stopped, and the hands looked across the table at each other with big and questioning eyes. They began to chew a whole lot slower. They poked at the meat hesitantly with their forks—and then the truth was known. Old Hunkus the wild cat was lurking amongst the mashed potatoes.

There was rebellion in the ranks. The cook screamed and quit her job on the spot without even touching the dirty dishes. Grown men cussed and growled and went outside to spit and puke. The lady who owned the ranch and her Colonel companion came over when summoned by the hysterical cook and they joined in the outrage.

The other, more dull and less entertaining story is that old Joe discovered the treachery when he took the cat ham into the house to clean it and cut it up. Joe, for all his shortcomings, had been a professional meat cutter, and I hate to admit that he probably would have noticed the minute differences in color, texture and smell. He had cut up a lot of deer. But then . . . you never know. It may not have been Joe who cut the meat at all. It was, after all, the Holiday Season, a time for celebration and social drinking, and Joe the dragon might very well have been drunk, sick, hung-over, or in such a cigar smoke fog that he couldn't see or smell anything.

Eldon, with his warped and perverted sense of humor, wanted Joe to eat the cat, and forty years later, I want him to eat the cat too—God forgive me.

There is a question about whether or not Virginia and the Colonel might have partaken of the tainted fare. It's something they probably wouldn't have been proud to admit and the surviving players are unwilling to commit themselves about that aspect of the incident. Judging from Virginia's reaction, I wouldn't be surprised if she and the Colonel had enjoyed a fine mountain lion fillet—that, or they came real close to a gastric encounter with old Hunkus and were rescued from the brink in just the nick of time.

When the cowboys came back from their holiday a few days later they were greeted with an icy hostility. Eldon tried to laugh and pass it all off as a fine joke, but he was outnumbered and he wasn't the big dog in the kennel any more. He was a lone wolf caught up in a great storm out on the prairie and it was time for him to hunt a hole.

One of the cowboy eyewitnesses told me that Virginia

confronted the Range Boss directly—like a man—with her hands on her hips and her eyes flashing fire. She told him in cold and measured words, "I do not appreciate your sense of humor," and she fired him on the spot. She told Arnold and Don to get the hell out of there too—they were all fired.

Virginia must have been very upset. From what I had seen with my own eyes, Eldon the Range Boss walked on water at the ranch and his many indiscretions had been forgiven him in the past. His perfidy must have hit very close to home. The boss lady seems to have taken it personal.

It was a cruel joke, made the more onerous by the season of the year and the fact that the players were all good friends. One of life's little truths is that the easiest people to screw-over are the people who trust you and count you as a friend.

Like the hero in a Louis L'Amour novel, Eldon rode off into the sunset. I heard that he worked for Charlie Redd in Southern Utah for a while, and then for another cow outfit on Gentry Mountain in Emery County. He even hung his spurs up for a time and did a short stint as a bartender in the Moose Club in Price.

I was told that he ended his days in a nursing home in the great State of Colorado, but he was a tough old Timber Wolf, and I'm sure he's still out there somewhere. He was far too crusty and too damn mean to ever die. He rode at the very end of a long line of cowboy range bosses, and I'll always remember him the way he looked riding that big black horse up the canyon, the last of the old-time cowboys. I wish him only the best, and I hope he rides forever with the ghost riders in the sky—he would have wanted it that way.

Speaking of timber wolves and bad dogs in general, I don't know what ever happened to the Colonel's soul mate, old Brody. He probably choked on a cantaloupe rind or innocently cocked his leg on an electric fence somewhere and went out with a flash and a bang. I can just imagine little tufts of burning dog hair floating away on a soft morning breeze.

He was such a good dog, and everybody loved him, and I'm sure he went to a better place. He's probably up there in doggie heaven somewhere, cocking his leg on the diamond-studded fire hydrants that line those streets of gold. I can see him in his little canine angel wings with ice cream slobbers on his fuzzy chin, a smile on his muzzle and a song in his heart. He's powdered and perfumed and he chases cantaloupe-flavored tennis balls and immortal peacocks who never quite learn to fly. I'm sure he's pestering all the white-robed harp players by putting his divine but leaky little nose in their silken laps, and by licking their harp-playing fingers with his celestialized, horse-biscuit-fondling and disgusting tongue.

I never spoke with Virginia Nutter again. I knew she was at the ranch several of the times I stopped to visit with Joe and Humbert, and I would have loved to talk to her, but I was still in the mindset of that young boy who was the hired help and I felt it would be very presumptuous of me to knock on her door just to say hello. She was still the boss lady to me, the officer's wife, the queen mother, and I felt like I should wait to be invited just to speak to her. I saw her in town a couple of times, but she was always in the suburban, or with a group of prominent people and I wouldn't be so brash as to interrupt just to say hello.

She was a woman of my grandmother's generation, but like a third-grader with a crush on a pretty teacher, I worshipped her from afar. I'm sure she never knew that I was her biggest fan and secret admirer.

Virginia died in October of 1977 and the ranch was sold to a Texas oil company.

The Colonel stayed in the canyon for a while after Virginia passed away. It took him almost two years to sell the ranch. He soon married a new wife, a young girl with curly hair who wore rodeo queen outfits. The Colonel was seventy years old at the time; his new bride appeared to be in her mid-twenties.

I sort of lost track of the Colonel and the happenings at the ranch after Virginia died. I saw him in town with his new wife a couple of times, and I saw him out in the canyon once, just before he left.

It was the last cattle drive of the Preston Nutter Corporation, the end of an era and the closing of the proud traditions of the Nutter family and the great ranching empire that had endured for a hundred years. It was the final curtain on the cowboy way of life, and I came upon it quite by accident.

I had heard that the ranch was sold, and I was truly surprised, when Jeannie, our little boys and I, came upon a herd of Nutter cows being driven down the canyon just the way Humbert and I had done so many years before. There were half-a-dozen men on horses pushing the cows and they had the portly bovines on the run. The old cows had their tongues hanging out and their sides heaving. They looked like they'd been run for miles. Jeannie, who knows and loves cows, was incensed, and she asked me what in the world was going on. I told her I had no idea. I'd never seen cows moved in such a rough and abusive fashion.

We got past the cows and the hypertensive cowboys, and just a little farther down the canyon we came upon the commanding general—the field marshal of the trail drive.

The Colonel was all scattered out on a reclining lawn chair with a pillow under his head and a cool drink in his hand, waiting for his cavalry troopers and heat-stressed cows to catch up. His young wife was sitting next to him, holding his hand. There was a large cooler sitting on the open tailgate of the pickup truck and I can only imagine that it was stuffed with crackers, fine wine and gourmet cheeses. Old man Preston Nutter never had it so good.

I winced and ducked my head, embarrassed for him. I waved and drove on past. I didn't stop to talk—what could I say?

Douglas McArthur, in his farewell speech to the U.S. congress, said that old soldiers never die—they just fade away. That's what the Colonel did after the ranch was sold; he just faded away. He died in 1982 at the age of 73 and was buried with full military honors.

The Nutter Ranch is in ruins now. The buildings are still there, but they stand vacant and have fallen into disrepair. The fields grow weeds and briars. The stupid peacocks are gone and the corrals have been torn down and tree limbs and weeds and trash have crept up against the buildings. The lilac bushes need pruning, the lawn is dead, and the gate to the yard is sagging on its hinges. The ditches are filled with silt and sagebrush grows in the old stack yards.

The ancient cottonwoods remember, and they hang their heads sadly. Even the fence posts don't stand up straight anymore.

In the early 1980s, I took Jeannie and our little boys back to the Sand Wash Hotel to show them around and tell them the story of my first visit there. The place had changed drastically; I could hardly recognize it. The old cabin was sinking into a lake of sand and greasewood. The gravelly, alluvial bench the cabin had sat on had turned into a mud flat and the greasewood had grown as tall as a man. The pole corral, the old trash pile and the stone inscription were all gone. Nothing remained inside the old cabin but a few boards that were sticking up out of the sandy mud.

There was a place to launch boats just a short distance fr(
the cabin, and a graveled parking area for cars. There we
portable toilets and a large trashcan. A large wooden sign with
a green BLM logo dominated the parking lot. It stood like a
pushy, overbearing traffic cop, a fat BLM ranger in a varnished
shirt, blurting out the official rules and regulations for the river
runners; a harsh reminder that big brother was watching and
keeping tabs on your "wilderness" adventure. The big, muddy
river floated past, diverting its eyes, embarrassed and humiliated by the unsightly intrusions.

No one was around the day we were there. It was wintertime and the river runners were home in L.A. and Denver. I walked around the old cabin again, and I was surprised that the ghosts that haunted the place were the ghosts of river runners past and not old cowboys. There were lipstick-stained cigarette butts and tennis shoe tracks in the soft dirt around the cabin, and a couple of spent wine bottles lounged in the nearby bushes.

I fled the dark shadow of the BLM sign, and we walked along the river on that strip of sandy beach where all tracks and traces of previous visitors had been erased by the muddy water. The river remembered, and she welcomed me back. The musty smells of the water, the tamarisk bushes and the mud hadn't changed at all. Even the sun came out and smiled.

Jeannie and I held hands and watched our little boys play near the water. They were so excited. They ran and jumped and bucked in the sand like a bunch of happy baby lambs. They threw sticks in the water, and we watched the little boats float away, innocent and unknowing, going down into the depths and shadows of Desolation Canyon to meet the mighty Colorado and eventually the deep waters of Lake Powell. I knew the little boats would run the same rapids and follow the same turbulent paths over the rocks and through the

The Split Sky

other little boats had followed just a few short
generation ago. I smiled and was happy it was such
 for my sons. I could see in their eyes that the river
 canyon, even the world itself, was new and exciting,
 free to them, just as it was to me once, and I rejoiced.

About the Author

Tom McCourt was born in Price, Utah. His father was a coalminer and later a Deputy Sheriff. Tom is the oldest of five sons and was a fourth-generation coalminer. He grew up in Wellington, Utah, a quiet little town of small farms and big-hearted miners.

Tom graduated from Carbon High School with the class of 1965 and was drafted into the Army in July 1966. He qualified for Officer Candidate School and was commissioned an officer and a gentleman in May 1967. In December of 1967, shortly after his twenty-first birthday and a month before leaving for Vietnam, he married his High School sweetheart, Jeannie Price.

In Vietnam he served as a forward artillery observer with the Fourth Armored Cavalry of the First Infantry Division - known as The Big Red One.

In 1969 Tom was honorably discharged as a First Lieutenant and went home to work in a coalmine. He graduated from Carbon College (The College of Eastern Utah) and from The University of Utah with a BS degree in Anthropology, the first step toward being an Archaeologist, which was his ultimate but unfulfilled goal.

wing family, Tom returned to the coalmines in
. went to work for the Plateau Mining Corporation
.y Control Engineer. He worked there for twenty-
.rs, until a catastrophic explosion and fire closed the
Creek Mine in mid-2000.

ɟm is now writing full-time, and he and Jeannie own and
ιage Southpaw Publications. They have four handsome
ns, four beautiful daughters-in-law, and eight precious
grandchildren. They live in Carbon County Utah. They have a couple of dusty acres, a nice pickup truck and an ugly dog. Tom says, "Life is Good."

Other Works by the Author

White Canyon: Remembering the Little Town at the Bottom of Lake Powell
ISBN: 0-9741568-0-9
Published and distributed by Southpaw Publications.
First printing 2003. (225 pages)
White Canyon is an autobiographic work about Glen Canyon before Lake Powell.